AMERICAN ICONOGRAPHIC

CULTURAL FRAMES, FRAMING CULTURE
Robert Newman, Editor

AMERICAN ICONOGRAPHIC

National Geographic, Global Culture, and the Visual Imagination

STEPHANIE L. HAWKINS

University of Virginia Press
Charlottesville and London

University of Virginia Press
© 2010 by the Rector and Visitors of the University of Virginia
Printed in the United States of America on acid-free paper
First published 2010

9 8 7 6 5 4 3 2 1

LIBRARY OF CONGRESS CATALOGING-IN-PUBLICATION DATA

Hawkins, Stephanie L., 1971–
   American iconographic : National Geographic, global culture, and the visual
imagination / Stephanie L. Hawkins.
      p.   cm. — (Cultural frames, framing culture)
   Includes bibliographical references and index.
   ISBN 978-0-8139-2965-1 (cloth : alk. paper) — ISBN 978-0-8139-2966-8 (pbk. : alk.
paper) — ISBN 978-0-8139-2975-0 (e-book)
   1. National geographic—History. 2. National geographic—Social aspects.
3. Discoveries in geography—Press coverage. 4. Photography in ethnology. I. Title.
   G1.N275H39 2010
   910.5—dc22   2009041710

For Ian and Audrey

Contents

Illustrations

Acknowledgments

My first encounter with *National Geographic* is etched indelibly upon my memory. I had lost my first tooth and was in my grandmother's care while my parents awaited my brother's birth. To occupy me, Gram let me paw through old issues of *National Geographic*. A cover with King Tutankhamen's golden sarcophagus caught my eye. As a result, the interior walls of Egyptian tombs with their hieroglyphic murals and stylized etchings form some of my earliest memories.

The origins for this book, then, are deeply personal, as well as intellectual, for it was in a graduate seminar at the University at Buffalo that I first took a scholarly interest in *National Geographic*. I wrote an essay that sat in a file drawer while I completed a dissertation. At the behest of a fellow traveler in academe, I later salvaged that essay, which, in the intervening years—involving a long-distance relationship and geographic migration, the deaths of two-fathers-in-law, and the birth of my daughter—has culminated in this book.

This book would not have been possible without the tremendous support of colleagues and friends, near and far, who have provided both inspiration and encouragement throughout this process. My thanks to Stacy Hubbard, whose graduate seminar "Primitive and Collecting Arts" inspired this project; thanks also to Laura Otis, Susan Schulten, and Douglas Kellner for their advice at various critical stages. From the start, *National Geographic* archivists Renee Braden and Mark Jenkins enthusiastically supported this project. I am grateful for their help tracking down materials as well as their knowledge of *National Geographic* institutional lore. Thanks to Ashley Parada for helping with *National Geographic* photograph permissions; and special thanks to Lisa Comrie ("Betsy Ross") and Deirdre Wall ("Sharbat Gula") for permitting the use of their snapshots from the "Intense Individuals" blog.

I am indebted to my University of North Texas friends and colleagues Jacqueline Foertsch, Evan Horowitz, David Kesterson, Walton Muyumba, Nicole Smith, Robert Upchurch, and Luis Velarde whose helpful feedback and thoughtful criticism have enriched the work. My thanks to Bonnie Lovell for her expert research assistance and to Diana Holt and Andrew Tolle for their help with matters large and small. Finally, the University of North Texas Junior Faculty Research Grant and Summer Research Fellowship provided invaluable support for this project in its many stages.

Portions of this book appeared previously in the following: "Savage Visions: Ethnography, Photography, and Local-Color Fiction in *National Geographic*," reprinted from *Arizona Quarterly* 64.2 (2008), by permission of the Regents of the University of Arizona; review of Tamar Y. Rothenberg's *Presenting America's World* (Ashgate, 2007), *American Studies Journal* 48.4 (Winter 2007). Permission to reproduce this material is gratefully acknowledged.

My gratitude to Robert Newman and Cathie Brettschneider at the University of Virginia Press for their interest in this project; and especially to the anonymous readers, whose criticism and expertise were so crucial to the book's contributions. Thanks, as well, to Susan Murray for her sensitive and careful copyediting and to the many individuals at the Press who have contributed to the final product.

As always, I am profoundly grateful to my family and my friends: Katherine Forrest and the late Leonard Salle, Betty Johnson, Jerry and Betty Hawkins, Sinikka Grant, Rachel Hall, and Mark Peters. My deepest gratitude goes to Ian Finseth, who first urged me to write this book and read its every page. His intellectual partnership, love, and boundless patience have made this book possible.

AMERICAN ICONOGRAPHIC

THE REDISCOVERY OF SHARBAT GULA

National Geographic in the Twenty-first Century

In the years since its 1888 founding as a scientific journal, *National Geographic* has become not just a cultural icon but a generator of icons. None, most likely, is more internationally recognized than *National Geographic*'s June 1985 cover photograph titled "Afghan Girl" depicting a nameless twelve-year-old with piercing green eyes, witness to the Soviet occupation of Afghanistan. Seventeen years later, in the aftermath of the September 11 terrorist attacks, the rediscovery of Sharbat Gula as a married woman caring for her children in the forbidding hills of Tora Bora only intensified the earlier image's sympathetic appeal. Like "Migrant Mother," Dorothea Lange's iconic Depression-era portrait of sharecropper Florence Thompson, the 1985 photograph of Sharbat Gula has helped to shape modern notions of global citizenship through its enormous power to express both victimhood and an ennobling courage amidst great hardship.[1]

Indeed, so widely has Sharbat Gula's image circulated that it has become the "Migrant Mother" of our own cultural moment. Her numerous sister images—tributes, parodies, improvisations—proliferate on the Internet. Her watchful eyes peer from a man's tattooed shoulder blade, and her replicas haunt costume parties. Each of these images testifies to how the original cover photograph has been orphaned from its original context in ways that highlight the complex relationship between sentimental identification and aesthetic commodification characteristic of our global civic culture.

Iconic images such as Sharbat Gula's are able to catalyze public sentiment precisely because they circulate freely from era to era in a variety of public forums and contexts. The icon, write the communications scholars Robert Hariman and John Louis Lucaites, triggers an emotional bond between the audience and the image. Because of this bond, the icon functions as a powerful means of public address, one that both expresses and renegotiates the cultural conflicts and political tensions at the heart of democratic society. In this respect, the image visually reenacts and thus "performs" recognizable moments of collective life for various audiences. Iconic images and their recycled progeny in popular media, then, can be regarded as "civic performances" that visually embody contradictions in attitudes, beliefs, and values held sacred by a particular culture at a particular historical moment.[2]

Those contradictions are encoded in the competing aesthetic principles in Sharbat Gula's 1985 image. Much of the photograph's power derives from its stylistic fusion of documentary and fashion photography with Renaissance painting. Her tattered veil and haunted expression recall the visual details of hardship captured in Depression-era documentary photographs. Her full lips and thick brows, on the other hand, resemble a look that Brooke Shields and Madonna brought into vogue in the 1980s, while her veil and slightly turned face also pay homage to classical paintings of the Virgin Mary. But it is photographic realism, finally, that lends her portrait its peculiar power—a realism symbolized by a trace of white paint or plaster that adheres to her veil, signaling her refugee status in the waning days of the Cold War.

A number of critics have argued that *National Geographic*'s photographs distance the magazine's readers from "social reality" through "sheer force of technique," via a predictable formula in which photographic art takes the place of journalistic substance. Sharbat Gula's disconcerting gaze, however, a gaze "that sears the heart," seems very directly embedded in a particular social reality.[3] Hers is an image that commands our attention and demands a sympathetic response—at least to her as an individual. That is, the photograph has been said to express the "politics of pity" in which spectator sympathy with the hardship of those photographed becomes a substitute for true justice. It is just this sort of "commodified sentimentality" in *National Geographic*, some have argued, that prevents a genuine engagement with cultural differences and global suffering.[4] Moreover, the idea that *National Geographic* has long reinforced an American cultural and political agenda has become commonplace among the magazine's numerous critics.

Certainly, *National Geographic*'s 2002 account of Sharbat Gula's rediscovery suggests some of the ways in which the magazine can serve that agenda. Her dramatic rediscovery, for example, seemed uniquely timed for President George W. Bush's post-9/11 call for homeland security, and for Americans to accept short-term curtailment of civil liberties in exchange for the administration's "war on terror." It was, after all, iris recognition and FBI facial analysis, the latest in biometrics and surveillance technology, which made her rediscovery possible.[5] As though she were a "wanted" fugitive finally "found," Sharbat Gula's rediscovery might actually be said to make personally invasive surveillance technologies seem like part of the ordinary fabric of global culture—and even a necessary means for preserving national security. Understood from this perspective, Gula's iconic image potentially mobilizes public sentiment around the containment of potential threats to national civic order.

Nonetheless, scholarly readings of the magazine that emphasize the dark political significance of photographic images and the fearsome power of the "culture industry" have not adequately accounted for the varied and complex responses of *National Geographic* readers throughout the magazine's 120-year history. While it may be true that "*National Geographic* accumulated power by virtue of [its] consistency," as one historian has argued, it does not follow that the *public* responded consistently to those images.[6] As well as suggesting the fundamental instability of the iconic image, the multitude of popular appropriations of Sharbat Gula's likeness expose the less visible, psychological transformations that global icons, like *National Geographic,* may inspire—and that form the broader context for this book.

In many ways, *National Geographic* readers have actually anticipated the magazine's cultural critics in recognizing the magazine's political biases. After Sharbat Gula's image first appeared, readers noted the "impression of Soviet brutality" conveyed by the issue's cover and its accompanying article, "Along Afghanistan's War-Torn Frontier." A Canadian reader speculated, "Perhaps that girl is a teacher and watching [the] destruction of her school by religious fanatics who want to maintain their power by keeping [its] population illiterate." This same reader, however, questioned the article's accuracy, since it left out crucial details: Afghanistan's history under British imperial rule and its many requests for aid to establish an independent government. "Please," continued the reader, "don't make [*National Geographic*] into a tool of military industrial complex propaganda."[7] Readers as far-flung as Mexico, England, and West

Germany urged *National Geographic* to dispense with "politically motivated" and "distorted" accounts. "Leave [politics] to the other media and their hate mongers," wrote another reader, echoing a sentiment expressed by many. "Hate and fear are powerful weapons today. If we can control hatred we can control our destiny."[8]

As these remarks suggest, identification with *National Geographic* as a reputable forum for scientific exploration and genuine cross-cultural understanding enhanced, rather than neutralized, the critical independence of its readership. They also suggest that, despite its flaws, the magazine helped readers negotiate their own complex feelings about globalization. Against that background, we can better understand how popular culture's appropriations of Sharbat Gula highlight the essential instability of iconic images—and cultural icons themselves—as vehicles for institutional or political agendas.

We need look no further than the send-up of *National Geographic* in the *Harvard Lampoon,* which devoted its 2008 April Fool's issue to spoofing both the 1985 and 2002 covers featuring Gula's photograph. In one parody, Paris Hilton's face is superimposed on the original, the surrounding text miming the tabloid-style journalism with which Hilton has become associated.[9] Its point is to suggest how the codes of fashion photography were manipulated in the original image to turn the traumatized gaze of a twelve-year-old refugee into a sexual commodity, a literal and figurative cover girl. A caption beneath the *Lampoon* image has Hilton remark that she "never posed for this photo" and "actually find[s] it really offensive."[10] Parody or not, these remarks have real bite because they call attention to the exploitation intrinsic to the global commodification of Gula's image.

Another parody, this time of the post-9/11 *National Geographic* cover that shows Gula concealed beneath a purple burka holding her 1985 image, with the dramatic caption, "Found." Now, however, she holds a photograph of Waldo from the popular "Where's Waldo?" series. Such seemingly banal trivializations of iconic images of human tragedy or suffering, it has been argued, actually bespeak "a deep fatalism about individual powerlessness."[11] Yet in their literal effacement of Sharbat Gula, the various adaptations of her iconic image achieve a level of critique that makes visible the exploitative visual rhetoric underlying the products of serious photojournalism.

Recasting Hariman and Lucaites's understanding of icons as fundamentally unstable sources of either ideological control or resistance in a global context, I see popular appropriations of Gula's image as enacting "a new global civic ethic."[12] This ethic invites our rethinking of the relationship between national identity and global interconnectedness as more than either a voyeuristic sentimentality or an exploitative commodification. Paradoxically, it is *National Geographic*'s commercialization of Sharbat Gula—and its readers' sympathetic response to her ubiquitous image— that has revitalized global activism, as evidenced by the $1,078,600 that *National Geographic* readers have given to the Afghan Girls Fund established by *National Geographic*.[13]

Gula's story resonates well beyond the nationalist agenda mobilizing the Bush administration's "war on terror." Living on the threshold of absolute poverty—earning less than one dollar a day, according to the United Nations Development Program (UNDP)—Gula's family puts the human cost of global economic disparity into sharp relief.[14] Gula's reappearance, then, speaks as much to the hope for a new global order based on the developing world's fair access to global resources and an equal stake in a global economy as it does to America's national security interest in defeating terrorist regimes. While the commodification of her image— an image of which she herself was unaware until 2002—might seem to reinforce her own powerlessness relative to the economic forces of mass production and distribution, it also highlights the failure of globalization to yield more inclusive avenues for economic justice, autonomous expression, and civic action.

Cultural appropriations of Sharbat Gula's image thus capture, consciously or unconsciously, the plight of Third World "losers" in a global economic equation that continues to privilege wealthy Western nations at the expense of developing countries. A medical student who had an image of Gula's eyes tattooed on his shoulder described his thinking in his blog. Her image, he wrote, "symbolizes the true [violent] nature of the world that we are so often blinded to and the ever-present need to be mindful of our fellow human beings, wherever or whomever they may be."[15] Rather than dismissing such remarks as platitudes, however, we should note that *National Geographic,* throughout its history, has been able to inspire, often in spite of itself, a kind of broad, critical, thoughtful humanism, which sometimes even manifests in readers' choices of various professional paths. Two of the magazine's more astute critics, for example, the anthropologist Catherine Lutz and the sociologist Jane Collins, acknowledge that their "life's work" resulted from their early reading

Fig. 1 *(left)* Deirdre Hall dressed as Sharbat Gula. (Courtesy Lisa Comrie). **Fig. 2** *(right)* Deirdre Hall and Lisa Comrie, dressed as Sharbat Gula and Betsy Ross. (Courtesy Lisa Comrie)

of the magazine.[16] Perhaps an overlooked positive attribute of nostalgia, then, is that it invites us to return more critically to the magazine as the source of some of our earliest and most formative memories.

While iconic images like Sharbat Gula's have been associated with the strategies of "othering" and the forms of escapism that have historically constituted *National Geographic*'s imperial "romance," their popular appropriations can also be powerful performances of a global civic culture. Understood in a broader anthropological context, cultural performances are restagings of social behaviors, which are "framed" or put on public display.[17] There is no better example of this performative cultural framing than the ironic use of *National Geographic*'s iconic yellow frame.

A 2007 blog displaying photographs from a fund-raiser for the arts offers a particularly evocative example of how the iconic detachability of *National Geographic*'s yellow frame enables a performance of global civic culture. In one photograph, a woman dressed as Sharbat Gula in her 1985 portrait holds a mock frame in front of her face to create the illusion of a cover (fig. 1). Subsequent photos of costumed characters entering and exiting the *National Geographic* frame throughout the evening reveal its power to transform even ordinary people into icons. One particularly evocative photograph, though, shows "Sharbat Gula" and "Betsy Ross" within the yellow frame, as the U.S. flag Ross carries forms a dramatic backdrop for the new "cover" the two created (fig. 2). However spontaneous and improvisational, this new *National Geographic* "cover" is an example of global civic performance that provocatively joins global and national myths. It heightens our sense of how the visual rhetoric of the war on terror and U.S. patriotism has since become wedded in the national imagination in the years following 9/11. In this way, appropriations of cultural icons can both call attention to and undermine their potential to supply a "rationale for our violence."[18]

Certainly, as the highly charged performances of "Betsy Ross" and "Sharbat Gula" make plain, global icons express both sides of an ongoing debate regarding the possibility of forging nonexploitative alliances in our ever-more-globalized world. As an icon forged during the early decades of globalization, *National Geographic* has expressed, almost from its inception, the conflict between an individual allegiance to the nation and growing awareness of collective membership in global cultural networks. Sharbat Gula's 1985 image embodies NGS president Alexander Graham Bell's 1904 ideal of "living pictures" that "touch the heart"; this iconic photograph and its various sympathetic and ironic appropriations highlight *National Geographic*'s positive potential to forge what sociologists describe as a "new global civic ethic" based on "new understandings, commonalities and frames of meaning without direct contact between people."[19] As subsequent chapters of this book demonstrate, *National Geographic* not only catalyzed public sentiment around powerful national civic narratives, but also helped its readers negotiate the quick and shifting currents of an emerging global culture.

1

NATIONAL GEOGRAPHIC

The Icon and Its Readers

In November 1896, *National Geographic* published its first nude photograph, a portrait titled "Zulu Bride and Bridegroom." This was the
first of many images to wed the magazine's reputation to the far-flung and
racially erotic. More than a century later, *Harvard Lampoon* parodied the
iconic magazine in its 2008 April Fool's edition. A comic send-up of *National Geographic*'s 120-year history, the *Lampoon*'s cover features tabloid
celebrity Paris Hilton posing with a phony elephant and ape in front of a
backdrop of an African savannah. Inside, a mock apology from the editor
acknowledges that "thousands and thousands of bare boobs have been
printed in this magazine. Boobs of every shape and color . . . all of them
right under my nose."[1] As if in tribute to those breasts, the magazine's
centerfold opened to a pixilated photograph of a lion composed of breasts
in varying hues.

Given the magazine's famed history as anthro-pornography, one could
hardly imagine a more apt parody, or a celebrity more fitting to grace its
cover than Paris Hilton, whose name conjures the magazine's long association with the tourism and travel industries, and whose appearance with
an ape invokes such *National Geographic* "cover girls" as the primatolo-
gists Dian Fossey and Jane Goodall. The *Harvard Lampoon* parody not
only affirms the magazine's iconic stature as a purveyor of ethnographic
erotica, but also reveals how *National Geographic*'s readership over the
years has found creative, and often critical, outlets for reimagining the
magazine's exotic oeuvre.

During the period of *National Geographic* cultural history this book
covers, 1888 to 1954, the magazine was, of course, more than a venue
for displaying women's breasts. It helped readers imagine themselves

in relation to diverse peoples scattered across the globe. Since evolving beyond the specialists' journal that it was at its 1888 founding, *National Geographic* has become commonplace in ordinary American households, medical waiting rooms, and schools. Historically, then, the magazine has belonged to a network of both informal and official educational media that have adapted and circulated visual narratives in which science and imaginative transport provocatively combine. As one of the world's most widely recognized distributors of global images, *National Geographic* has filled an important role in what Arjun Appadurai has termed the global "mediascape." Mediascapes, writes Appadurai, are like fiction in that they provide "image-centered, narrative-based accounts of strips of reality"; they furnish "characters, plots and textual forms" from which "scripts can be formed of imagined lives, their own as well as those of others living in other places." By disseminating images of distant lands and peoples, *National Geographic* fostered a sense of what social theorists call "complex connectivity" among nations and cultures, a global connectivity ushered in by media that bring "distant images into our most intimate local spaces."[2]

This powerful combination of science and imaginative transport, it is well known, often promoted a Western, and imperialist, view of the world. However, while *National Geographic*'s imperial narratives could be persuasive, they also contained tensions that encouraged critical engagement with the magazine's institutional mission and its role as public icon. For this reason, I want to emphasize another aspect of the potentialities of the mediascape in relation to global interconnectedness. Appadurai's concept is especially useful, not just because it helps us understand the magazine's global influence, but because it also suggests how readers can "experience and transform" what they see and read, precisely by virtue of their exposure to multiple "imagined worlds."[3] This emphasis on how readers transform images and texts is one key point of distinction between this book and previous studies of *National Geographic,* many of which take for granted that readers wholeheartedly endorsed the magazine's imperialist worldview.

As one of the most visible and widely available purveyors of images of the non-Western world, *National Geographic* has understandably received considerable critical attention. Philip J. Pauly's 1979 *American Quarterly* essay "The World and All That Is in It: The National Geographic Society, 1888–1918" opened up serious engagements with the magazine's representational strategies by commenting on the magazine's departure from geography as an academic discipline. *National Geographic*'s expansive definition of geography as the "world and all that is in it" not only offended the nation's official geographers and spurred the formation of the more scholarly and reputable American Geographical Society, it also placed the magazine in the more quaint category of natural history and made it a cousin to the museum by including human beings among its visual repertoire of the world's flora and fauna.

After Pauly, perhaps the most well-known study is *Reading "National Geographic"* (1993) by Catherine Lutz and Jane Collins. Their study of *National Geographic* from 1950 to 1986 examines its photographic repertoire of non-Westerners in the context of the magazine's institutional culture and editorial policies, devoting two chapters to a relatively small sampling of fifty-five readers' reactions to uncaptioned photographs. Theirs is one of many critiques: of the Society's promotion of male explorers in Lisa Bloom's *Gender on Ice* (1993); of its national imperialist ideology in Julie Tuason's "The Ideology of Empire in *National Geographic Magazine*'s coverage of the Philippines, 1889–1908" (1999); of its production and distribution of maps in Susan Schulten's *The Geographical Imagination in America, 1880–1950* (2001); and of its portrayals of Middle Eastern women in Linda Steet's *Veils and Daggers* (2003). As with Howard S. Abramson's *"National Geographic": Behind America's Lens on the World* (1987)—a scathing account of faked photographs and institutionalized anti-Semitism, racism, and sexism—criticism of the institution repudiates the self-aggrandizing narratives contained in the celebratory tomes written by National Geographic Society (NGS) insiders.[4] More recently, Tamar Rothenberg's *Presenting America's World: Strategies of Innocence in "National Geographic" Magazine, 1888–1945* (2007) focuses on *National Geographic*'s cultural and political implications, maintaining that the magazine serves as a "case study" of the "manufacture of consent" regarding U.S. imperialist attitudes and policies.[5]

The assumption of much scholarship on *National Geographic* is that readers are not *reading* the magazine so much as treating it as a picture book, mindlessly flipping through the photographs without pause for critical reflection. In their assessment of *National Geographic*'s cultural influence, for example, many reproduce a common criticism of early-twentieth-century mass-consumption magazines. These magazines, it is argued, fostered a culture of passive readership in which "political spectatorship" substituted for "active citizenship."[6] So pervasive has this critique become that it is almost a foregone conclusion that "the world [*National Geographic*] gave its readers was a world they wanted to see."[7] This assumption has had a major, and rather misleading, impact on our understanding of *National Geographic*'s role in modern American culture—indeed, on our understanding of that culture itself.

This book questions just how much the so-called "manufacture of consent" is a consequence of the manufacture of the public *perception* of consent and not true consent. By choosing to publish only laudatory letters in the magazine and its numerous institutional histories, for example, *National Geographic* editors consciously shaped its public image of respectability and popularity, while the great number of reader criticisms remained unvoiced because they were unseen by the magazine's broader readership. My study draws upon the Society's archive of unpublished readers' letters to show that a culture of dissent existed alongside the magazine's manufactured image of consent. That readers did in fact read the magazine's articles and its photographs critically and rigorously is a major contention of this book, a perspective that casts new light on the relation between the consumption of popular media and the nature of political and cultural consciousness. Archival materials that have been neglected in scholarship on *National Geographic,* including letters from readers and the magazine's promotional leaflets for advertisers, together with parodies of the magazine in fiction, cartoon caricature, and film, necessarily complicate our understanding of the magazine's role in fostering visual cultural literacy.

I approach *National Geographic* as a literary scholar and educator invested in understanding the ways in which readers imaginatively engage texts and form judgments independent of, and often at odds with, ideological narratives. This is a book about *National Geographic*'s rise to iconicity in the first half of the twentieth century and how its thousands of readers, who saw themselves as "members" of the NGS, responded to its public image—one that was both national in its interests and allegiances and international in scope. It is about the magazine's early educational role in visual literacy and its deft management of science and art in its photographs and texts. It is also about how the tensions between science and art, and between such visual and textual domains as pictorial and documentary photography and literary realism and romance, complicated its reception and fostered a critical readership alert to discrepancies and quick to note their magazine's failure to adhere to their ideals or standards. Finally, and most broadly, this book addresses the evolution of attitudes toward globalization and national citizenship when the world was becoming more closely knit than ever before.

As the testimony of five hundred unpublished readers' letters—one hundred in each decade between 1912 and 1954—reveals, *National Geographic* not only offered visual spectacle, but also supplied genuine knowledge about the world. Despite the magazine's national focus, American and foreign readers alike continued to value the magazine's potential to promote global understanding. These readers believed, as a reader from Alberta, Canada, put it, that *National Geographic* would "do more to foster international understanding and consequent good-will than any other single agency."[8] Readers sought escape through imaginative travel, but the magazine also fulfilled a desire for self-improvement, a need for belonging, and an urge to contribute to humanitarian causes. If *National Geographic*'s educational mission nurtured nationalism, it also fostered global consciousness. Of course it reflected the cultural biases of its time—but that also makes *National Geographic* a vital means of examining the processes of icon formation and the complex dynamics of acceptance and resistance expressed by its readers.

American Iconographic

In 1990, a Ralph Lauren ad for a line of men's clothing featured in the *New York Times Magazine* showed the interior of a hunting lodge littered with the accoutrements of masculine outdoor exploits—rubber boots, flannel shirts, a Native American rug—and, under a wicker chair, a stack of vintage *National Geographics*.[9] What this ad reveals is *National Geographic*'s role as a repository of a vital cultural memory, one grounded in a mythic American past encapsulated in the ad's frontier images. The "American iconographic" of this book's title signals the magazine's mobilization of these uniquely "American" motifs and ideals for its iconicity. These include the primitivism and rugged individualism of the "strenuous life" popularized by President Theodore Roosevelt, and the regional peculiarities of place, or "local color," captured in dialect or costume. These are the visual emblems of an ethnographic impulse to "salvage" lost, forgotten, or recovered fragments of a mythic national past. These fragments survive in *National Geographic*'s photographs and heighten the magazine's potential to secure readers' emotional identification. Its readers were participants not just in science but in an ongoing narrative of American nationhood and the place of global cultural difference within that narrative.

This book's title, *American Iconographic,* is meant to signal *National Geographic's* role as an object of reverence, as well as reference, for many Americans in the early twentieth century. While not all of its photographs can properly be termed icons, the magazine nevertheless embodies the icon's modern transformation from the sacred relic to the secular artifact.[10] *National Geographic* does not circulate in the same way as a singular iconic image, like the 1945 photograph of Marines raising the U.S. flag at Iwo Jima. Instead, and perhaps more powerfully, *National Geographic* is an icon that produced other iconic "types": images of the far-flung and exotic, women of color, photographer-adventurers, and picturesque nature photography. Its distinctive yellow-bordered cover denotes the magazine's all-encompassing "window on the world" theme of global exploration and human cultural variety. Moreover, the magazine adapted to the shifting values and attitudes of its cultural moment and reflected those attitudes back to its thousands of member-readers. While many of those readers were both stimulated and soothed by the magazine, others responded critically to the attitudes and values it reflected.

Although iconic images can be powerful agents mobilizing collective action and reinforcing certain long-held stereotypes, their effects on a given public are less pervasive and more complex than critics of popular media might assume. As it circulates in the public media, the iconic image grows ever more visible, but its meaning also grows increasingly unstable in response to its history of popular appropriation.[11] Because of this fundamental instability of meaning, the role of iconic images—and, one might argue, cultural icons like *National Geographic* in general—is a mediating one rather than a controlling one. Iconic images help audiences identify themselves in the various public roles they inhabit, those of "citizens, consumers, imperialists, dissenters, Americans, Canadians, moderns, members of the 'family of man.'"[12] Not only do they give audiences a vital means of recognizing and coming to terms with the social norms and complexities of their cultural moment, they can supply new visual terms of cultural critique.

In contrast to previous studies of *National Geographic,* which have examined the institutional strategies by which the Society and its magazine mobilized nationalist consent, this book traces how inconsistencies within *National Geographic's* institutional aesthetic encouraged debate and dissent. Some might argue that dissent goes against the very essence of icon formation by which communities coalesce around its shared symbolic meanings. Certainly icons demand allegiance, but, as in the case of the American flag, the ideas for which an icon stands or fails to stand invite contestation. While the icon might operate as narrative shorthand for a constellation of ideas and symbols, it does not follow that this iconicity cancels out critical or innovative responses and uses.

The meaning of a cultural icon is more than the sum of its parts. Rather, any individual icon represents the fluid, unpredictable processes by which cultural meanings are assigned to—and gathered from—objects, people, and ideas. In its decades-long effort to promote geographic knowledge, *National Geographic* was diffusing not just ideas about the unknown regions of the world, but ideas about the *known,* about American values, assumptions, and beliefs about the United States' global role. In this way, *National Geographic* educated its readers in ways unanticipated by its earliest founders. While readers praised the magazine's artistic photographs and humanitarian mission, they also challenged the American exceptionalism writ large in its pages. By reflecting those attitudes back to its readers, *National Geographic* opened the way for readers to confront and challenge their nation's most tenacious myths and preconceptions.

Vicarious Travel: *National Geographic's* Cosmopolitan Citizenship

National Geographic's emergence as an influential American institution in the early twentieth century has generally been attributed to the fortuitous combination of the 1893 magazine revolution, the 1898 Spanish-American War and U.S. imperialism, the early founders' political connections and business savvy, and, of course, innovations in photographic technology. Certainly, all of these were crucial factors in the magazine's transformation from a scientific journal to a popular illustrated monthly. This same period, however, saw the proliferation of communications technologies that helped overcome geographic distance, bringing people into ever greater closeness, if not physical proximity. The telephone, invented by NGS president Alexander Graham Bell, was a harbinger of the leading role *National Geographic* would assume in the global "mediascape" as it brought images of the world abroad into ordinary American households. Advertising pictures that "speak their own story," *National Geographic* promoted the illusion of face-to-face contact with the subjects of its photographs. In its efforts to collapse geographic distances into the space of a photograph, the magazine was distinctively modern, yet its emphasis on romantic timelessness simultaneously made it an escape route from modernity through vicarious travel.

For many of *National Geographic*'s first-generation readers, vicarious travel was indeed one of the magazine's main attractions. Watson R. Sperry of Hartford, Connecticut, spoke for many *National Geographic* readers in declaring that *National Geographic* "takes me to all parts of the world, many of which I have visited without having to leave my chair." Another reader observed, "should one happen to visit strange lands I think it would seem more like re-visiting [them] after reading the wonderful descriptions in the *Geographic* and looking at the pictures." Others felt they had grown more worldly and "cosmopolitan" as a result of *National Geographic*.[13] In this sense, the term "cosmopolitan" invokes both the cultural sophisticate as well as the individual who is both open to and actively engages cultural variety and difference.[14]

Sociologists who study the impact of the modern global media have debated whether armchair travelers of this sort can gain anything beyond a superficial understanding and appreciation of cultural difference. Letters from *National Geographic*'s first-generation readers cannot resolve that question, but they do shed light on some of the earliest attitudes that formed in response to widely circulated images of the world's peoples. In particular, they demonstrate how the magazine did not simply promote Western global dominance but encouraged a reflective self-consciousness about cultural attitudes and beliefs.

Nude photographs, for example, called forth objections that revealed the magazine's ability to offend cultural sensibilities and inspire race prejudice. "Can't you give us something besides those everlasting pictures of naked heathens?" wrote Horace R. Sturgis of Riverside, Maine, who also enclosed a check for his membership dues. A reader from Wyoming considered it "quite a loss" that he had to "cut out a number of the pictures because of their impure nature" before he could set out the issue for guests. "Repulsive barbaric tribes of the earth," complained a teacher from Brooklyn, are "useless in the classroom" or "on the reference shelf of a school of eastside girls." If the magazine's images of racial diversity upset some readers, its reproduction of pejorative terms conversely offended the cosmopolitan sensibilities of others. One reader criticized the magazine for its racial epithets, writing, "In volume XXXVI—No. 1—page 29 you use the words Southern Darky—These are the words of the lower Stratum of the white South—The word 'Darky' is very offensive to the refined and educated colored man. We expect better language from a first class magazine."[15] If the magazine has seemed, in one sense, a national "cultural standard-bearer," as Rothenberg has it, readers' letters complicate our understanding of just whose "culture" the magazine represented by locating culture as the site of contestation and debate.[16]

Much attention has been given to *National Geographic*'s nationalism to the exclusion of its readers' expressions of divergent cultural ideals. For many readers, the magazine fulfilled a profound longing to be part of something bigger than themselves, particularly through an organization they believed would promote the common good. On April 28, 1926, Wayland Ramsey of Los Angeles wrote to praise the altruism of the NGS. "All my life I have longed to be associated with an organization of just such a character—and many have been my disappointments in my efforts to seek such association. At last," he wrote, "I have found an organization existing solely for the 'enlightenment of humanity,' free from the taint of commercialism."[17] For every reader who desired *National Geographic* to be more national, there was another who identified with the magazine's international scope.

Like other late-nineteenth-century institutions that trafficked in the collection and exhibition of cultural phenomena—world expositions, natural history museums, and ethnographic cinema—*National Geographic*'s presentation of the exotic "Other" involved a form of narrating national allegiance while negotiating cultural differences and international connectedness. In many ways, therefore, the magazine disordered its readers' ideas of the world as much as it shaped them according to national aspirations. The contents of a "typical" *National Geographic* could be downright disorienting. A reader glancing through the September 1900 issue, for example, would have first encountered an article titled "The Colorado Desert," followed by "The Chinese Paradox," "Colonial Government in Borneo," and "The Water Supply for the Nicaragua Canal," before rounding out the issue with articles titled the "Forest Reserves of the United States" and "The Great Wall of China." Readers encountering this issue may have taken pride in their nation's vast resources, but the dizzying juxtaposition of Colorado and China, Borneo and Nicaragua, would have also invited a more speculative ordering of the globe, where the boundaries separating vast geographic distances collapsed with a flip of the page.

My emphasis on readers' imagined identifications with the magazine invokes the well-known theory of the "imagined community" as the basis for nationalism. Nations and national affiliation have historically been formed in part through the "synchronous time" of newspaper reading, in which people can imagine many others engaged in the same task.[18] Today, in newspapers, magazines, and the complex digital media networks that crisscross the globe, readers encounter a multiplicity of national stories. Within these national narratives, writes the cultural theorist Homi K. Bhabha, "the people" are constructed as both "the historical 'objects' of a nationalist pedagogy" whose authority derives from an originary historical moment or event and as "subjects" in a narrative process that has to portray the disparate qualities of individuals' daily lives as part of an ongoing national story. National discourse, writes Bhabha, turns the "scraps, patches, and rags of daily life . . . into the signs of a national culture."[19] In so doing, national discourses reduce people and their complex social interactions to mere emissaries of nationhood.

We cannot fully apprehend *National Geographic*'s nationalist impulse apart from the readership that it claimed to represent. As we have seen, however, this readership was far from uniform in its values and allegiances. For that reason, Bhabha's discussion of the ambivalence within nationalist forms of address—which continually have to assert their power through narratives affirming the universal consensus of "the people" in the face of a variety of "cultural differences and identifications"—is instructive for examining how *National Geographic* and its readership illuminate tensions between nationalist and more diverse and distinctive cosmopolitan values.[20] The lived experience of people going about their daily business, such as reading magazines, confronts and challenges nationalist and theoretical discourse that attempts to resolve "the people" into a uniform entity that represents "the nation." Similarly, in speaking of global consciousness we have to avoid using "globe" in ways that unconsciously overlook or deliberately disregard geographic and cultural specificity.

In order not to reproduce a sense of *National Geographic*'s readership as a similarly uniform body, I anchor my discussion of *National Geographic*'s relationship to its readers in the context of the everyday reading practices, cultural values, and rituals of consumption: when and how readers' read and where they displayed the magazine in their home. What results is a complex picture of the ways in which narratives of American identity and America's place in the "family of nations" are formulated, circulated, and continually revised.

Beyond Nation: "Cultural Cosmopolitanism"

For Bhabha and a number of social theorists, the term "culture" relocates such big, abstract concepts as "citizenship" and "nation" into the complex realm of individual daily practices and social interactions.

"Cosmopolitanism" and "culture" have become watchwords in a debate over whether internationalism can serve as "a shared universal value, applicable across different cultural contexts."[21] Scholarship has dwelt equally on the utopian possibilities for cosmopolitanism to bring about global cultural understanding and peace—as opposed to its dystopian counterpart: a Western-dominated "McWorld" owned and run by multinational corporations and media conglomerates whose homogenizing influences threaten local cultural attachments. In this dystopian nightmare, cultural commodities are bought and sold with little regard for the economic forces and social particularities from which they arise. Cosmopolitanism, from this perspective, amounts to little more than an insidious form of economic imperialism, its media representations another manifestation of a "culture industry" complicit with Western global domination through commercial enterprise.[22]

Scholarship seeking a middle ground between these competing visions of a global utopia and its dystopic counterpart has found that the term "culture" can play a mediating role. Social theorists have tended to embrace an anthropological understanding of culture as both active, "the order of life in which human beings construct meaning," and inclusive, one that addresses "all manner of everyday practices."[23] Writing from a sociological perspective, Gerard Delanty offers "cultural citizenship" or "cosmopolitan citizenship" as a model that "shifts the focus of citizenship onto common experiences, learning processes and discourses of empowerment." In the aftermath of September 11, and amid the challenges of global terror and mass migration to concepts of citizenship, he stresses the need to recognize citizenship as an active process. Delanty calls for an approach that would illuminate the "cultural dimension of citizenship" as it is learned in the "informal context of everyday life."[24] By taking into account readers' letters, this book explores how the ordinary contexts for reading *National Geographic* informed its members' identification with certain aspects of the magazine as well as their resistance to others. Examining the various contexts for reading and the uses to which readers put the magazine provides insight into how complex and unpredictable their identifications with a national or international citizenship were—so dependent were they on visual experience and other cultural narratives. While it is beyond the scope of this book to engage contemporary debates regarding global citizenship, contemporary sociological perspectives inform my understanding of *National Geographic*'s historic role as a forum for negotiating the complex cultural dimensions of national and global citizenship.

The challenges to citizenship sociologists identify as part of our own cultural moment, for example, also resonate with similar crises at earlier moments in U.S. cultural history treated in *National Geographic:* the 1898 Spanish-American War and the emergence of the United States as an imperial nation, the second wave of immigrants from southern and eastern Europe, the "great migration" of African Americans from the agrarian South to northern industrial centers, the First World War as a catalyst for internationalization, and the retreat, following World War II, from international affairs through a new "cult of domesticity."[25] Despite the magazine's editorial policy of nonpartisanship, each of these major passages in history was captured thematically in *National Geographic,* from its emphasis on geography as a component of progressive education and visual literacy (chapter 2); to its articles on insect and plant "immigrants" from 1900 to 1910 (chapter 3); to its role in educating foreign-born soldiers during the First World War and its coverage of fascism before the Second World War (chapter 4); to its genre of "jungle housekeeping" articles, spanning the interwar period to just after the Second World War (chapter 5); and finally, to popular spoofs of *National Geographic's* iconic pantheon of photographer-explorers and exotic women of color (chapter 6). *National Geographic* does not just present a transparent window on the world; it opens a window on the shifting attitudes of the magazine and its readers toward national civic ideals and global citizenship.

What social theorists point out, and what *National Geographic* readers make especially vivid, then, is that people travel conceptually, even more so than they do physically. The annihilation of physical time and geographic space does not require a train, boat, or plane. The imagination's allies are the photographic image and the easy chair. In training its gaze on the various cultures of the world, *National Geographic* has played a vitally important part in globalization, or the processes of "complex connectivity," as the sociologist John Tomlinson would have it. This sense of proximity to otherwise distant peoples and regions is enabled by mass media that make expanded cultural awareness possible without having to leave home. At the same time, writes Tomlinson, "complex connectivity" is a "troubling phenomenon" because it involves the "deterritorialization" of cultural space, "the simultaneous penetration of local worlds by distant forces, and the dislodging of everyday meanings from their 'anchors' in the local environment." A key implication of Tomlinson's argument is that a corresponding psychological sense of dislocatedness, or conceptual "deterritorialization," results from the "penetration" of media images into our most intimate cultural spaces in ways that disturb and unsettle familiar notions of self-identity and collective belonging. To quote Tomlinson again, it is not just "family life that is threatened by the penetration of the outer world into the inner: there is also an implied challenge to the 'boundary' which constitutes the self."[26] In describing their distaste for *National Geographic*'s portrayal of nude or nearly nude "savages," therefore, the magazine's readership was also signaling its discomfort with the forced intimacy with racial and cultural difference that global "complex connectivity" entails.

To take a literary example, Elizabeth Bishop's "In the Waiting Room" suggests how *National Geographic*'s images of cultural and racial difference presented just such a threat to self and, by extension, cultural identity, illuminating the utopian dreams and dystopian anxieties stimulated by globalization. In the poem, a child occupies herself with a *National Geographic* while awaiting her aunt's return from the dentist's chair. The child's perusal of images of a "dead man slung on a pole," "babies with pointed heads," and "black, naked women with necks / wound round and round with wire" stages a dramatic encounter with cultural difference that provokes a vertiginous loss of self. Destabilizing the boundaries between self and other, the magazine plunges the child into a collective human sea in which she loses her identity in a larger human collectivity. She feels as though "I—we—were falling, falling, / our eyes glued to the cover of the *National Geographic*, / February, 1918."[27] Exemplifying the "troubling phenomenon" of deterritorialization that dislodges individuals from their comfortable "anchors," the one cultural anchor in the poem is the magazine itself. We do not, however, have to see the child's momentary loss of self as entirely negative.

In spite of its power to dislocate the child from the cultural space of the waiting room and the familial proximity of her aunt in the doctor's office, the magazine's deterritorializing force also brings awareness. Witnessing dramatic human difference, the child wonders: "What similarities— boots, hands, the family voice . . . or even the *National Geographic* . . . held us all together / or made us all just one?"[28] Her figurative fall from self-absorbed innocence into a knowledge of human diversity points to a more positive aspect of deterritorialization as it shifts "the boundary between the 'private self' (say, the self of the insular familiar structure) and the self imagined in relation to a wider horizon of human belonging."[29] Bishop's poem calls attention to the magazine's role in the child's experience not only of space but of her own humanity; the *National Geographic* photographs may disturb the child's comfortable cultural moorings, but they also promote self-awareness.

Though a literary artifact, the poem underscores the importance of seeing the act of reading *National Geographic* as embodied and culturally embedded. Within the space of the magazine, the potential exists for reflective engagement with its representations—or what sociologists have come to call "reflexivity"—rather than passive absorption. From this perspective, reading *National Geographic* in a waiting room, an act typically thought of as passive absorption, a means of forgetting or escaping the anxiety of a doctor's visit, can also promote other, more self-conscious, forms of cultural engagement, creating a "heightened sense of awareness towards what seemed common-sense" behaviors.[30] Moreover, against the backdrop of the First World War, the poem also functions as a form of "civic performance" described by Hariman and Lucaites, in which Bishop's reconstruction of a child's imagined encounter with representations of cultural difference dramatizes questions of national and international affiliation.

As Bishop's poem demonstrates, there can be positive consequences of globalization through expanded possibilities for identification with those beyond one's own nation and an increasing awareness of one's civic obligation to those outside our nation's geographic boundaries. In our own cultural moment, the Internet and television have made it almost a routine matter to get information about other societies or peoples (whether or not such information leads to greater enlightenment), but in the late nineteenth century, *National Geographic* was the principal means for conceptual travel. It was the first magazine to focus exclusively on bringing images of the world not just to ordinary American households but to an international readership abroad. It stood at the forefront of how twentieth-century media, and the visual strategies they employed, evolved in relation to the concept of a global "family of nations."

The magazine with its distinctive yellow border and visually arresting photographs brought before its readers' eyes entirely new possibilities for picturing the world. As a case in point, on December 1, 1940, a Mrs. Elisabeth Howe Terflinger wrote to the NGS to praise an issue of *National Geographic* that had appeared twenty-seven years earlier. Inspired by an April 1913 issue on Machu Picchu in Peru, she and her husband traveled, magazine in hand, to the ancient Incan ruins. "We spent the night there," she wrote, "to see a full moon, behind a mackerel sky, shooting shafts of silver at random all over the peaks and we knew then that *National Geographic* had pointed the way to a wonderful experience. Most of those we met knew nothing of the ruins and devoured the contents of the 1913 issue—too late."[31] Until *National Geographic* "pointed the way," the ruins of Machu Picchu simply did not exist for the Terflingers. More than that, the couple relied upon *National Geographic*'s photographs and articles to make Machu Picchu's ruins culturally legible once they were there. For Terflinger and her husband, it was not enough to see the ruins: they had to be read. Taken as a representative document, this letter testifies to the magazine's formative impact on the nation's visual literacy: its cultivation of a pictorial imagination, a sense of the world as already-pictured and thus completely accessible through images.

A hallmark of visual literacy is the "educated" gaze, a gaze that not only identifies images of importance but knows how to read them for cultural meaning. Terflinger's letter underscores *National Geographic*'s role in tutoring the individual eye and "I" to recognize places, people, and objects worthy of cultural attention. In one sense, the magazine fostered what the sociologist John Urry has termed a "tourist gaze," a roving eye that seeks as its objects the unusual, the typical, and the representative, as well as the unfamiliar in the midst of the ordinary and commonplace. The Terflingers' experience, then, reveals the ways in which the magazine paved the way for a modern pilgrimage to the sights disclosed in its pages. The magazine, I argue, hastened a modern sensibility by which "twentieth-century pilgrims in some senses 'know' each other before they arrive."[32] Like Urry, who sees the "tourist gaze" as one conditioned by a welter of other discourses, I understand *National Geographic*'s educational role in the late nineteenth and early twentieth centuries in terms of a confluence of cultural, visual, and textual paradigms that shaped its representational strategies and informed its readers' interpretation of images.

National Geographic and Visual Literacy

The Society's numerous institutional histories fondly credit the inventor Alexander Graham Bell (1847–1922) and Gilbert H. Grosvenor (1875–1966), who came aboard as magazine editor in 1899 and retired as the longest-reigning president of the NGS in 1954, with the magazine's rise from obscurity in the late 1800s to international recognition by the early 1900s. Although these two men were the architects of many of the magazine's most recognizable visual and textual motifs, my narrative focuses principally on the educational philosophy behind the magazine's founding as well as the visual and literary context that provided the crucial aesthetic framework for its success in bringing the world to its readers.

That context involved a host of late-nineteenth-century visual media that objectified cultural differences as "exotic" commodities. Lantern slides, stereographic images, collectible tobacco cards, and postcards issued by photographic studios made images of the globe's inhabitants commonplace goods in the lives of late Victorians. Natural history dioramas and world's fairs presenting indigenous peoples in constructed villages similarly catered to the era's thirst for images from abroad. The same period saw the birth of the "ethnographic novel," which catered to male audiences and featured the spectacle of imperial conquest and racial difference.[33] As Edward Said has observed, such mass-produced images of the exotic were often Westerners' first exposure to racial and cultural difference, thereby conditioning certain ways of seeing non-Western "Others."[34] In the classic narrative pattern, cultural fantasies and private imaginings lead the lone adventurer to seek new lands, new peoples, and novel experiences.

What makes National Geographic so significant to the cultural historian is its unusual success at using photography to make these themes come alive in the minds of its readers—even if these readers did not always subscribe to the colonialist narrative. In an era when visual literacy was a growing part of school curricula, progressive educators used pictures not only to provide information but to cultivate aesthetic taste and moral virtue. National Geographic's success derived, in large measure, from the creative blend of scientific and aesthetic modes achieved in its photography. Even as turn-of-the-century ethnographers used photography as a medium for documenting racial difference, amateur and professional photographers attempted to overcome its association with institutionalized science by experimenting with photography as an art form. As these educators revolutionized the teaching of geography beyond the rote study of land forms, National Geographic both stimulated and met the demand for visual materials to help students better imagine the peoples and places in different geographic regions.

The "imagined worlds" to which National Geographic gave its readers access were thus aided by the flexible epistemological boundaries between science and art, and between the realistic and romantic dimensions of photography. Yet by the same token, this flexibility also generated tensions, fractures, and indeterminacies within the photographs that readers were often quick to point out. Fluid ideas about what counted as authentic, reliable science, and correspondingly about what role the photograph would serve, artistic or documentary, played themselves out in the pages of *National Geographic* and in the many letters from readers writing to commend—and also to contest—its vision of the world.

Beyond simply embracing photographic realism, therefore, Bell and Grosvenor enlisted the romantic imagination in the creation, and reception, of *National Geographic* photographs. "Romance," and all the associated images, concepts, and themes that it conjures up, appears repeatedly in readers' letters and the magazine's institutional lore. As the word is used in this book, "romance" encompasses elements of both the early-nineteenth-century movement termed "romanticism" and of the venerable literary genre, dating from the medieval period, having to do with the courtly heroics of knights errant and their rescue of comely maidens.[35] A term that has changed with the times, "romance" has meant different things to its audiences at different historical junctures. In the late nineteenth and early twentieth centuries, it often connoted the masculine pursuit of distant and unfamiliar lands, adventures in "virgin" wildernesses, exotic spectacle, and fantastic trials and escapes. The popular genre of romance adventure, with its stereotyped "noble savages" and its emotional idealism, invited Americans to project themselves in imagination into distant places around the globe. It also invited them, however, to project themselves *literally* into other lands, and has thus been identified with the imperialist ideology underlying U.S. territorial acquisitions abroad. This encounter with wilderness and racial difference, however, also carried older associations with the terror and beauty of the romantic sublime, embodied—in the case of *National Geographic*—in panoramic vistas, volcanoes, earthquakes, and natural disasters.

At the same time, even the magazine's romantic images contain contradictions that prevent their complete fulfillment of the myths they seek to represent. Edward Curtis's photographs of Indians astride horses, bearing spears and wearing feathered headdresses, for instance, appeared in *National Geographic* at a time when Native Americans were swiftly going the way of the buffalo. Or, Wilhelm von Gloeden's homoerotic photographs of young Italians featured in *National Geographic* in December 1909 embodied a romantic narrative of empire and a youthful aesthetic that Mussolini's fascist iconography would later exploit in John Patric's "Imperial Rome Reborn" (March 1937). Such "dynamical pictures," in Bell's phrase, revealed the human inconsistencies and contradictions that make photographs, like literary works, impossible to reduce to a single meaning—that is much of what made them dynamic. While these examples underscore photography's romantic underpinnings and its nostalgic function, they also remind us that photographs, despite their utility as instruments of social control, invite complex forms of identification and provide ways for spectators to come to terms with cultural change.

This study, then, works at the juncture of postcolonial theory and cultural studies by considering how the audiences of imperialist visual representation responded to what they saw. Taking consent as a given, critical approaches to popular culture have tended to deny the power of Western audiences to adopt skeptical positions toward *National Geographic*'s imperialist representational strategies. Such approaches are traditionally more invested in locating resistance from positions of marginality within the imperialist system.[36] Yet scholars of popular culture suggest that the process of cultural consumption necessarily involves multiple layers of interpretation, translation, and reappropriation. Even mainstream audiences, they maintain, are active participants in constructing cultural meaning from media.[37] This book suggests that "ordinary" readers and consumers are as capable as imperialism's discontents of creating new visual and textual forms that comment critically or cast an ironical gaze upon institutional practices and dominant cultural narratives.

If one's membership in the NGS conferred special spectatorial privileges, it also promoted a particular orientation toward the institution itself. As patrons of scientific exploration and research, readers felt entitled to comment on and freely criticize the magazine's content and style, either when it did not adhere to their values or when it seemed to depart from its professed goals. In a very real sense, members were joint stockholders in the magazine and played a significant role in its content. Annual surveys upon the renewal of membership dues solicited candid commentary on the magazine's content, and members, in turn, expected the magazine to respond, as in the case of the magazine's curtailment of advertisements for cigarettes and alcohol.[38] Believing themselves active participants in scientific progress, NGS members are far removed from scholarly accounts of late-nineteenth-century magazine consumers as mere passive spectators. NGS members frequently read the magazine's texts and photographs with an eye toward inaccuracies and discrepancies between the two.

Although this study does not aim for systematic quantitative analysis, it does locate broad patterns of reader identification and dissent, and assesses these responses in relation to the magazine's thematic preoccupations. In doing so, I join ongoing debates in American studies and cultural studies regarding citizenship and nationalism, and am keenly aware of the value of magazines as primary resources for cultural history. As the magazine historian Judith Yaross Lee suggests, magazines "capture moments in time and document cultural processes as they unfold."[39] In presenting for American eyes little-known parts of the world, *National Geographic* documented America's national and cultural unfolding. Yet a complex magazine like *National Geographic* not only records the prevailing attitudes and beliefs of its historical moment, but, when examined issue by issue, reveals thematic patterns and cultural concerns that do not predictably adhere to the editorial dictates of its founders. This study aims, then, for a contrapuntal analysis in which readers' commentaries are read both within and against the magazine's recurring motifs and the period's central cultural concerns.

By 1919, some twenty thousand letters from readers poured into NGS headquarters each day.[40] Many were geographic inquiries, while numerous other readers wrote to praise or criticize "their" magazine. The Society's archives of these letters dates back to 1912 and are stored on more than twenty-five rolls of microfilm. The late-nineteenth-century convention of signing one's name by initials persisted well into the twentieth century and frequently obscures gender. When readers explicitly identify themselves as male or female, I have made note of it, as I also do in cases where readers identify themselves by race or ethnicity.

By highlighting a savvy readership's capacity for independent and critical response, however, I do not mean to embrace a militant strain of reception studies that mistakes superficial "resistance" to consumer culture for politically engaged and efficacious resistance. Mindful of *National Geographic* scholarship that has focused on the magazine's promotion of conservative ideologies, I also reconstruct broader late-nineteenth and early-twentieth-century cultural contexts that illuminate how the audiences for these narratives actually responded to what they read (and saw). In adopting a "multiperspectival" approach advocated by media scholars, some of my findings may in fact reinforce the conclusions of my predecessors.[41] But they are complicated by close attention to what readers' letters reveal about the everyday consumption of dominant cultural narratives and about the extenuating cultural and historical factors that influenced how they interpreted the magazine's photographs and texts; that is what primarily distinguishes this book from important postcolonial interventions in visual studies.

In *National Geographic*'s earliest decades, its readership included immigrants, African Americans, and rural Americans as well as the cultural elite associated with the nation's urban centers. By closely attending to the diversity of *National Geographic* readers' letters, this book demonstrates what happens at the moment of consumption and illuminates the intricately negotiated process of reading images and texts. Indeed, such rituals of consumption—the practices of home display and varied public and private contexts for reading the magazine—are almost as important to this study as are the magazine's representational strategies; for the dynamic relationship between the visual and the literary, and between the magazine and its audience, reveals inconsistencies between the magazine's mission and its message. As importantly, this book endeavors to answer the question of how immigrants, African Americans, working-class Americans, and cultural elites alike could all identify as "members" of a national society and felt empowered to critique its editorial policies. Finally, where others have contributed to our understanding of the magazine's aestheticization of ethnographic racial "types," this study highlights a greater range of photographic genres in *National Geographic,* from self-consciously artistic photographs and portraits of ordinary Americans to photographs documenting the photographer on assignment. The magazine's lens was trained as much on American subjects as it was on European and non-Western ones. The "local" and the "global" were not sharply demarcated within the magazine. Domestic and national issues often overlapped with broader cosmopolitan, global concerns.

National Geographic's ethnographic vision manifests itself in other ways, too. It reveals the history of a nation seeking to solidify its sense of a national tribe. Beyond constructing a sense of privileged insidership for those who discovered little-known places through the *Geographic,* membership in a national society inculcated a pictorial consciousness, whereby *National Geographic* texts and photographs cooperated to shape readers' perceptions of the world but not to determine them. By capturing and diffusing images of a world in transition, *National Geographic* provided a means for Americans to imaginatively negotiate national, ethnic, and cultural identities within a rapidly changing modern world.

2

TRAINING THE "I" TO SEE

Progressive Education, Visual Literacy, and
National Geographic Membership

Long before Edward Steichen's famous 1955 exhibit, Family of Man,
debuted at the Museum of Modern Art, *National Geographic* promoted global images of the family. The photograph "Zulu Bride and
Bridegroom" (fig. 3) in *National Geographic*'s November 1896 issue not
only inaugurated the iconic nude images historically associated with the
magazine, but also established a visual grammar for its educational mission.[1] In this case, marriage and family supplied one of its most enduring
motifs—that of "universal" human endeavor—and helped to domesti-
cate the more estranging aspects of cultural and racial difference. Unlike
ethnographic head shots of the nineteenth century that highlight human
difference, "Zulu Bride and Bridegroom" suggests vital points of identification. Despite the couple's nudity, the full-length shot reproduces the
conventions of formal wedding portraiture. Attired in tribal finery, husband and wife face the camera, their hands ceremonially clasped in front
of a long wooden staff. Behind them looms the jungle.

The photographic theorist Marianne Hirsch has observed how institutions have long drawn upon the conventions of family portraiture and
photo-album snapshots as "family frames" that translate "global issues
into domestic concerns" (50). Like Steichen's photographs, "Zulu Bride
and Bridegroom" invites a "familial look" that translates "a global space
of vast differences and competing interests into a domestic space" (53)
wherein the commonalities of human nature seem to transcend culture.
Yet, while allowing for a "humanism of differences," in Hirsch's phrase,
such photographs stop short of political engagement by refusing to extend
"absolute civic equality" to the human subjects they portray (58). Looking

Fig. 3 "Zulu Bride and Bridegroom." (Unknown photographer/ National Geographic Image Collection)

at "Zulu Bride and Bridegroom," American or European *National Geographic* readers sitting comfortably at home, surrounded by family photographs, could simultaneously interpret marriage as a universal human activity while feeling affirmed in their belonging to a "civilized" culture.

At first blush, "Zulu Bride and Bridegroom" might seem to reinforce all that cultural historians have taught us about *National Geographic,* but if we examine this iconic first photograph in context, we can discern another way in which it manages readers' cultural identifications. The article in which the photograph appears, "The Witwatersrand and the Revolt of the Uitlanders," chronicles not a Zulu attack upon Dutch and English colonial settlers, as one might expect, but a violent—one might even say "savage"—dispute between the Dutch and English over the control of South African resources. Its author, George F. Becker of the U.S. Geological Survey, expressed his divided allegiance as he described the encroachments of English "foreigners," or "Uitlanders," as the Dutch called them, upon South African gold reserves. "While there is a natural sympathy in the United States for Anglo-Saxons taking up arms for their rights," Becker maintained, "we, as Republicans, also sympathize with the South African Republic in the endeavor to maintain its independence" (352). Becker portrayed the conflict as the result of innate racial antagonism between the "highly intelligent, and perhaps somewhat impatient men" represented by the English, and "the pastoral pioneers" represented by the Dutch Boers (351–52). The Teutonic Boers, he maintained, were "ignorant of the refinements of life so dear to advanced Anglo-Saxons" and "backward as a race, according to our standards" (353–54). So focused is Becker on tracing the discord to *European* racial conflict that he mentions South Africa's native inhabitants only in passing, and in the clichéd terms of sensationalist ethnographic accounts. The "the Zulus, Matabili, Basutos," he noted, "possess some excellent traits, but are horribly cruel when once they have smelled blood" (356). Whether *National Geographic* readers consciously identified with the sophisticated cultural tastes of the English or the humble agrarian roots of the Boers, they must have been struck by how little the photograph "Zulu Bride and Bridegroom" had to do with the article's content. Posed for the camera at the height of ritualized matrimony, and against the backdrop of warring imperial factions, the Zulu couple exemplifies the kind of family-minded civic virtue that *National Geographic*'s first generation of readers would have taken to heart.

In fact, "Zulu Bride and Bridegroom" was one of many stock images that *National Geographic* reproduced in its early years. Although not taken by the magazine's own photographers, "Zulu Bride and Bridegroom" wonderfully illustrates how the magazine's photographs instructed readers in unexpected ways. Broadly speaking, *National Geographic* trained the individual gaze to recognize cultural and racial differences while constructing its readers' sense of "membership," not just in the NGS but in a collective global community. As a portrait of family solidarity, the Zulu couple reflects the progressive educational emphasis on family and home as stable sites for the nurturing of a national civic culture. At the same time, the familiar ritual of marriage emphasizes human unity over human diversity, and thus serves to ease tensions between the local and the global, and between national and cosmopolitan forms of identification.

More than a "strategy of innocence" designed to cloak imperialist ambition, *National Geographic*'s photographs of the world's diverse peoples did not always reinforce prevailing stereotypes, and could forge unpredictable lines of cross-cultural identification.[2] As a reader in Cincinnati, Ohio, remarked in 1914: "Surely no such splendid and wide-spread means of education tending to 'make the whole world kin' was ever set in motion, or attained such worthy results, as the *National Geographic* . . . which by the way, should be called the 'International,' or, better still, 'The Interracial' Magazine."[3] The magazine's visual repertoire invoking familiarity and "kinship" taught readers to "place" themselves within other domains: Science, the Nation, and Government, but also, increasingly, the Globe.

Critical accounts of *National Geographic* have tended to emphasize its nationalist and imperialist visual content while overlooking or downplaying other, equally powerful, symbolic meanings and attachments it allowed its readers. These readers treated the magazine not only as a kind of geography textbook, but also as a field guide, a portable university, even a classic of literature and art. Unlike other illustrated monthlies, its readership model was based on membership in the NGS. Each month, the magazine encouraged its member-readers to feel as though they were part of an exclusive community and participants in scientific discovery. The certificate they received with their nomination was a matter of pride. "I don't know when I have been so proud of anything as the little certificate which I hold as a member of the Society. It is second to my college diploma," wrote Margaret Wilson from Burma, India.[4] In crucial ways, membership invoked an understanding of citizenship beyond national borders. While for some readers NGS membership marked one's "American-ness," national allegiance, and racial purity, it also indexed one's moral and social aspirations and fostered a sense of belonging to an international community.

This chapter addresses the complex ways in which *National Geographic* both facilitated and troubled its readers' identification as "members" within the NGS, the nation, and the world by encouraging certain reading practices. It explores the educative aims of the NGS at its 1888 founding in the context of progressive educational reform and pictorial education between 1880 and 1914. *National Geographic* was in the vanguard of this educational movement, as changes in geographic education supplied additional narrative paradigms for reading the world and its people as a world of iconic signs. In response to the proliferation of visual images, lessons in visual literacy were incorporated into school curricula as educators encouraged the critical consumption of magazines and mass media. Progressive educators schooled readers in the interpretation of images as morally edifying stories, while also instituting practices that shaped a critical readership alert to the kinds of contradictions between text and image that we have seen in "Zulu Bride and Bridegroom."

Carefully attending to how the magazine's member-readers in fact "read" *National Geographic* photographs and articles, I tell the story of what *National Geographic* meant to its many thousands of member-readers in the first half of the twentieth century. The institutional goals and imperial aspirations articulated by the magazine's founders often ran against the grain of its member-readers' imaginative identifications, and the aesthetic tensions between *National Geographic*'s national goals and its international scope fostered a critical engagement with the magazine and, arguably, with mass culture more broadly.

An "Epic Story": Progressive Education and Visual Literacy

National Geographic's visual aesthetic has its origins in late-nineteenth-century storytelling technologies, commercial stereographs, ethnographic exhibits, natural history museums, and touristic excursions. In the process of bringing visual spectacle to American eyes, institutions also sought to guide, even discipline, American vision. The American Museum of Natural History, founded in 1881, compensated for the visual "drunkenness" viewers might experience in response to overwhelming spectacle by propelling them through a maze of carefully choreographed exhibits.[5] Historian Steven Conn's imaginative reconstruction of a "stroll" through a typical late-nineteenth-century museum illustrates this storytelling impulse:

> As visitors moved (horizontally) through the galleries, they saw objects which had meaning inherent in themselves. Combined together from case to case and exhibit to exhibit, the objects formed coherent visual "sentences." That coherence, however, was achieved only after those objects had been deliberately selected, quite literally from the basement storehouse, and ordered properly within the galleries. Meaning was thus constructed visually, with objects, like words in a text, as the fundamental building blocks of the museum language.

What Conn terms an "object-based" epistemology of museum curation, in which individual objects bespeak larger cultural narratives, was additionally heightened by explanatory legends evoking geographic excursions or chronicling an evolutionary narrative. Museum exhibits thus participated in a cultural mission aimed at "civilizing" the public. Lettered and unlettered masses alike could gaze upon images or scenes of human progress and place themselves on the imaginary rungs of an evolutionary ladder, from the lowliest "savage" tribe to the most civilized nations.[6]

Such institutions not only made cultural difference part of an evolutionary framework, but also narrated what NGS president Gilbert H. Grosvenor described, in his 1936 institutional history, as the "epic story" of human progress. Writing at a time when the telegraph, telephone, and radio had collapsed geographic barriers to communication, Grosvenor observed: "The day when history was formed by events that could be localized is gone. News and thoughts are now exchanged among nations almost instantaneously, so that the whole world is sensitive to important events in any of its parts. The epic story of these parts—and their ever-changing human and economic geography—is told in the *Geographic Magazine*."[7] In its earliest decades, the magazine's global traffic in cultural commodities, practices, and sign systems did not offer its readers the same narrative coherence as museums of natural history. Instead, the magazine's range of "geographic" issues and events presented what might be called a cosmopolitanism of form, which disrupted as much as it reinforced prevailing beliefs.

In contrast to the narrative coherence of the natural history museum, *National Geographic*'s visual and textual arrangements could appear arbitrary and discordant. If the magazine was "to be American rather than cosmopolitan, and in an especial degree to be national," in the words of then editor-in-chief John Hyde in 1896, the actual contents of the magazine often blurred this nationalist focus.[8] A single issue, for example, could contain articles on subjects as disparate as the Badlands of South Dakota, hurricanes in the West Indies, commercial development in Japan, and expeditions to the polar regions.[9] Despite its ostensibly national focus, the magazine disordered the map and rearranged the globe. Its scattered geographic subjects accomplished what amounts to a breaking up of conventional temporal and spatial locations, highlighting the world's ever-increasing interconnectedness.

National Geographic articles comparing individual nations' resources and trade routes reinforced this sense of connectivity at a time when immigration to the United States brought the issue forcefully home, as the influx of peoples from southern and eastern Europe dramatically transformed what one *Geographic* contributor later termed the nation's "racial geography." In the 1890s, immigrants from non–English-speaking nations in eastern and southern Europe flooded the nation's ports, reaching an unprecedented 1 million in 1907 alone, and remained steady until the outbreak of the First World War. Public institutions promoted a national effort to assimilate the newcomers. Schools, in particular, assumed the traditional role of families and neighborhoods in inducting children into the processes of work and industry as well as social life. The expanded curricula included language education, cultural literacy, and citizenship as well as practical vocational training. It was in this democratic spirit of progressive education that *National Geographic*'s vice president, William James (W. J.) McGee, an ethnographer for the Smithsonian's American Bureau of Ethnology, described the Society's public mission. "In accordance with the plan of government by the people, of the people, and for the people," he wrote, "our educational facilities are brought within reach of every citizen, our educational methods adapted to the needs of the masses."[10] By broadening what qualified as geographic study and appealing to lay audiences, the magazine aligned its educative aims with the democratic goals of progressive educators.

The progressive spirit included more than assimilation, however. It revitalized education by valuing hands-on experience and orienting education toward everyday life. Abandoning traditional coursework based on rote memorization, teachers put education in the context of real-world experiences. Children read newspapers and magazines, ventured into the countryside for their geography lessons, and expressed themselves through art and drawing. Within this context of rising immigration, industrialization, and growing demand for visual materials to inform geographic education, *National Geographic* was responsive to the progressive educational requirement that schools extend beyond the "three R's" model that had been in place since the widespread adoption of public school systems in the 1860s. The educational mission that *National Geographic*'s early founders envisioned "for the increase and diffusion of geographical knowledge" reflects this general educational ferment and its drive toward breadth, contextual learning, and pragmatic reform.[11]

For the magazine's early founders, geographic education represented a vital means of negotiating racial and cultural diversity, both nationally and globally. In keeping with the citizen-making aims of progressive education, editor John Hyde, a statistician for the Department of Agriculture, envisioned *National Geographic* as a vehicle for civic ends. By supplying

NGS members with "a knowledge of the conditions and possibilities" of their "own country," the magazine, Hyde affirmed, would take a leading role in cultivating "an enlightened patriotism."[12] This nationalizing mission found its most vivid expression in the aftermath of the 1898 Spanish-American War as the magazine devoted numerous issues to educating Americans on the nation's assets at home and abroad in the newly acquired Philippines, Cuba, and Hawaiian Islands.[13] Offering more than a geography of current events, however, the progressive educational methods advocated by NGS founders touched deeper registers of imaginative and comparative vision, and of national and international identification. First, children were taught to develop a mind's-eye view of the world by comparing geographically similar land masses, regardless of their disparate locations or diverse human inhabitants. Second, this comparative method was deployed as children read about, and subsequently imagined, distant lands and peoples. By learning to project the mind's eye outward, across distant lands and spaces, students acquired visual literacy in imagining the globe as a coherent whole.

The 1888 inaugural address by Society founder Gardiner Greene Hubbard, delivered before an elite corps of Washington, D.C., businessmen and government geographers, anticipated this global vision by representing the earth's geography in terms of both telescopic verticality and panoramic, horizontal sweep. Hubbard began by defining geography as etymologically derived from the Greek ή γῆ, for "the earth," and γράΦω, meaning "I write." The story of epic global progress, "the geography of man," had been vividly rendered in the conquests of modern India and Russia by Alexander the Great, the fall of Rome, and the geographic "spirit of discovery" of Columbus (5–6). Following Columbus, a vision of the world as spheroid became standard, and by 1865, advances in telescopic photography had made possible the first photograph of the moon.[14] Speaking to his audience from the perspective of this modern, telescopic imagination, Hubbard envisaged the earth "as an enormous globe suspended in empty space, one side in shadow and the other bathed in the rays of the sun" (4). Future *National Geographic* readers, he promised, would see the planet whole, from the "unbroken ocean of air" composing its atmosphere to its "solid surface . . . which teems with countless forms of animal and vegetable life" (4). From such a global perspective, geography, as Hubbard conceived of it, anticipated the pronouncement more than a decade later by his successor, Alexander Graham Bell, that "the world itself and all it holds" would be the magazine's theme.[15] This godlike perspective positioned the spectator as the privileged witness to humanity's epic story played out upon a global stage. The earth's teeming variety, as expressed by Hubbard, could be recognized as of a piece with Darwin's aesthetic appreciation of the "beautiful ramifications" of diversity in natural selection.[16]

The magazine promoted a way of seeing that combined global distance with immersive proximity, teeming variety with visual containment. In this way, National Geographic's visual strategies reflect the Progressive Era's desire to manage racial and ethnographic variety.[17] Hubbard's vision of the globe spinning through space embodies the anthropological "view from above" that the media scholar Ellen Strain characterizes as "distanced immersion," the effect of visual technologies like the stereoscope, camera, and cinema to present spectators an illusion of total immersion in exotic geographic and cultural space while remaining detached outsiders with the conceptual freedom to move between both registers of intimacy and distance.[18] The conceptual freedom associated with distanced immersion resembles National Geographic's visual aesthetic of what I term "vicarious participation," a manner of seeing in which readers identified with the photographed subjects as though they were real, as though looking by itself amounted to firsthand geographic exploration. The magazine's promotion of photographs as a form of imaginative transport enlisted the scientific comparative method to educate the reader in dramatic new ways.

When applied to recording geographic forms, the comparative method offered itself as the conceptual model for imaginative transport. In an address before the NGS in 1893, William Morris Davis, professor of physical geography at Harvard and a member of the magazine's editorial board, outlined a plan titled "The Improvement of Geographical Teaching" (July 1893), based on a systematic comparison of geographic forms in disparate quarters of the globe. According to his methodology, New England's geography would be compared to other similar regions around the world. The Deerfield, Connecticut, and Berkshire valleys, for example, would find their companion districts in the German Rhine and the Thames at Norwich, England.[19] Geographic education of this sort fostered an associational way of thinking in which identifying physical geographic similarities across national boundaries also primed the mind for taking the imaginative leaps necessary for thinking globally.

In National Geographic's new kind of geographic education, readers were not just schooled in the comparative method, but in the proper use of the imagination for civic ends. Geography was not just a series of disparate facts, but a storied account of human struggle and progress. The essential groundwork for *National Geographic*'s early visual strategies was set forth at the Chicago World's Exposition by W. B. Powell, Washington, D.C., superintendent of public schools, and was published in *National Geographic* as "Geographic Instruction in the Public Schools" (January 1894). For Powell, seeing geographically was an acquisitive process that involved meticulous schooling in deliberate acts of repeated looking, naming, and assigning meaning. Powell maintained that the ability to "read" a landscape's geographic features would both improve geographic education and foster the interpretive skills necessary to understand the nation and its unique cultural productions.

Quite literally, for Powell, seeing *is* reading, a process of identifying geographically what the "casual, uncultivated reader does not see, cannot see" by interpreting physical forms. The reading strategy Powell urged, that of "training the imagination" and "comparing the unknown with the known" (147), steeped the child in the comparative method, the cornerstone of positivist science. Powell elaborated a system by which a child's training in visual literacy would first begin with hands-on contact with individual natural phenomena and then gradually come to describe the place of each element in its larger natural and cultural context. Children are "taken to the fields to observe the decay of rocks, the making of soil, the running of streams, the washing of hillsides and the numerous other phenomena which the casual, uncultivated reader does not see, cannot see, but which the student of geography should be trained to see before he is allowed to proceed further in the study" (145). In moving "from the things" themselves "to the symbols of things," geographic education would train young readers to see the world iconographically, to "gain power to see things in symbols" (141). In 1896, *National Geographic* editor W. J. McGee echoed Powell when he defined geography as "the reading of world-history from geographic features."[20] Powell's treatment of geographic landscape as a storied succession of symbols placed *National Geographic* in the forefront of educating for visual literacy, whereby children learned to interpret pictures as symbols of "universal" truths as well as to cultivate aesthetic taste and moral sensibilities.

Beyond simply supplying positivist lessons in the comparative method, then, geographic education for Powell provided equally important aesthetic training that had implications for the formation of a national and cosmopolitan consciousness. Stemming from this process of geographic comparison, still another level of reading was made possible, that of imaginative transport through books. Powell wrote, "If [the child] does not travel from home he takes journeys in imagination, for books are put into his hands for that purpose. He thus, in imagination, visits other cities in distant states" (147). Schooled in the nation's geography, the child advanced to imagining the circumstances of the world's inhabitants. Having grown "strong enough to look upon the world as a whole," wrote Powell, subsequently the "imaginations of the children are called on in picturing the lives and homes of the people of these countries in comparison with their own lives and their own homes" (148–49). Geography served as a stimulus to the imagination, preparing the child for better visualizing the metaphorical world of the written word and the literal world beyond.[21]

Powell's method of reading a landscape symbolically anticipated progressive educational efforts to foster an educated consumption of the nation's burgeoning print culture. The onslaught of images spurred a shift in American educational curricula, which increasingly relied on pictures to cultivate the "imagination and aesthetic sense."[22] *National Geographic's* transformation from specialized journal to popular magazine through a philosophy of vision demonstrates how, in an ever-expanding visual marketplace, art, ethics, and science were not mutually exclusive, but harmonized within a humanistic educational paradigm in which their disciplines communicated through visual symbols.[23]

From an educational perspective, then, the subjects of pictures were believed to function iconically as reflections of spiritual and moral ideals, and students were trained to read pictures iconographically, not just as static symbols, but as stories that prompt moral reflections.[24] It is a "fearful thing," wrote the progressive educator Estelle Hurll in "Picture Study in Education" (1899), "to dissect a picture and be left to gaze upon the dismembered fragments." Great works of art were believed to be permeated by "a vital force." For Hurll and other educators, "the Madonna and Child are not intended as historical figures, but as idealized types," the embodiment of the "universal ideas of motherhood and childhood." Hurll's example of the "Madonna and Child" as models of spiritual and familial fidelity, appropriately, recalls the sacred origins of the word "icon" in religious devotion. Historically, icons, from the Greek *eikon* for "likeness, image, portrait" (*OED*), were objects of meditation and reflection, symbols of religious devotion based on copies of religious figures so true to their originals that they were believed to partake of their spiritual essence. Photographs similarly operate as "secular icons," participating in an existing "pictorial cannon" and acquiring greater cultural resonance with repeated display.[25]

In *National Geographic,* photography operated like a system of secular icons in focusing readerly sentiment and associating the magazine in the popular imagination with both storytelling art and objective science. But while icons are typically static figures whose movement depends on cultural circulation, *National Geographic's* photographs were conceived of as "living pictures" that appealed to both the emotions and the imagination. As Alexander Graham Bell wrote in an April 4, 1904, letter to Grosvenor, "living pictures" had an artistic dynamism that was the crucial element for infusing "LIFE" into the magazine. In photographs and texts, Bell wrote, "[t]here is something . . . that touches the *heart.* An article that appeals to the head alone without any appeal to the emotions is dry and uninteresting to the general reader, however important and valuable it may be." Bell also deemed pictures "dynamical" if they could "arouse in the mind a chain of thoughts" and "stimulate the mind to self activity."[26] This emphasis on photographic distinctiveness and variety helps to explain why the magazine, in its promotional literature, would characterize its images as "so human that they literally 'talk' their own story."[27] *National Geographic* photographs thus participated in the icon's aesthetic qualities while having greater immediacy than traditional icons, which represent ideals based on people from remote antiquity. In other words, *National Geographic's* photographs thwarted photography's long association with mortality, as mementos of deceased loved ones.[28] Its stories were powerful precisely because they offered readers tantalizing glimpses of current events, while also revivifying occurrences from the remote past.

In some ways, the liveliness of the image and the variety of genres— self-consciously artistic photographs, postcards, tourist snapshots, government collections, and stock photographs—made the magazine visually inconsistent. Photographs contributed to the magazine's rise to iconic stature, and certain iconic "types" emerged, such as the bare-breasted woman of color and the male photographer-adventurer. If a landscape or a portrait could render epic story visible, so too could immigrant or otherwise "alien" bodies, which supplied a veritable landscape of signifiers that could be "read," decoded as harbingers of danger or safety. Thus emerged the vogue of criminal and "type" photography, in which eyes, nose, chin, and all manner of physical features were external markers of one's place within an evolutionary hierarchy that could also map internal, moral dispositions and intellectual capabilities. Such visual technologies of containment allowed for the so-called "scientific" sorting of individuals into racial, ethnic, and moral "types."[29]

As has been shown, *National Geographic*'s photographs of racial types are especially vivid examples of visual synecdoche, where representative snapshots of individuals come to represent entire races, professions, or classes of people, often reinforcing existing cultural stereotypes from nineteenth-century evolutionary discourse.[30] A far greater number of *National Geographic* photographs, however, run counter to the dictates of photographic realism based on empirical "types." In keeping with *National Geographic*'s emphasis on geographic diversity, the magazine offered photographic variety rather than uniformity, and this practice invited a more deliberate, and more self-conscious, consumption of its images. There is thus a kind of instability or unpredictability in the *National Geographic* icon, a potential multiplicity of meaning, suggesting that precisely because dynamical pictures were dynamical, they were also resistant to unitary definition.

Progressive education likewise emphasized variety and breadth over disciplinary specialization. As geography became increasingly specialized in universities, in public schools it grew to resemble social studies in its scope and function. Rather than merely list a chronology of landforms, newer geographic textbooks sought to account for a nation's regional and racial differences, commercial resources, and overall progress on the basis of a narrative of environmental determinism. A nation's success or failure to exploit its available resources was deemed the result of either fortuitous or unfortunate geographic circumstance or superior or inferior racial attributes.[31]

The magazine itself reflected this broader progressive educational tendency to yoke geography to current events. Alexander Graham Bell conceived of *National Geographic* as a "text book to illustrate current events" and, particularly, places of "historical" interest to the "public mind."[32] Accordingly, *National Geographic* articles like "Dealings of the United States with the Nations of the World" (April 1904) and "Useful Facts about the Countries of the World" (June 1907) published government statistics showcasing American economic might through its distribution of imports and exports compared to those of other nations.[33] Others highlighted the nation's industrial modernity. "How the World Is Shod" (September 1908) took its readers on a visual tour of the world's footwear, from Breton peasants cobbling shoes outdoors to Asian markets featuring straw-soled shoes, culminating in an overhead shot courtesy of the Regal

Shoe Company of its "more than 4,000 skilled shoe workers" processing "heels and shoes cut out by perfected machinery" (657–59). "Queer Methods of Travel in Curious Corners of the World" (November 1907) took readers on a tour of South America, India, Korea, China, and Japan to survey their "peculiar conditions" for travel, atop burro, camel, and elephant and, finally, on conveyances shouldered by men. In this way, photographs and text visually compared region with region, while carefully fitting each within an environmentally deterministic narrative.[34] In the pages of *National Geographic,* observes Philip Pauly, "America was known for its industry and scenic wonders; Europe and the rest of the world for the integration of people into a 'natural' landscape of rural villages, old towns, and ancient temples. America was the future; the rest of the world, the past."[35] Readers from the early twentieth century to the present have critiqued the magazine's persistence in portraying the West as modern and "the rest" as backward and quaint.

Subsequent cultural appropriations of the magazine's iconic features, for example, draw on its capacity simultaneously to disorient perception and to engage in unintentional self-parody. Unlike natural history museums or geographic textbooks, *National Geographic* greeted viewers with a seemingly random and discordant array of geographic subjects. The same issue in which the laudatory "Useful Facts" (June 1907) appeared also contained the following: "Our Fish Immigrants," by Dr. Hugh M. Smith, deputy commissioner, U.S. Bureau of Fisheries; "The Big Horn Mountains," by N. H. Danton, of the U.S. Geological Survey; "Picturesque Paramaribo: The City That Was Exchanged for New York," by Mrs. Harriet Chalmers Adams; "An Impression of the Guiana Wilderness," by Professor Angelo Heilprin of Yale University; "Fishes That Build Nests and Care for Their Young," by Dr. Theodore Gill; "Notes on the Remarkable Habits of Certain Turtles and Lizards," by H. A. Largelamb, an anagram for Alexander Graham Bell. This discordant array of "geographic" subjects is at odds with the conventions of carefully orchestrated museum curation. Yet geographic discord produced a consistency all its own, whose repetition decade after decade approached self-parody. The fortuitous pun of Dr. Theodore "Gill" writing on fishes, for instance, anticipates spoofs of *National Geographic* that would appear decades later. One can also take pleasure in how the repetition of certain motifs within titles over several decades lends itself to parody, as in "Vienna: A Capital without a Nation" (January 1923); "Hungary, A Kingdom without a King" (June 1932); and "Bulgaria, Farm Land without a Farmhouse" (August 1932). This work's concluding chapter addresses how *National Geographic*'s earnest appeal to its readers' curiosity became, in later years, the object of cultural ridicule.

Magazines and the Masses: *National Geographic* and Its Peers

If photographic variety to a degree undermined *National Geographic*'s visual narrative coherence, the magazine's physical form reinforced the high-toned cultural associations of "epic story." Unless an issue is dedicated to a specific topic, magazines—by the nature of their genre—are composed of disparate and disconnected content. More episodic than epic, magazines, unlike novels, are designed for sporadic reading and easy digestion. They are taken up from the coffee table during transitory moments of leisure and just as quickly discarded. *National Geographic*, however, was not a typical magazine. Its unique status as a physical object may offer one way to account for the critical attention it has received as well as the iconic stature it achieved just after the First World War. Unlike other illustrated monthlies, *National Geographic*'s articles were lengthy (a frequent subject of reader complaint), intended not for quick perusal but for extended study and reflection. *National Geographic*'s distinctive physical appearance, the fact that it could literally and not just figuratively stand on its own, like a book, reinforced its reputation as a repository of human knowledge, an object worthy of display in libraries, and invited readers to preserve old issues for later reference rather than throw them away. The magazine was thus "epic" in scope. As has been remarked of the epic genre, it is the "monumentalization of the ruling authority, the highborn singing their own achievements to themselves."[36] By placing the magazine within public view, families could in some ways be seen to identify with the "highborn" cultural and scientific "achievements" the magazine represented. In displaying the magazine, families were literally exhibiting their own cultured-ness, as well as the culture of the "exotic" peoples displayed in its pages.

As a result of its formidable combination of science and aesthetics, *National Geographic* far surpassed the typical four-year lifespan of magazines published between 1865 and 1918.[37] Initially, however, its dry professional content and steep price, at fifty cents a copy, placed it out of the intellectual and financial range of most American households. In this regard, *National Geographic* resembled most other magazines in the 1880s, whose readership, according to the magazine historian Frank Luther Mott, was predominantly "aristocratic." In these years, Mott notes, magazine reading "was leisurely in habit, literary in tone, retrospective rather than timely, and friendly to the interests of the upper classes."[38] Within a decade, however, world events and technological advancements would dramatically alter the scope of magazines and expand their readership. The Spanish-American War launched the United States into world prominence, the advent of halftone photoengraving and a dramatic drop in the typical price of magazines from thirty-five cents to ten and fifteen cents, transformed the landscape of American magazines and their readership. In an age of emerging internationalization, magazines were not just a luxury for the wealthy, but a vital source of news and information for all classes of Americans in a rapidly changing world.

Now in direct competition with newspapers, magazines updated their contents from culture and the arts to timely subjects and pragmatic concerns. While the prices of *Century* and *Harper's* were kept at thirty-five cents in order to retain the magazines' air of exclusivity, the onslaught of ten-cent monthlies like *Ladies' Home Journal, McClure's*, and *Cosmopolitan* pressured the elite magazines to lower their prices. In 1899, *Harper's* dropped its issue price to twenty-five cents, like *Scribner's* and *Munsey's*.[39] That same year, *National Geographic* halved its price from fifty cents to twenty-five cents. This price differential is crucial to understanding *National Geographic*'s position as somewhat more modest than other high-class monthlies, but nonetheless a cut above lowbrow dime magazines. Faced with dwindling membership, in January 1896 magazine editor John Hyde repackaged *National Geographic* as an "Illustrated Monthly." The inaugural issue was both national and global in scope, featuring articles titled "Russia in Europe," "The Arctic Cruise of the U.S. Revenue Cutter, 'Bear,'" and "The Scope and Value of Arctic Exploration." Both its reduced price and enhanced visual appeal made the magazine more accessible to a growing middle-class readership that identified with sophisticated cultural values.

The magazine owed its dramatic expansion following 1896 not just to its coverage of the nation's territorial acquisitions stemming from the 1898 Spanish-American War, but to NGS membership, which endowed it with a cultural cachet unlike any other magazine of the period. Much of the credit for this strategy of amassing members rather than mere subscribers is owed to Bell, who reluctantly assumed the Society's presidency in 1897 after the death of his father-in-law, Gardiner Greene Hubbard. Bell shared Hubbard's vision for popularizing geography. Accordingly, he sought to bolster revenues by expanding the magazine's membership to include those he considered "ordinary" Americans.[40] To attract broader audiences, he filled the magazine with articles on timely subjects of national and world geographic import. In 1898, Bell hired the young Gilbert H. Grosvenor as assistant editor and charged him with the task of soliciting advertising and expanding the magazine's membership.

What constituted *National Geographic*'s appeal, what set it apart from its competitor magazines, and what became the chief means by which it generated cultural recognition and prominence, was the concept of "membership" in the NGS. Especially in the magazine's formative decades, readership was nearly synonymous with membership in the NGS. New NGS members were nominated by other members and then "elected" to membership. A 1905 letter congratulating nominees listed such NGS members as the U.S. president, Supreme Court justices, senators and congressmen, as well as various statesmen. The muckraking journalist Ida Tarbell, Harvard president Charles W. Norton, and the psychologist G. Stanley Hall, all leaders in progressive educational reform, were among those on the membership roster.[41] Crucially, however, the illustriousness of the initial membership pool was designed to lure new members rather than to communicate exclusivity. As Bell wrote in a July 13, 1899, letter to Grosvenor, "pressure must be brought to bear so that it shall always be easy for a member to nominate another."[42] Membership provided the psychological appeal of exclusivity, yet without putting people off and without inhibiting growth. For three dollars a year, membership conferred special privileges, including a certificate, invitations to lectures, and a monthly issue of *National Geographic.* For many of its member-readers, *National Geographic* democratized knowledge previously confined to the arid atmosphere of university lecture halls and offered a vision of the world hitherto available only to the most affluent and well-traveled cosmopolite. Membership in the NGS came to connote both national belonging and a sophisticated, cosmopolitan view of the world.

By 1903, when Grosvenor became *National Geographic* editor-in-chief, Bell had identified a magazine that would serve as its model: "a magazine like the *Century,* of popular interest and yet scientifically reliable as a source of geographic information," he wrote Grosvenor. "Our efforts, therefore, should be to enlarge the magazine, have it bright and interesting, with a multitude of good illustrations and maps."[43] In the 1880s, the *Century* "epitomized secular high culture," publishing essays and criticism, fiction and poetry by the "nation's leading authors," including works by such luminaries as William Dean Howells, Mark Twain, and Henry James. In the early 1900s, *Harper's, Century,* and *Atlantic Monthly* formed a triumvirate of "upper-class" magazines whose higher price and more elevated content, compared to the cheap ten-cent monthlies like *Mc-Clure's* and *Munsey's*, secured a predominantly middle-class readership, an emerging "professional managerial class."[44] The heightened interest in politics and world affairs of the *Century* in the 1890s was the "current events" format Bell envisioned for *National Geographic* in his 1903 letter to Grosvenor.

By 1912, *National Geographic* headed the list of "the best" American magazines and was hailed as a refreshing alternative to popular magazines "with their pictures of actresses, their terrible drawing by 'artists,' and their love stories."[45] Educators, in particular, upheld *National Geographic* as "the better sort" of magazine around which lesson plans could be designed that would expose students to edifying and culturally enriching reading as an antidote to mass culture. For progressive educators, the ability to read both popular and highbrow literature, to develop a more catholic taste or sensibility, represented an important cosmopolitan value. To narrate the national and international epic, Bell and Grosvenor had to create a magazine that would rise above the period's proliferating visual ephemera, the unedifying mass production of photographs and cheap illustrated magazines.

Despite *National Geographic's* embeddedness in the era's print culture, Society founders sought to create a new aesthetic object, one of enduring value that in time would stand for the institution itself. To do so, they had to eschew the culture of the "throwaway" image. In February 1910, the magazine's cover appeared for the first time framed by the familiar yellow border with acorns and oak leaves. The following year, *National Geographic* rolled out the official slogan in its advertising pages: "Mention the *Geographic*—it identifies you." With its artistic illustrations and accounts of the latest scientific expeditions, the magazine appealed to the eye as classic and to the intellect as modern. Showcasing this modernity just before the First World War, *National Geographic* highlighted the technological efficiency of its new headquarters in the center of the nation's capital; smiling schoolchildren, seated in desks, hold issues of *National Geographic* (fig. 4).[46] As a magazine received by NGS members who shared its mission, *National Geographic* signified economic prosperity and the republican virtues of enlightenment and civic responsibility. It was both cosmopolitan and middle American, mainstream and exclusive, a product of both Progressive Era and Victorian values. "Every member of my family, except the baby in the cradle, takes an interest in the Magazine

Fig. 4 "Sight-Seeing in School." (Normal School St. Cloud, Minnesota/National Geographic Image Collection)

and is benefited by it," wrote the Reverend J. W. Schoech to the NGS in 1914.[47] The magazine's timeless beauty and its technological modernism together forwarded its democratic goal of educating the nation's masses through pictures.

The idea of educating young readers to be more discriminating and conscientious consumers of mass culture began to play a significant role in progressive education as early as the 1890s. Before the First World War, educators had already begun incorporating magazine study into middle and high school English curricula in order to "arouse the interest" in the reading of "the best magazines" and thereby instill a lifelong "love of reading." In a 1913 paper presented to the National Council of Teachers of English annual meeting in Philadelphia, Sarah E. Simons lamented that the "modern magazine" dominated "the literary life of the average American." While magazines were credited with democratizing the reading of literature and expanding the reading public, rapid perusal of short articles seemed to pose a threat to the sustained effort and "quiet concentration" required by literary masterpieces. Overall, the rise of the magazine, which "adapts itself to the rush and hurry of American life," was seen by many to portend the demise of Arnoldian cultural values, prompting Simons and others to ask, "Are we, indeed, already missing something of sweetness and light in our literature because of constant catering to the prevailing magazine taste of the reading public?"[48]

By 1917, the belief that "outside-reading habits may have much greater educational significance" than "any or all of the specific textbook lessons assigned in school can possibly have" inspired educators to have units on "current events."[49] The war in Europe had catalyzed a desire to ensure that students were staying abreast of contemporary issues. J. O. Engleman, the superintendent of schools for Decatur, Illinois, maintained:

> We are wholly justified, I think, in giving the place we give to Greek and Roman, mediaeval, modern European, and early American history, but to do this and to permit students to close their eyes to history in the making, when Congress is in session, when most of Europe is at war and the rest of it is compelled to preserve an armed neutrality, when treaties are broken, and other earlier treaties and alliances first written in ink are being written anew in blood, when ships are being sunk daily, when waters troubled in 490 B.C. and in 1453 A.D. are again disturbed, when even the United States is feeling the effects of the war in countless ways, is to miss one of our greatest opportunities to vitalize both modern and mediaeval history.

The "epic story" of the redrawing of geopolitical boundaries occasioned by the First World War thus invigorated educators' desire to acquaint students with "the character of different magazines" in order to have them graduate with "a reading habit and a discriminating taste that ought to persist." As a result of the expanded availability of mass-market magazines, educators published formal and informal surveys of students' preferred outside reading, including magazines and popular fiction. With its emphasis on timeliness, *National Geographic* was precisely the sort of magazine to which teachers and students turned for knowledge about current events.[50]

In 1915, Grosvenor instituted seven editorial principles that contributed to the magazine's "quality" status, while further complicating how the public perceived it. Combining aesthetic sensibility with an emphasis on journalistic objectivity, he refused to publish anything he deemed of "a trivial character" or with "partisan or controversial" content. Instead, the magazine would publish only items of a "kindly nature" and nothing "unpleasant or unduly critical." For Grosvenor, each issue of *National*

Geographic should be an aesthetic object that would retain "permanent value" at least "five or ten years after publication." Its photographs had to blend science and aesthetics by being both "instructive" and "artistic."[51] Grosvenor's aspirations for the magazine's timeless beauty inevitably conflicted with—and ultimately superseded—Bell's earlier vision for the magazine as an "interpreter to the public of the work of the Government Departments." Despite his emphasis on artistic value, however, Grosvenor wanted to retain the magazine's scientific authority and historical currency. He wrote, "Whenever any part of the world becomes prominent in public interest, by reason of war, earthquake, volcanic eruption, etc., the members of the NGS have come to know that in the next issue of their Magazine they will obtain the latest geographic, historical, and economic information about that region, presented in an interesting and absolutely non-partisan manner."[52]

That the *National Geographic*'s announced goals amply satisfied the needs and values of its readers is evidenced by the magazine's remarkable circulation and membership statistics. It is important here to distinguish between membership, which comprises subscribers, and circulation, which is more extensive and indicates overall visibility, as magazines are privately shared and distributed among friends and families or publicly displayed in waiting rooms, schools, and libraries. In 1885, only four monthlies had subscriberships of 100,000 or more. By 1905, however, twenty such magazines carried a combined subscribership of over 500,000.[53] In 1904, NGS membership numbered 2,800; by 1914, that number had risen to 250,000. Membership then doubled by 1916, soaring to 500,000, and by 1920, the NGS's membership of 713,312 equaled the total combined subscription rate of its rivals: *Atlantic Monthly, Century, Harper's, Outlook, Review of Reviews, Scribner's,* and *World's Work.*[54] A relative latecomer compared to *Ladies' Home Journal,* whose subscription rate topped 1 million by 1903, and *Cosmopolitan,* whose subscribership was over 1 million by 1918, *National Geographic* did not surpass 1 million in member-subscribers until 1925. In 1926, *Library Journal* ranked *National Geographic* among the nation's top-five magazines, including *American Magazine, Saturday Evening Post, Literary Digest,* and *Cosmopolitan.* Even then, it lagged behind *Saturday Evening Post,* whose subscribership had already topped 2 million by 1918. *National Geographic* would not achieve this lofty milestone until 1954, at which point its supremacy as the nation's foremost purveyor of photographic images was superseded by *Life* magazine, whose subscriptions in 1956 peaked at 5.8 million.[55] Despite the magazine's status as a late bloomer, *National Geographic*'s debut as an illustrated monthly in 1896 made possible a dramatic expansion of its readership from specialists and government bureaucrats, to middle- and lower-income readers.

The magazine's policy of nonpartisanship, together with editorial tenets in which romantic beauty and scientific truth coexisted, allowed the magazine to combine professional and amateur, "high" and "low" culture with ease, paving the way for its ready acceptance as an American cultural icon. Even so, the irreconcilable conflicts between artistic permanence, political nonpartisanship, and geographic timeliness produced inevitable tensions and inconsistencies within the magazine. These tensions were not, fortunately, lost on contemporary readers, who had been trained to read magazines with critical care.

National Geographic's Member-Readers

Progressive geographic and pictorial education, as argued above, trained early-twentieth-century Americans in the interpretation of landscapes and images. In so doing, they contributed to a public understanding of the interdependence, not the incompatibility, of the visual domains of science and art. Photography's unique history as a medium for both private and public consumption, both middle-class leisure and visual mass culture, meant that images could promote personal identification and emotional response while didactically reinforcing cultural norms. Thus we find *National Geographic* readers praising the magazine's photographs for both their artistry and their scientific authenticity. In their words, *National Geographic* satisfied "an itch in society" for knowledge through "pictures, lectures and reading" while providing a "regular thrill of adventure."[56] But if the founders themselves revealed an ambivalence about narrating a national epic, so too did the magazine's readers express an ambivalence about consuming one, in letters that poured in by the thousands per day in the early 1900s, when *National Geographic* first began preserving them for editorial use. While a laudatory handful eventually found publication in the NGS's institutional histories, a far greater number were unpublished. These unpublished letters, both adulatory and critical, are those I draw upon here and throughout the book to establish a candid glimpse of the magazine from the perspective of its earliest readers—and to demonstrate how its representational strategies existed in a complex give-and-take with public attitudes.

As we have seen, membership was by far *National Geographic*'s greatest asset and what most distinguished it from its rivals, assuring its survival amid cutthroat competition. The magazine's visual iconography and scientific mission generated the aura of sophisticated exclusivity, but Bell and Grosvenor both desired to attract what they considered "ordinary" Americans. As Grosvenor would write in 1935, "The lonely forest ranger, the clerk tied to his desk, the plumber, the teacher, the eight-year-old boy, and the octogenarian, cannot, like a Carnegie or a Rockefeller, send out their own expeditions, but they do enjoy having a part in supporting explorations conducted by their own Society and reading the first-hand accounts in their own magazine." After serving four decades as NGS president and editor of *National Geographic,* Grosvenor observed, "I would rather get another barber or bricklayer for a member than a college professor." The NGS promoted the democratic breadth of its readership, listing among its members two cigar makers, one poet, seventy-one ranchers, four writers, and thirty-five photographers. Teachers (637), lawyers (181), housewives (164), and mechanics (106) made stronger showings.[57]

Who were *National Geographic's* readers? Despite its overt appeal to "ordinary" citizens, the magazine's advertising materials suggest that, in addition to "ordinary" people, it attracted a more affluent and upwardly mobile population. As early as 1919, *National Geographic* advertising circulars promoted the magazine's access to "homes of unusual intelligence and income." By 1924, it claimed a readership in which 65 percent were above average in annual earnings. Professionals accounted for 43 percent of its membership, followed by skilled laborers and employees in business or industry. The remaining farmers, educators, housewives, and students accounted for 23 percent of the magazine's readership. Even in the depths of economic depression, *National Geographic* promoted itself as the "Open Door" to "the million or more families whom good fortune, intelligence and energy have put at the top." By 1955, this readership was nearly 80 percent male and 77 percent married, with a median age of forty-one years. More than half were employed in business. Of its readers twenty-five years old and younger, 53 percent were male and nearly 30 percent were female.[58] A 1953 distribution analysis by geographic and political divisions identifies the magazine's strongest circulation with the predominantly white portions of the globe, in western European and Anglophone nations.[59]

While statistics do not lie, they tell only a partial story. Letters from readers indicate that *National Geographic's* readership included many immigrants and people of color, even as its promotional materials imagined a homogeneous readership of "like-minded" people. Moreover, membership in the magazine made its readers unusually responsive to its failure to express their cultural and moral ideals. In a 1946 letter to a disgruntled reader, Grosvenor bragged that the magazine had a 96 percent renewal rate.[60] This persuasive-sounding index of loyalty, however, obscures the fact that readers' letters indicate declining satisfaction with the magazine's content from the 1930s onward. And indeed, the magazine's readership in the 1940s and 1950s did not keep pace with the membership boom that occurred between 1910 and 1929.

The most adulatory letters appear between 1915 and 1926, when the magazine cleared 1 million member-readers, the period I consider the high-water mark in *National Geographic*'s romance adventure. The magazine suffered a wave of membership cancellations in response to its anti-German sentiment during the First World War and then, seemingly paradoxically, its sympathetic treatment of fascist nations in the 1930s. Between 1915 and 1920, growth flagged as the result of economic downturn, rising dues, and reader dissatisfaction with the magazine's war coverage.[61]

Yet despite its occasional departure from editorial "kindliness" and nonpartisanship, *National Geographic*'s iconic visibility and appeal did not diminish in the twentieth century's first three decades. These were the years in which *National Geographic* published its popular adventure articles on the giant sequoias, Theodore Roosevelt's African safaris, and romantic journeys by sea and land.[62] Many of these partake of that variety of nineteenth-century armchair ethnography George Stocking has playfully termed the "Amongthas."[63] Articles titled "Among the Cannibals of Belgian Kongo" (November 1910), "Life among the People of Eastern Tibet" (September 1921), and "Among the Hill Tribes of Burma—An Ethnological Thicket" (March 1922), among others, offer vivid examples of a *National Geographic* genre that persisted well into the 1950s.

In the first decade following *National Geographic*'s self-reinvention as a magazine for the masses, readers associated membership with the democratic values of inclusiveness. Writing in 1920 just after the magazine raised its membership dues, a reader praised NGS membership as "distinctly American and democratic" because the "ordinary man of the masses could be, and remain, a member." Others identified with the exclusivity of membership, finding it more genteel than "the promiscuous solicitation of subscriptions." For some readers, however, membership was not exclusive enough. "If the National Geographic Society represents anything worth mentioning," complained one reader, "the fact that persons can become members by having the magazine 'wished' on them for a Christmas present has made me feel that it is scarcely an organization that I care to belong to."[64]

Nor did all readers approve of the Society's practice of seeking members by nomination. In 1915, a reader from California found the practice distasteful and fundamentally antidemocratic. "Why do you not quit taking *only* 'distinguished' members and launch an *aggressive campaign* to do the most good for the greatest number of American citizens, most of whom are your peers if they are not ex-presidents," he complained. "Do you know, your nomination scheme strikes me all wrong, and rubs me the wrong way. However, I suppose you run your paper with the idea—every man to his own nation! Not much nation." But only a handful chafed at the tone of exclusivity. Other readers were so honored to be nominated that they often mentioned the nominating member by name. A man from Scotland wrote, "I am grateful to Mrs. Mather, who recommended me as a member, and to your Society for accepting my nomination." He continued, "I shall do anything I can to further the interests of the Society in increasing its membership, and thereby taking a small part in helping the objects of the Society," and signed himself, "Yours Faithfully, George M. Jenkins."[65] Not until the 1930s did readers begin to consider membership a commercial scam. Although Ishbel Ross's 1938 *Scribner's* article "Geography, Inc." publicly exposed the magazine's use of membership as a clever ruse to secure subscribers, readers well into the 1950s continued to view membership as an honor.

Membership in the NGS seemed both to confirm one's citizenship and to communicate cosmopolitan belonging in a diverse national family. The metaphor of "family" held additional resonance for the magazine, not just because it was produced for families by the Bell-Grosvenor family, but because the single-family home is where the magazine achieved its greatest visibility. As a 1920 advertising circular noted, the family home was a primary site for attracting new NGS members. It detailed the magazine's circulation from "old subscriber homes into new homes and then among their friends too." Tellingly, the circular refers to *National Geographic* readers as "subscribers" rather than "members," a revealing admission of the philosophical divide between the image projected and its economic bottom line. A 1925 circular lauded *National Geographic*'s circulation of 1 million. "Read by the Men, the Women, the Children of the Solid Families who call it 'Our Magazine, the *Geographic*,'" *National Geographic*, it claimed, commanded "steady, year-after-year growth without use of can-vassers, premiums or club offers." A 1935 circular boasted of homeowner-ship as the basis of the magazine's solid membership, reporting that "15 out of every 100 *National Geographic* families will build or buy homes averaging 7.1 rooms each," underscoring the relative affluence of the mag-azine's "first million" readers.[66]

After 1926, and particularly throughout the 1930s, 1940s, and into the 1950s, readers' letters reveal a marked decline in satisfaction with the magazine. Bored by articles on birds and natural history, they urged a return to the magazine's golden years of romance adventure. Still others were tired of what they perceived as the magazine's persistent focus on the exotic, notably Africa and the Orient. Nonetheless, a good number of members both at home and abroad, many identifying themselves as sec-ond-generation readers, continued to take pride in their membership. By and large, *National Geographic*'s member-readers saw their membership status as a marker of democratic civic values. Even more importantly, as those who saw themselves engaged in a shared endeavor of public impor-tance, they also felt free to critique and challenge the magazine's represen-tational strategies and its political allegiances. Readers' letters disclose a cultural milieu in which dissent played as significant a role in the maga-zine's livelihood as public consent.

Rereading *National Geographic:* Varieties of Spectatorship and the Rituals of Readership

An examination of the rituals of consumption—when and how the maga-zine was read and displayed in the home—that emerged among its read-ership in its early years reveals just how closely the NGS was allied in readers' minds with *National Geographic* as an aesthetic object. These rituals tended to reflect the magazine's status as "art." *National Geographic* readers attributed its value to the aesthetic quality of its photographs, ac-cording the magazine a place of honor in their households. It was cor-respondingly hoarded, preserved, and bound for posterity. As early as 1914, *National Geographic* photography had become synonymous in read-ers' minds with the aesthetic value of the magazine: "the most beauti-ful photographic art production I have had the pleasure of viewing." "I know of no other magazine published that I would regard worth preserv-ing," wrote another reader that same year. By the 1920s, readers contin-ued to lavish praise upon the magazine as "a real marvel in literature and art." Another ranked *National Geographic* among Western culture's great literary achievements, writing, "I value the magazine as much as some of the classics I have."[67] Clearly, the magazine prompted an aesthetic response from its readers by reproducing iconography recognized as having high-cultural import. While there might be tensions between scientific and aesthetic uses of pictures, for *National Geographic*'s earliest readers there was apparently no conflict.

These letters demonstrate a number of persistent imaginative appropriations of the magazine: as a geographic textbook and guidebook, providing visual authentication for that which was previously only known through texts; as a literary "classic" on par with the Bible; as an object of culture worthy of display alongside family photograph albums; as a valuable collectible; and, most important, as vicarious travel, allowing readers of modest economic means more affordable access to imaginative transport. Each of these uses indicates how the magazine's unique blend of scientific authority and aesthetic beauty contributed to its iconic stature; I consider the following four throughout the book:

Textbook and Guidebook ▪ Teachers were among the first readers to praise *National Geographic* as a valuable resource for classroom use. Letters from educators describing the magazine as, for instance, "the most interesting and most read periodical on the reading table in my school room" are representative of the bulk of correspondence the NGS received from teachers.[68] A common practice among educators was cutting up *National Geographic* to construct pictorial teaching aids. The Rev. R. Cahill of St. Ann's School in Le Sueur, Minnesota, requested duplicates of a 1915 issue containing hand-tinted autochromes: "We set up these colored pages in our school especially for the Junior Grades. We paste them on calico and put them in cases on rollers like maps." In this way, the magazine provided a visual apprenticeship in acquiring knowledge of the nation's and world's biodiversity. As a naturalist's guide, *National Geographic*'s articles on wild birds and regional plants served the purposes of visual authentication. Readers seek in the world what they found in *National Geographic*'s pages. A reader from Columbus, Ohio, gave copies to a schoolteacher and described how "the nature copies are taken with the pupils to the fields and the woods and are put to practical use."[69] The magazine alternatively served as a tourist's handbook, indicating which local landmarks, monuments, and cultural events were worthy of interest and providing visual witness to cultural differences. Anticipating *National Geographic*'s "Pictorial Geography" educational initiative in 1919 (see chapter 3), educators and lay readers reveal how the magazine in official and unofficial ways fostered a cosmopolitan receptiveness to cultural variety and global complex connectivity.

Display ▪ Where readers chose to display *National Geographic* reveals much about the elaborate cultural meanings with which the magazine had been invested. By the First World War, *National Geographic* had become a "secular icon," rivaling the revered place of the family Bible and the photograph album in American households. In 1917, Benjamin R. Landis declared, "I think it is the greatest book I ever got my fingers on except the Great Book, the Bible." Indeed, readers repeatedly compared *National Geographic* to the Bible, reinforcing its resonance with the sacred origins of the word "icon."[70] Yet readers' public display of the magazine, and their elevation of the *Geographic* to near-equivalence to the Bible, built upon earlier, nineteenth-century practices of photographic display in family albums. In the nineteenth century, photograph albums took over the traditional genealogical function of the family Bible, supplying a photographic narrative of descent that marked a shift from oral to textual means of recording ancestry. Like the family Bible, "albums occupied a relatively public place in the home, on the center table of the parlor, where visitors would be received."[71] Having an honored place among family photographs, *National Geographic* symbolized both personal and public memory. Moreover, its near-sacred status alongside the family Bible allowed it to straddle the domains of provincial and cosmopolitan feeling by calling forth local attachments to church and family and the impersonal aspects of a "global" community.

Collecting ▪ Perhaps the most persuasive evidence for the *National Geographic*'s cultural and artistic authority is its readers' reluctance to throw them away. Reading *National Geographic* was an investment of time more than of money, although the magazine came to possess a tangible currency of its own. On July 8, 1918, O. R. Goldman of Alabama wrote, "I value my Geographic more than money." Following the Great Depression, the magazine had become a collector's item in its own right, one that operated as both aesthetic object and financial investment. A reader from South Africa despaired at having discovered the magazine belatedly: "I guard my copies jealously and have them bound in the best covers obtainable and my only regret is that I did not become aware of the Magazine's existence until two years ago. . . . I never see them for sale in secondhand book shops, which itself is a commentary on the value placed by your subscribers on their copies."[72] In 1935, Edwin C. Buxbaum published a slender little guidebook titled *Collector's Guide to "The National Geographic*

Magazine" in which he declared purchasing *National Geographic*s "far safer" than "buying stocks and bonds," adding that "no depression can make them worthless." At that time a complete set of *Geographic*s sold for from $1,200 to $1,500. Perfectly articulating *National Geographic*'s blend of realism and romance as the cornerstone of its success, he declared it a "veritable encyclopedia of travel, of foreign custom and dress, of strange and exotic people, manners and things different from the humdrum of our daily lives," as well as a "real referencework [*sic*] for the student."[73] The *National Geographic*'s public respectability and scientific authority made possible its literal and figurative transformation into cultural currency. Like any other collectible, the more it was hoarded and preserved, the more it acquired an aura and a mystique.

Vicarious Travel ▪ By far the greatest number of commendations from readers had to do with the magazine's capacity for democratizing travel. By the 1920s, a consensus was building among readers in which *National Geographic* photographs were the "best possible substitute" for travel. As a reader from Canada noted: "Your splendid illustrations and graphic descriptions bring before us parts of the world very little known, if known at all, by the most of us. And also the inhabitants of those parts, their physical features, primitive customs, ignorance and superstition, so clearly put before us that it is second only to a visit in person to those places." In a similar spirit, a reader from Australia wrote: "I find it so stimulating to the imagination that I seem to have actually visited most of the places described and pictured. I know them, far more intimately, probably, than if I had been there in person." The magazine's photographs and articles succeeded in establishing feelings of vicarious participation, thus contributing to its readers' conceptual mobility, and facilitating to a large degree an interest in cultural difference, despite limitations to experiencing it firsthand.[74] Readers' letters attest to the "dynamical" quality of *National Geographic*'s photographs as well as to how the "living picture" gave readers who otherwise could not afford travel the feeling of having been there. After reading a November 1930 article, "This Giant That Is New York," a man from California mused, "[I] have never been to New York, nor very far inland from the Pacific Ocean, yet after looking at the pictures and reading the statements as set down by this author I feel that I know as much, or more, at this moment about New York City than my wife does, who has lived there." Other readers found the mental images created by the text inspiration for their own literary efforts. "While reading your delightful contribution to this month's issue," wrote a young woman from

New Orleans, "I was interested in your word-painting beginning, 'Moving vans bumping,' out of which I have made the enclosed verses, using your own words and swinging rhythm." For each of these readers, visual experience, by simulating international travel, enabled the imaginative transport that presages global complex connectivity. By democratizing travel, and thus transforming the foreign into the familiar, *National Geographic* "word-paintings" evoked in readers' minds visual images that inspired new ways of perceiving themselves in relation to the larger world. Despite its overt embrace of national interests, the magazine's international content also promoted, intentionally or otherwise, an "openness" toward the world that is the essence of cosmopolitanism.[75]

Pictorial education in public schools and visual training in the magazine's institutional aesthetic served as much to create a critical readership as they did to encourage an acceptance of images as moral truths. Although early twentieth-century readers did indeed experience *National Geographic* photographs in an immediate way, their reactions to photographs were neither uniform nor predictable. Thanks to American spectators' early training in the aesthetic appreciation of images, photographs were received as more than a straightforward transcription of the real world.

Consequently, the magazine's broad appeal led to divergent critical responses among readers, precisely because they had been educated to read images and texts with considerable care. Given the magazine's classical aesthetic, a consistent ritual among readers was to examine the magazine with the thoroughness of attention given to contemplating a work of art—unlike popular entertainment, which was merely "consumed" as distraction. As a California reader remarked, "I never try to read it until I really feel like it as I want to enjoy every line." The magazine's photographs invited frequent perusal, and its lengthy articles necessitated extended periods of leisure for contemplation; read with devoted attention, the magazine fulfilled the aesthetic function of art in its demand for "sustaining engagement over repeated encounters."[76] Art commands active seeing, rather than passive consumption, and provides precisely the training necessary for an active and critical readership.

This attentiveness to textual and visual detail alike, however, did not always foster readers' willing belief in the authority of the image or of the magazine. For the earliest readers of *National Geographic* in its popular form, this awareness of pictures as aesthetic objects constructed for the purpose of communicating ideas established a means not just for appreciating the image, but for critical debate about the competing meanings the image communicated. Although Powell's methodology for identifying direct correspondences between the geographic elements in a landscape and their symbols cultivated an attitude of transparency, such an attitude was inconsistently reflected among *National Geographic* readers themselves.

National Geographic's violation of its editorial nonpartisanship during the First World War, for instance, heightened readers' uncertainty about the photograph's status as an authoritative source of knowledge. Puzzled by the caption to a photograph of a World War I plane flying over Jerusalem in a January 1918 issue ("No bombs were dropped by this airman in his flight over the holy city of Jerusalem while it was still in the hands of the Turks"), an Australian reader could not understand how, during wartime, the photographic firm Underwood and Underwood could procure such a photograph. The reader went on to point out an even more glaring discrepancy: "Neither could I understand why, although the reflection of the buildings could be seen in the pool of water that of the aeroplane did not show, although it appeared to be flying very low. My speculations were set at rest however, by turning to the January 1918, number of the American *Review of Reviews*. In that number, on page 49, is shown the identical photograph appearing in your magazine, but without the aeroplane [*sic*]. I experienced a feeling of great disappointment to think that the magazine which I had looked upon as an educational benefactor, could have been guilty of publishing a 'faked' photograph."[77]

National Geographic's occasional failure to adhere to its editorial standards was not lost on its readers, and its authority as a reliable source of global knowledge was subtly undermined as a result. As well as demonstrating an alertness to the photograph as a narrative document, intended not just to illustrate text but to convey an idea or story, readers often interpreted these images in ways radically different from the "reading" intended by the caption. They expressed skepticism about the "truth" that the photograph (and the magazine) was apparently meant to communicate, either because the image had already been used elsewhere or because of inaccuracies in the caption. They expressed dissatisfaction when captions were misleading, inaccurate, or utterly failed to account for the content of the photograph. Finally, they showed an awareness of when the NGS editorial claim to "kindly" nonpartisanship was at odds with articles that revealed a clear political agenda.

From its inception, *National Geographic* was conceived as having a crucial role to play in shaping the nation's visual imagination, but a meticulous apprenticeship in reading images as constructed narratives could also work against the idea of the photograph as a consistently reliable document of truth. Far from being anesthetized by beautiful photographs, readers criticized the sometimes glib tone of *National Geographic* articles and photographic captioning. A reader in 1914 complained that the legend below "some of the admirable photographs in the *National Geographic* does not seem to further explain the photograph, and sometimes seems to be quite foreign to it." The charge that readers had grown tired of the "flippant, cheap, and yellow-journal style of some of the captions under the pictures" was thus well earned.[78]

National Geographic also received frequent complaints about photographs that had been recycled, either from other magazines or within the same article. In "Our Foreign-Born Citizens" (February 1917), a photograph titled "Wallachian Children from Austria" and another photograph depicting the same children with an entirely different title, "A Russian Mother and Her Flock," was enough to make Elizabeth Sutton Brown of Denver, Colorado, remark, "I could not finish that article with quite the confidence that I have always before had in the *National Geographic*, just on account of that one inconsistency!"[79] Letters like these were not anomalous. Readers who had firsthand knowledge of places or events depicted in photographs frequently complained of mistakes, as was the case with a Japanese student studying business at Columbia University, who noted that the photographs in an article on Korea in the October 1924 issue were in fact taken in China. The September 1925 issue received a volley of letters reporting that the Chinese flag appeared upside down in a photograph.[80] Numerous readers' letters reported this error, testifying to the thoroughness, even caution, with which *National Geographic* photographs were read.

It follows that *National Geographic* readers' emerging cosmopolitan sensibilities would conflict with and perhaps even confound national identification. This conflict between nationalism and cosmopolitanism came to the fore during the First World War, when German Americans criticized the magazine for portraying the Germans as a race of "Huns," the subject of chapter 4. The American nation forming in the pages of *National Geographic* embodied tensions between its cosmopolitan citizens and an emerging national identity. The crucial components of *National*

Geographic's iconicity—its photographs of racial and cultural difference— promoted cosmopolitan sympathies in addition to national pride. Such criticisms persisted, with varying frequency.

Despite the magazine's flaws and inconsistencies, readers continued to take pride in their membership and felt a responsibility to extend the *Geographic* family by nominating additional members. Although the magazine's revenues by 1925 were far beyond what one would expect of a "nonprofit" educational institution, *National Geographic* published comparatively fewer ads than other popular monthlies.[81] That, combined with its scientific content and educational mission, helped protect the magazine against charges of commercialism—a perception, however, that readers increasingly expressed by the late 1920s and that by the 1930s no longer really held.[82] Still, the earnestness with which most early *National Geographic* readers took the magazine as a reliable source of knowledge about the world was matched by their conviction that the magazine could promote lasting peace within a larger international community.

While the NGS trained its readers to view images as realistic stories, the record shows that it also invited challenges to its own interpretations of its photographs. As well as undermining the supposed "realism" with which photography in its early years has been associated, readers' letters reveal that they literally "read" *National Geographic* photographs, studying them as carefully as if they were the printed word. Such a response accords with Neil Harris's account of the period's anxiety about the proliferation of illustrations and images in general, a phenomenon that contributed to a sense of human inefficacy, falling literary standards, and fear that the malleability of images made them prone to distortion.[83] *National Geographic* readers' status as "members" authorized them to express their doubt and uncertainty about the authenticity of the magazine's photographs or to register distrust when photographs did not adequately fulfill their pictorial obligation to give "expression" to an article.

While it is impossible here to convey the sheer number, variety, and complexity of readers' responses to the magazine, it is clear that its images have never been received in uniform fashion—whatever the camera's power to construct and assimilate an interpretive community. It may be valuable, then, to think of these letters as invaluable commentary on what anthropologists identify as the many "visual systems" of signifying narratives that cultural institutions put into circulation.[84] *National Geographic* provides an astounding array of such systems, while letters from individual readers expose just how malleable are the narratives within any given issue. As readers' letters attest, *National Geographic* photographs and captions render otherwise unseen cultural narratives visible, inviting the "eye" to see what the photographer may not have intended and thus prompting individuals to question the photograph's documentary authority. The contradictions between photographic image and written text, between the photographer as participant-observer and self-conscious artist, create the space for the reader's self-conscious exploration of the processes—technical and otherwise—that produce the image. These tensions form a crucial part of the story of the visual imagination as experienced by *National Geographic* readers in the twentieth century, a counterweight or contrast to the often deterministic view of the culture industry and the imperialist machine.

In the chapter that follows, it becomes clear that what *National Geographic* photography shares with romantic pictorialism and literary realism is an attraction to the firsthand authority of the autobiographical, more colorfully termed the "romance of the real."[85] The impulse to document a vanishing culture, to recover the "lost" or "forgotten" civilization of a distant geographic past, while at the same time educating "new" Americans, is what compels the visual and literary romance at the core of *National Geographic*'s science. In each example of the pictorial imagination, the photographer serves as guide. Through the photographer's lens, the *National Geographic* reader could experience the illusion of stepping through the open window of the photograph into a world of spectacle and romance adventure. But the ideas, feelings, and attitudes that photographers brought back from that other world were far from predictable, for they became part of magazine's "epic story" in ways that also called attention to its self-conscious artifice.

3

SAVAGE VISIONS

Ethnography, Photography, and
Local-Color Fiction in *National Geographic*

G ive us the romance of geography—the lands and the peoples, in little
or unknown places," cried a reader in 1921.[1] Tellingly, "romance" here
embraces not only the unusual and exotic but the more modern concept
of "culture" as pluralistic variety. Before the term "culture" entered the
public lexicon as a term denoting human variety—rather than a hierarchy
of taste or "civilized" behavior—*National Geographic* photographs turned
an anthropological gaze on regional, ethnic, and racial differences.[2] Yet
this gaze was trained not only on far-flung people and places, but also
on the United States' own regional, cultural, and racial diversity. Articles
on such homespun subjects as native grasses, backyard insects, and the
Indians of North America were as much a staple of the "romance" of geography in *National Geographic* as its more exotic—and erotic—content.
In this regard, *National Geographic* had as much in common with its
literary contemporary, local-color fiction, and with the artistic precepts
of pictorial photography as it did with standard forms of ethnographic
representation.

National Geographic's forceful presence in the popular imagination—
its status as icon—is in large measure a result of its masterful management of the textual and visual signs of cultural difference. The magazine
illustrated what literary historians have called the "ethnographic imagination," a fascination with cultural differences as markers of regional,
or "local," distinctiveness, in the nation's literature from the 1890s to the
1920s. The diffusion of cultural geography throughout the American literary and visual marketplace, and in *National Geographic* in particular,
gave these visible differences of skin color, body markings, and "native"

or local regional dress the consistency and the power of icons. As signs of regional, racial, and cultural distinctiveness, they could be detached from their cultures of origin and circulate freely in a variety of historical and cultural contexts.[3] This abstraction of culture from geographic place allowed *National Geographic* to escape the fixed categories of "race" and "nation" to instead highlight global cultural mobility, detachment, and disjunction.

If a single *National Geographic* could disorder conventional geographic relations and invite new ways of imagining global connectedness, then its blending of visual genres reinforced the magazine's cultural variety. The visual discord among scientific, photojournalistic, and artistic photographs, sometimes within the same article, furthermore, undermined *National Geographic*'s appeal to "universal" aesthetic values and cultural timelessness. The magazine's photographs of ethnographic and cultural "types" displayed elements of self-consciously artistic photography that contradicted the magazine's editorial principles of scientific accuracy associated with a realist aesthetic. Its decontextualization of cultural variety also created a visual dissonance that disordered conventional nineteenth-century narratives based on social Darwinian racial hierarchies.

In addition to the magazine's visual discord, another photographic genre complicating the production of "type" was that of *National Geographic* photographers in the field. In these "self-documentary" images, as I call them, the institution trains a lens on its agents of photographic production. Photographs like these constitute a genre wholly unique to *National Geographic.* Snapshots of photographers break the conventions of type in that they highlight the photographer's dual role as both witness and artificer. In this way, the confluence of visual and textual genres in *National Geographic* arrives at nothing less than an artistically "modern" form.

By calling attention to the systems of photographic reproduction, the magazine had much in common with the "modernist" artistic movement in literature and the arts, which self-consciously called attention to the various means and methods of artistic representation. In staging the production of yet another photographic type—that of the intrepid *National Geographic* photographer—"self-documentary" photographs thereby exposed how "types" are culturally made.

Overall, *National Geographic* shows how the cultural diversity before and after the culture concept was in play expressed itself in contradictory ways. On the one hand, the magazine reflected the rapacious energy with which the nation's museums, world's fairs, and ethnographic exhibits collected exotic peoples and artifacts from abroad for display. On the other hand, however, the magazine also turned its gaze inward, upon the nation's growing cultural diversity as foreign peoples entered U.S. ports in the hope of becoming Americans. By revealing the migration taking place within U.S. borders, *National Geographic* portrayed America as a geographic space "filled with moving," to quote modernist poet Gertrude Stein.[4] In so doing, it performed a double movement of going out into the world to gather images of the foreign and exotic, while it also looked inward and educated its readers on managing cultural difference at home. Each month *National Geographic* chronicled the "epic story" of global human progress, while producing new relations between the global and the local.

Local-Color Fiction and the "Local Exotic"

In the early decades of the twentieth century, *National Geographic* was one of a handful of national institutions in the business of cultural display. The Smithsonian Institution (1846), the Museum of Natural History (1880), the popular midway attractions that featured reconstructed native villages at national and international expositions, the Chicago World's Fair (1893), and the Pan American Exposition (1901) in Buffalo, New York, heightened the vogue of displaying the primitive for popular entertainment and scientific edification. Local-color fiction was one other cultural institution that joined their esteemed ranks.

Visibly mainstream between the 1880s and the 1920s, local-color fiction and *National Geographic* shared similar representational terrain. "Local color" documented the minute details of place, the distinctive features of a landscape, and the equally distinctive racial types, vernacular speech, and customs understood to have sprung from its soil. In addition to surpassing the specialized content associated with academic geography, *National Geographic* embraced specifically "American" flora and fauna, regional manufacture and economics, as well as the quaint customs peculiar to a specific place.

National Geographic participated in the local-color fascination with the primitive, portraying geography as the "epic story" of human progress and producing iconic images of ordinary folk as well as of the savage and the culturally exotic. Both venues reflected popular beliefs concerning evolutionary biology's role in producing essential racial and cultural differences. Placing *National Geographic* alongside its literary contemporary local-color fiction foregrounds their larger instructional uses and their mutual investment in identifying and documenting ethnographic and regional types.

Primitivism is the conceptual hinge that joins *National Geographic*'s visual emblems of ethnographic romance to the evolutionary narratives of local-color fiction. "Primitives are free," writes the literary historian Marianna Torgovnick, only to occupy the "lowest cultural levels."[5] Local-color fiction, it has been argued, could "be pressed into the service of a primitivism that has more in common with the evolutionary scheme of a ladder of cultural stages" than with the more progressive model of cultural pluralism.[6] In this regard, local-color fiction and *National Geographic* both had a great deal in common with the "romantic revival" in literature of the 1880s and 1890s, which expressed contradictory ideas about "ancient instincts." On the one hand, these primitive instincts were valued as an antidote to modern decadence and artifice. On the other, it was feared that these instincts might rise up unexpectedly if not given an appropriate emotional release.[7] *National Geographic*'s local exotic satisfied these preoccupations regarding primitive instincts. It served the edifying aims of local-color fiction, on the one hand, while supplying a psychological outlet for the modern reader's internal savage through adventure and the romance of exotic racial difference.

For the literary establishment, as well as for *National Geographic,* local color also meant literal skin "color" as well as ethnographic culture. Early ethnography shared local-color fiction's preservation of "authentic group-based difference" through dialect—as, for example, in fiction geographically focused on the plantation aristocracy of the agrarian South by Joel Chandler Harris, George Washington Cable, and Charles Chesnutt—and representation of racial "types."[8] Supplying a visual supplement to literary description, *National Geographic*'s photographs similarly fulfilled the ethnographic imperative to document "type" and the local-color mandate that they be aesthetically pleasing, or visually "picturesque."

Though *National Geographic*'s founders hoped the magazine would inspire an "enlightened patriotism," it also encouraged a global, cosmopolitan worldview by blurring the boundaries between the "local," or close at hand, and the far-flung, or "global." In so doing, it combined local-color fiction's emphasis on the picturesque charm of the "local," or regional, with the exotic and culturally diverse, in what I term the "local exotic." Drawing upon the familiar, ordinary, and scenic attributes of local color, the "local exotic" made the estranging elements of the exotic less threatening.

More importantly, it enlivened the more mundane aspects of modern, national life with the piquant flavor of the Orient and popular romance adventure. To encourage settlement in the Southwest, for instance, an article dubbed the state of Arizona "America's Egypt." In an era preoccupied with racial difference and national destiny, the "local exotic" also projected comforting images of America onto continents charged with threatening primitive associations. In the African nation Liberia, its capital, Monrovia—named after the fifth U.S. president, James Monroe—and Southern plantation-style architecture wed American patriotism to economic enterprise. In this way, *National Geographic* produced a complex and nuanced portrayal of what constitutes the "local" and the "global," as well as of regional, racial, and cultural difference.

With its peculiar blend of the sensational and the commonplace, *National Geographic*'s representations of a "local exotic" responded to national concerns regarding race and cultural assimilation. The magazine was read by an emerging professional class of Americans, and the nation's newcomers, immigrants who sought literacy. In broken English, a Polish minister expressed his hope that *National Geographic* would promote cultural assimilation: "Allow me to suggest to you that future of this country depends also on education of millions of foreigners pouring through all ports to America. . . . Could I suggest to your institution to issue several lectures with slides, patronizing thus thousand of people seeking education?" A native from Bavaria similarly remarked, "Since I am in this country I always like to look over the pictures in the *NGM* and, as far as I could master the language to read the text."[9] In *National Geographic*, both image and word fueled a national literacy movement.

National Geographic's geographic "diffusion," then, was modeled on the ethnographic concept of "cultural diffusion," an anthropological theory linking civilization's transmittal to the processes of "cultural mixing and communication, whereby the cultural achievements of one society are grafted onto another."[10] Redefining geography as "the World and all that is in it," *National Geographic* simultaneously transformed geography from a science of landforms to a cultural backdrop against which to present what most attracted its readers: regional cultural and racial differences both at home and abroad.

As part of its educational mission, then, *National Geographic* filtered such "local" and domestic concerns as the dangers of overcivilization and the future impact of geographic migration upon the national cultural and racial landscape through "local-exotic" metaphors linking the frontier ideology of Manifest Destiny to the far-flung exoticism of the Middle East, Polynesia, the African continent, and the visibly different new immigrants arriving in the nation's ports.

The "local exotic's" dynamic fusion of the western frontier with Orientalist tropes appears dramatically in the 1909 *National Geographic* article "The Call of the West," which is indebted in more ways than one to Jack London's *The Call of the Wild* (1903). Its portrayal of life and conditions in the Yukon and its cast of characters with distinctive accents reflecting regional and cultural differences align *The Call of the Wild* with contemporary local-color fiction. Like local-color fiction, the novella also reflects the nation's preoccupying domestic concerns: the dangers of overcivilization and the future impact of geographic migration upon the nation's cultural and racial landscape—themes Blanchard's "The Call of the West" further complicates by projecting the Asiatic East onto his imagined U.S. West.[11]

London's narrative of Manifest Destiny chronicles the adventures of Buck, a mixed-breed dog raised comfortably on a sprawling California fruit plantation, then stolen from his wealthy owner and sold up North to toil in the traces as a sled dog during the 1897 Klondike Gold Rush. Throughout the journey, Buck "progresses" from a civilized aristocrat to a lean, virile beast, a transformation that indicates a cultural preference for the "savage" and primitive against overcivilization. Buck's "call," his atavistic reversion to primitive instincts, allows him to transcend his mongrel status and ascend to his place as wolf pack leader and grandsire of a revitalized wolf progeny. Like much local-color fiction, London's novel reflected the nation's obsession with the dangers of overcivilization and migration upon its cultural and racial landscape. Blanchard's "The Call of the West" filters these same issues through its romantic association with the Asiatic East.

An article whose purpose was to promote irrigating and settling the arid and less populous southwestern frontier, C. J. Blanchard's "The Call of the West" builds upon *The Call of the Wild*'s themes of romantic mysticism and the gritty realism of Manifest Destiny. Its opening lines, "The Call of the West comes to us today insistent and inviting . . . a voice from out [of] a vast wilderness of mountains, deserts, and plains" (403) recalls London's romantic portrayal of "primitive" indigenous groups as "mystics, in tune with nature, part of its harmonies."[12] The trope of the "vanishing" primitive that cultural anthropologists identify with "salvage ethnography" similarly finds its analogue in the article's Orientalist allusions.[13] Arizona, for example, is a "land of mystic dreams, of lost races and crumbling ruins," a land just "awakening to the touch of modern civilization" (425). Within this feminized space, Arizona is "America's Egypt." It is a sleeping beauty awaiting "the quickening kiss of canal-borne water to yield abundant harvests and to provide homes for millions" (403). In keeping with the romance genre, Arizona is a virginal land "awakened" by civilization's masculine "touch."

Moreover, the West becomes a geographic space where utopian fantasies await full realization and where democratic principles might be more fully achieved than in crowded urban centers. Blanchard writes: "The cradle of our civilization was rocked in the desert. . . . May not our own desert develop new systems of ethics and morals to lead us back from the material to the spiritual, into ways of gentleness and simple living?" (403). In this belief that the vitality and simplicity of primitive, rural life might rejuvenate a modern industrial culture enervated by machines and urban crowding, the article has the flavor of the "antimodernism" that cultural historians attribute to the early twentieth-century's fascination with the "primitive" as a beneficent counterforce to refinement and decadence.[14] By projecting the iconic markers prevalent in the Western fantasy of the Middle East—ruins, pyramids, vanished civilizations—upon the southwestern landscape, *National Geographic* conjures a modernist spirit creatively energized by primitivist archetypes. "The Call of the West" trained readers to populate the unknown spaces of a national landscape with the "local exotic," imagined signifiers of exotic racial and cultural difference.

In the pages of *National Geographic,* then, cultural diffusion was not just an anthropological theory; it was an educational mission put into aesthetic practice. Its editorial principles of "absolute accuracy" and "timely" information emphasized both nineteenth-century science's descriptive method and local-color fiction's educative social aims.

By drawing upon local-color strategies of representation, then, *National Geographic* could provoke powerful intellectual and emotional responses from its readers. Beyond its serviceability for nationalist purposes, however, the "local exotic" had the unintended effect of allowing for global cross-national forms of identification—identification, that is, with nonwhites or non-Westerners. Although the magazine strove for visual immediacy through a kind of universal language of the image, the aesthetic and ideological tensions between scientific accuracy and romantic universality within *National Geographic*'s particular development of the local-color genre also worked to denaturalize *National Geographic*'s narrative strategies of vision. When the magazine's gaze was turned outward on the world, therefore, the ostensibly stable representations of culture and "type" enabled various kinds of readings and responses, various forms of imaginative human relation.

National Geographic's efforts to create a coherent visual narrative based on "type" originated with its editorial practice of selecting pictures and stories that spoke a "universal" language. This language was one that had a particular grammar of type in the form of synecdoche, the symbolic detachment of a part, or fragment, to represent or stand in for a larger whole. Photographs of representative "types," then, formed their own basis for a visual language that strove for universal understanding. At the same time, photographs themselves could function synecdochally by detaching their subjects from their individual cultures of origin. This process of decontextualization, facilitated by the photograph, then allowed the image to circulate in a variety of other contexts and accumulate different meanings.

Capitalizing on the popular assumption that photographs were an immediate and transparent means of communication, *National Geographic* advertised its first coffee-table book, *Scenes from Every Land* (1913), by celebrating photography's promise to democratize vision, to unite lettered and unlettered, American and foreigner alike, through the "universal language" of the image. The NGS's marketing materials to potential advertisers reinforced this connection by proclaiming the "universal appeal" of photographs "so human that they literally 'talk' their own story" a primary selling point.[15] It is this emphasis in *National Geographic* on photography as an analogue to speech and cultural authenticity that most vividly connects it to local-color fiction.

Photographic color in *National Geographic,* for example, could supply a sort of visual realism, or authenticity, that accorded with local color's focus on the quaint and picturesque details of cultural difference. The diversity of colors was of a piece with cultural variety. "Glimpses of Korea and China" (November 1910) occasioned the magazine's first use of color in thirty-nine hand-tinted images of "street scenes" in Seoul, which "offer great variety for the Kodak." In *National Geographic,* photographic color also illuminated the "local color" of "unusual scenes, and customs so strange."[16] The strange, the unusual, the exotic all appealed to an emerging modernist aesthetic that decontextualized—or otherwise dislocated from their cultural origins—the distinctive features of cultural difference, allowing them to circulate freely in a visual marketplace.

National Geographic photographs and texts, then, share local color's use of visual synecdoche—taking one part or visible attribute to represent, or stand for, a whole—as a method of decontextualization. While photographs of individual types in *National Geographic* use one person to secure the whole group in a static image of cultural timelessness, synecdoche also makes the circulation of images and their global cultural diffusion possible.

This power of visual synecdoche to decontextualize attributes of cultural distinctiveness, and thus lend them iconic significance, is most visible when *National Geographic* photographers seek photographic subjects who resemble characters from popular culture and literature. *National Geographic* staff photographer Maynard Owen Williams described the failure of a photographer—"who *had read somewhere* that the habit of carrying heavy jars of water on their heads gave the women of the Holy Land a queenly carriage"—to find a Middle Eastern woman who could resemble her fictive counterpart. A telling example of visual synecdoche, this familiar visual formula of women bearing water jugs on their heads evokes the "Arabian Nights" motif in *National Geographic,* the persistent portrayal of the Middle East and its women as historic throwbacks to biblical days.[17]

In keeping with the magazine's "local exotic," its Orientalism also has some unexpected "local" origins. Williams attempted to conjure up local color in a street scene in India by encouraging his subject to "look more like Tom Sawyer and less like a monument."[18] More than merely a passing reference to Mark Twain, the period's local-color fiction provided crucial representational strategies and motifs for *National Geographic.* In *National Geographic,* the visual markers of cultural distinctiveness—whether culled from fiction or elsewhere—helped fulfill its advertising's promise to publish photographs that "'talk' their own story."

National Geographic's promotion of the photograph as an equivalent to speech as a form of storytelling powerfully emerged as racial iconicity in *National Geographic* photographs and descriptions of people of color and immigrants. Local color's fascination with regional distinctiveness, or "color," is on display in a 1922 photograph of Egyptian women entitled "Local Color for the Egyptian Picture" (fig. 5). In an effort to direct the reader's eye to visual details denoting regional "color" as well as cultural difference, the caption reads, "Bare-foot women go back and forth between their mud-walled huts and the slippery banks of the muddy Nile, with earthen water jars perched at rakish angles on their steady heads."[19]

Fig. 5 "Local Color for the Egyptian Picture." (Kodak, [Egypt] Ltd./National Geographic Society)

As invested as it is in bodily geography as a visual marker of regional difference, or "local color," *National Geographic* participated in the photographic production of "a physiognomic code of visual interpretation of the body's signs."[20] In this image, bare feet function synecdochally as markers of the picturesque; the River Nile conjures the primitive and exotic, while the water jugs held at "rakish angles" function metonymically to evoke stereotyped images of the Middle East as well as the casual and carefree lifestyle commonly associated with the period's local-color fiction.

To take a literary point of comparison, bare feet play a no less picturesque role in Kate Chopin's *The Awakening* (1899), while becoming a refreshing counterforce to repressive Victorian sexuality. Early in the novel, we see the brazen-eyed Mariquita walking barefoot on the beach at Grand Isle; her slime-covered toes simultaneously mark her as closer to humanity's evolutionary origins. Mariquita's bare feet are not only picturesque, but they also make her a fitting exemplar of a "primitive" female sexuality that Edna later appropriates, a transformation of regional and racial distinctiveness into aesthetic commodity, thus marking the modernist turn toward regional writing in the 1890s.[21] Watching the barefoot Mariquita flirt openly with unmarried men at Grande Isle prompts Edna to loosen her confining stays and corsets, the trappings of Victorian culture.

Chopin's elegant description of Mariquita's unshod feet bespeaks why indigenous bodies held such visual appeal for modernist writers and painters as a refreshing counterforce to the restrictions of urban life and industrial civilization. Photographs from "The Romance of Polynesia" (October 1925), considered by readers to be an "arresting article," reveal the influence of Paul Gauguin on its composition, as in this image (fig. 6), whose caption attempts to disavow any deliberate artistry: "These young women are not 'posing,' but were photographed unawares at their task."[22] This visual homage to Gauguin, however, places *National Geographic* within the context of an international aesthetic arts movement whose exotic imagery circulated so widely that it emerged in fiction by local colorists Kate Chopin, Lafcadio Hearn, and Stephen Crane, among others, and was visually rendered by illustrators Aubrey Beardsley and Maxfield Parrish.[23]

The importance of the nude for an international aesthetic arts movement places *National Geographic*'s famed nudes in a broader global context, rather than an exclusively national one. Editor John Hyde, for example, contradicted his own "American" vision for the magazine by publishing in 1896 its first nude photograph, "Zulu Bride and Bridegroom." Although Hyde was the first to initiate the genre, Grosvenor made the publication of nudes a matter of policy in 1903. Just how Grosvenor's policy departed from Hyde's is unclear. What is clear, however, is that photography, and the specific *National Geographic* "policy" of photographing nudes, in particular, increased membership. By 1904, membership rose to just over 2,800.[24]

The languorous nudes in *National Geographic* and in Parrish's poster illustrations for the *Century* were part of this broader cultural context of an emergent modernist sensibility that embraced the primitive, not as evolutionary backwardness, but as a progressive departure from restrictive Victorian social mores.[25] In 1897, advocates of pictorial photography celebrated the nude's freedom from artificial constraints: "any one [sic] who knows the scarcity of well-formed feet, owing to their being cramped in leather from childhood, and other deformities wrought by wearing

Fig. 6 "Coffee Pickers of Bapa." (Rollo Beck/National Geographic Image Collection)

clothes, can supply a hundred instances of failure to [one nude photograph] of even modified success."[26] In this view, the Victorian disciplinary sartorial regime was as detrimental to the natural physique as to the modern psyche. The period's attraction to primitivism as a way of closing the distance between humankind and nature helps account for the appeal of *National Geographic*'s images of nude people of color.

While nude photographs fueled *National Geographic*'s popularity, its readers were often unnerved by their frequency, which are "not setting us a good example." Wrote one female reader, "The boys of a friend of mine have enjoyed looking at the magazine very much, but one or two numbers had too many nude figures, their mother agreed with me there was altogether too much on that line to be good for them to see; indeed, I felt a little queer myself looking them over alone."[27] Both the tone and the self-consciousness of the letter hint at *National Geographic*'s power to offend cultural sensitivities, tapping such domestic fears as miscegenation, as well as such repressed "local" anxieties as the dangers of transgressing conventional sexuality.[28] *National Geographic* photographs could simultaneously occupy the scientific space reserved for traditional ethnographic photography while fulfilling the romantic aesthetic requirements of the artistic photographer, who sought bodies not yet disfigured by restrictive clothing.

Global images, then, could powerfully tap into more domestic or provincial preoccupations. Conversely, local concerns could be symbolically redirected outward, projected onto a global stage. Even in *National Geographic's* numerous articles on Liberia, which are on one level undeniably racist, we can see this other dynamic at work—one in which biological racial differences between Liberians, Africans, and Americans are less important than a shared Euro-American cultural heritage. That heritage seems to be "shared" insofar as the global is imagined *in terms of* the local.

The linking of color and culture is most vividly expressed in *National Geographic's* articles on Liberia between 1907 and 1920, where firsthand accounts of Liberia's situation negotiated U.S. cultural anxieties about the potential of biological inheritance to determine a nation's economic destiny. In such articles as "The Black Republic—Liberia" (May 1907), "Conditions in Liberia" (September 1910), "Notes on the Only American Colony in the World" (September 1910), and "The Land of the Free in Africa" (October 1922), ethnographic stereotypes regarding race, biological inheritance, and national destiny play out in particularly fascinating and complex ways. The efforts of "American" blacks to forge a democratic republic from a colony on "foreign" soil were of special interest to *National Geographic.* As well as listing Liberia's natural resources of lumber and rubber, each article chronicles its national history as an American colony initiated in 1822 by the American Colonization Society, founded by former slaves and freed blacks who declared national independence on July 26, 1847.[29] As well as reflecting Americans' domestic preoccupations with race and economic destiny, however, articles on Liberia show the magazine emphasizing cultural similarities over so-called "biological" racial differences.

Hinting at more cultural similarities than genetic differences between Liberians and their American and European compatriots, these articles acknowledged that black European immigrants to Liberia fared no better than white European colonizers in the region. In "Liberia—the Black Republic" (1907), for example, Sir Harry Johnston and U.S. Minister Lyon of Monrovia describe Liberia's history as one of "constant struggles" between "Americo-Liberian invaders and the native blacks."[30] A 1910 report undertaken by a U.S. commission to Liberia further complicated racist narratives that associated blackness with atavistic degeneracy by declaring that "the Liberians have advanced, not retrograded, in their civilization."[31] Depictions of a modern black republic stood apart from the magazine's iconic images of a primitive Africa.

Even the imperial assumption that it was the white man's "burden" to govern disorganized black "natives" was called into question. As Kentuckian Edgar Allen Forbes frankly admits in his "Notes on the Only American Colony in the World" (1910), "I had gone to Liberia with the understanding that it was the final, unmistakable evidence of the black man's inability to govern himself" (723–26). Nonetheless, his article chronicles Liberia's geographic distance from Africa's "primeval" jungles as he encounters Western civilization's signifiers, "Standard Oil, and Singer sewing machines" (719), and strolls its picturesque streets named after Southern cities: Baltimore, Greenville, and Lexington (720). American place-names provide the occasion for Forbes to meditate on the similarities between Liberian and American culture, a meditation that ultimately undermines his earlier preparedness to have his racial stereotypes reinforced.

Even as Forbes prepares to be surprised by Liberia's civilization, he represents an encounter with a local in dialect, using verbal synecdoche to conjure more familiar and reassuring stereotypes. He writes, "I shall not soon forget the feeble, gray-haired Negro who hobbled up the steps and held out a hand that trembled with excitement," just before he has his protagonist strike the caricatured pose one might expect in a work by Joel Chandler Harris: "'I seed you on the porch,' he said, apologetically, with that old-time Negro deference, 'an' I knowed you waz sum o'mine—an' I'm some o' yourn'" (723). Forbes and the local instantaneously recognize each other as American "types." The historian Ernest Gellner has written that mutual "recognition" of one's compatriots is the basis for national identification; here, the old Liberian's recognition of their shared national (and perhaps racial) origins has transnational overtones as the Southern plantation dialect resurfaces in Liberia to make them both "locals," despite geographic distance.[32]

Of course, cultural identification could also facilitate exploitation of Liberia's natural resources. Harry McBride's "The Land of the Free in Africa" (1922), for example, provided a racial taxonomy of Liberia's native tribes in terms of their relative potential to cultivate the region's rubber and lumber. Following the First World War, Liberia was vulnerable to rival British and French colonial interests. Its national resources were held as collateral for debts incurred during the First World War. A U.S. buyout of $5 million, backed by rubber magnate Harvey S. Firestone to cover European loans in 1926, literally and figuratively paved the way for the materialization of literal plantations on Liberian soil. As the historian Richard West has observed, "[i]t was the destiny of Liberia to become not a colony of the United States, but of one American enterprise, the Firestone Rubber Company."[33]

Nonetheless, even *National Geographic*'s exposure of the darker side of cultural identification and global connectedness is instructive. It reveals how, with unpredictable consequences, cultural "types" are detached and transferred into other geographic and cultural contexts not just symbolically, as by visual and verbal synecdoche, but literally, through global economic and political forces. Furthermore, *National Geographic*'s narrative mobilization of "type" did not consistently affirm cultural timelessness. Rather, it complicated its own use of type by acknowledging cultural change and the signs and symptoms of an encroaching global modernity.

Photographic Pictorialism

By the end of the twentieth century's first decade, photography was chief among *National Geographic*'s strategies for "diffusing" global geographic knowledge. *National Geographic*, it has been argued, strove for "photographic realism," favoring images that created the illusion of direct contact with the photographed subject.[34] But its emphasis on "living" and "talking" pictures anticipated film and in many ways predated the photographer Henri Cartier-Bresson's concept of the "decisive moment"— defined as a photograph "whose composition possesses such vigor and richness" that it "is a whole story in itself."[35] In its earliest years, *National Geographic* mingled fanciful elements of self-conscious pictorialism with "realistic" photojournalistic and ethnographic shots. Pictorial photography, whose cultural ascendancy between 1889 and 1923 coincided with the rise of local-color fiction, shared with its literary counterpart the strategy of manipulating reality to distill a cultural essence or mood.[36]

National Geographic's earliest photographs are indebted to the pictorialist tradition of self-consciously "artistic" photography more so than to any other photographic genre. The magazine's pictorial photographs invoke familiar narratives of the frontier, exhibiting painterly composition and lighting as well as pastoral and classical themes. Edward Curtis's aesthetic photographs of Native Americans, Lewis Hine's portraits of immigrant children and the working class, Wilhelm von Gloeden's homoerotic shots of adolescent boys in classical Greco-Roman tableaux appeared alongside ethnographic "types" in *National Geographic*.[37] The juxtaposition of these imaginative and artistic images alongside ethnographic "types" often disrupted the magazine's pretensions to "realism" or scientific accuracy.

Photographic historians have characterized the photograph as a product of scientific positivism, an instrument of social surveillance, and part of a sophisticated disciplinary regime in which images of criminals, of the mentally ill, and of racial and ethnic types all reflected and reinforced the social Darwinian philosophy of biological determinism.[38] Nonetheless, there are other, equally important ways in which the photograph lent itself to more imaginative appropriations than those inspired by science and that introduced new possibilities for expanded visual horizons. Proliferating world exploration fueled the popularity of commercially produced "stereographs," in which two overlapping images created the illusion of three-dimensional depth. This heightened realism of the image, however, was popular precisely because it extended the existing possibilities for storytelling, and the ready availability of stereographic images fulfilled a desire for knowledge and leisure. Featuring actors or models in elaborate costume posed against artificial tableaux, such images provided vivid retellings of popular stories, chronicled the social rituals of romance and courtship, and brought images of a foreign world before the eyes of those for whom travel was an unaffordable luxury.

The photograph may have fueled the scientific rage for taxonomic order, but it also supplied the means to manipulate the distinguishing features of race, class, and culture and that sealed one's place in a social system. The photograph established a new means for achieving (and inventing) individual autonomy, if only through manipulating one's image. Individuals posed for daguerreotypes, fashioning the very likeness of themselves that they wanted to be seen; photographed in studios fitted to look like sumptuous parlors, those of lowly economic status could appear affluent in mass-produced visiting cards, or *cartes de visites*.[39] In many ways, the photograph satisfied, if it did not necessarily fulfill, the American dream of progress and prosperity.

Photography, then, was as much a medium of fantasy as it was of disciplinary authority. Capitalizing on the heightened demand for images of the foreign and exotic, commercial photographers posed models in ethnic dress and fabricated elaborate props and settings to evoke faraway locales in stereoscopic slides, which gave spectators the illusion of three-dimensionality. By extending the possibility for viewers to adopt the photographer's point of view, the stereoscopic image "simulates the role of transport device as the spectator adopts the position, posture, and lines of sight of the photographer."[40] *National Geographic*'s educative aims were indebted to this early cultural context of the commercial stereograph and artistic "pictorial" photography. These new visual technologies and genres prepared the magazine's readership for the imaginative transport *National Geographic* offered.

Like progressive educators advocating pictorial literacy, artistic, or "pictorial," photographers maintained that artistic vision required meticulous cultivation and training. One of pictorial photography's earliest advocates, Henry Peach (H. P.) Robinson, saw the photographer as one who "has learnt to see." Pictures of the same object taken by different photographers would inevitably produce quite "different pictorial results," Robinson wrote, "because there is something different in each man's mind, which, somehow, gets communicated to his fingers' ends, and thence to his pictures." The pictorial photographer sought not just to record but to "interpret" and "translate" both landscape and subject into works of art.[41] Pictorialists consequently emphasized the photographer's agency in mastering the atmospheric conditions of light rather than the camera's technological superiority to the human eye. For Robinson, as for Alfred Stieglitz, Clarence White, and other early-twentieth-century pictorialists, photography was not a purely mechanical or scientific process but an art form originating in the individual photographer's unique artistic vision.[42] In *National Geographic,* the juxtaposition of ethnographic and pictorial shots reminded readers that photography was an art form that, in turn, interpreted its subjects aesthetically, and, in this sense, was perhaps more idealistic than realistic.

Pictorial photography worked alongside local-color textual narratives as influential genres informing *National Geographic*'s trademark representational strategies. Indeed, *National Geographic* photography and the cultural vogue of photographic pictorialism came into being at the same historical moment. The year *National Geographic* billed itself an "Illustrated Monthly," in 1896, the Smithsonian hosted America's first salon of "pictorial," or artistic, photography at the Cosmos Club, the historic birthplace of the NGS, where Hubbard addressed the select group of government scientists who comprised the Society's early membership.[43] Between 1896, when photographs first appeared in *National Geographic,* and 1910, when it began hiring its own staff photographers, the magazine relied on independent photographers, stock collections, and, after the Spanish-

American War, photographs from federal employees.[44] As it depended on these stock collections in its early years, *National Geographic* published commercial and artistic photographs often side by side with journalistic or more scientifically styled "ethnographic" photographs. Occasionally, as in the example of photographs by Wilhelm von Gloeden, such images worked at cross-purposes to the magazine's scientific typology.

In a 1909 *National Geographic* article educating Americans about the flood of Italian immigrants arriving on the nation's doorstep, the author's journalistic-style photographs appear alongside those of the renowned pictorial photographer Wilhelm von Gloeden, whose work featured child nudes evocative of the pastoral allure of classical Rome and Greece. Photographic critics praised the aesthetic virtues of von Gloeden's photographs, likening their artistry to that of pastoral painting: "Here amid ruins of amphitheatres and fountains and terraces overlooking an exquisite bay, with an old town on the hills sloping to the water, the young figures—whether draped or undraped—for the most look as natural as in any painting of the Golden Age, or of classic times."[45] While von Gloeden's photographs were recognized as art, *National Geographic* captioning sometimes co-opts the images as ethnographic evidence documenting "the variety of race and romantic charm of that island 'where going to America is an industry.'"[46] Yet these images are so fanciful that they are far from entirely legible within the codes of ethnographic realism. More surprisingly, their overt homoerotic content works against the magazine's usual "type," the exotic woman of color.

In keeping with von Gloeden's sexual attraction to young men, adolescent boys and nudes reminiscent of ancient Greece predominate in the *National Geographic* article. "A Sicilian Youth," a close-up shot of a youth with a roguish expression, provocatively opened shirt, and cigar in his mouth, hints at von Gloeden's now well-known sexual preference. "A Sicilian Troubadour" and "Dreaming: A Singer of Old Sicily," both photographs of adolescent boys, follow a similar eroticizing code, where unbuttoned shirts expose hairless muscular young chests. Two others, "Summer Time in Sicily" and "A Shepherd and His Lute under the Almond Trees" (fig. 8) depict boys wearing nothing but provocatively draped loincloths against bucolic classical Greek settings. Yet another homoerotic image entirely resists easy readability. "Watching Mount Etna" (fig. 7) shows a nude man in a submissive crouch. His eyes, noticeably outlined in makeup, gaze beseechingly at the camera. His nails show the faintest trace of polish.[47]

It is difficult to speculate on the effect of such photographs on the magazine's readership since *National Geographic* does not possess archived letters prior to 1912. What is clear, however, is that they violate the codes of ethnographic realism and stand strikingly apart from the magazine's oeuvre of nude women. Posed and artful, each of these photographs reflects the pictorial photographer's creative agency in determining the aesthetic effect of the image. In insisting upon the documentary value of von Gloeden's photographs in ethnographically recording racial diversity, however, *National Geographic* could educate its readers to perceive the new arrivals through an aesthetic lens that would salvage the "lost" origins of the preindustrial past von Gloeden's photographs would evoke.

In *National Geographic,* pictorial and ethnographic photography were complicit with local-color textual representation in aestheticizing racial and cultural differences. While scholars have typically perceived *National Geographic* photographs as primarily documentary, and thus more closely aligned with science and photographic realism, from its inception photography at *National Geographic* fulfilled a more aesthetic purpose. Ethnographic language and pictorial photography cooperated aesthetically to promote a "universal language." In this way, *National Geographic* anticipated modernist literary and visual appropriations of the "primitive" for aesthetic purposes, while its captioning insisted upon the photographs as scientific documents of "authentic" group-based differences. These same differences could then be anchored textually through captioning that directed the reading eye to note specific differences and assign them larger, culturally symbolic significances. This strategy is particularly powerful in the case of photographs of individuals classed as representative types, or groups of individuals in which photographic captioning places them in the context of a broader social issue.

National Geographic's more self-consciously scientific photographs adhered to the dictates of the "type" photograph. Detached from their cultural contexts, subjects functioned as representative "types" and were photographed for the purpose of linking racial variation to evolutionary history. Such photographs assumed an "iconographic power" that popular demand for the primitive and exotic only reinforced.[48] In these images, the racialized culture embodied in *National Geographic* has consistently been rendered visually explicit. Ethnographic portraiture typically portrays an expressionless human face materializing from a white background, with the whiteness of the backdrop compelling the eye to note gradations of skin color. A 1912 *National Geographic* photograph titled "Typical Men

Fig. 7 "Watching Mount Etna." (Baron Von Gloeden/National Geographic Image Collection)

Fig. 8 "A Shepherd and His Lute under the Almond Trees." (Baron Von Gloeden/National Geographic Image Collection)

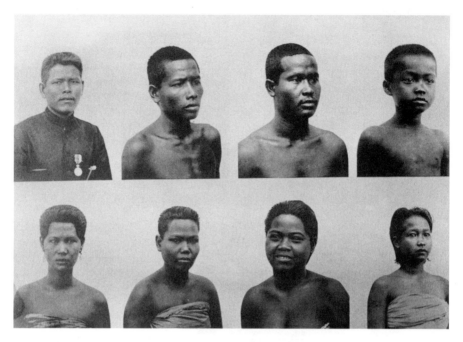

Fig. 9 "Typical Men and Women of Cambodia." (Jacob Conner/National Geographic Image Collection)

and Women of Cambodia" (fig. 9), in which human figures materialize ghostlike from a white backdrop, is one of many examples of more traditional ethnographic photographs featured in *National Geographic*.[49] Abstracted from their cultural contexts, the subjects of the type photograph function synecdochally, much like local-color fiction, in that they treat racial distinctiveness as timeless cultural essence. Despite, or perhaps because of, its scientific classificatory function, ethnographic photography also has the effect of aestheticizing its subjects by dislocating them from the cultural specifics of place.

In this way, photographic types are complicit in reproducing what has been termed the "museum effect," a process whereby the simple fact of exhibition transforms an ordinary object into art. The museum effect turns its subjects into art objects by dislocating them from their geographic cultural contexts. It invites the same "attentive looking" we typically associate with the serious contemplation of artworks.[50] More crucially, however, such iconic objects can then serve as "a model for experiencing life outside its walls."[51] They invite more self-aware forms of experiencing cultural difference.

Fig. 10 "Seeing Himself as Others See Him." (Members Citroen-Haardt Central African Expedition/National Geographic Image Collection)

National Geographic photographs can be understood to reflect both aspects of the "museum effect." On one hand, they detached subjects from their cultural origins and reordered them for aesthetic display in the magazine. On the other hand, the photographs themselves could also promote recognition of the artistic and ideological assumptions governing the production of photographic types.

A photograph of an African chieftain that is more self-consciously "artistic" than many of *National Geographic*'s more conventional ethnographic photographs, such as "Men and Women of Cambodia," offers a compelling study in the deconstruction of type itself. "Seeing Himself as Others See Him" (fig. 10), from a 1926 article, juxtaposes "primitive" un-self-consciousness and "modern" self-consciousness in ways that prevent the chieftain's easy assimilation into primitivist narratives.[52] Photographed against a white background upon which a series of lifelike sketches of him are arranged, the chieftain appears similarly "decontextualized." Here, he stands in tribal finery, yet closely scrutinizes a lifelike sketch of himself arranged with other drawings, as if in an art gallery.

The photograph has much to tell us about how ethnographic science has historically reconstituted its subjects. The white walls upon which the chief's portrait is displayed amid other representations of his jungle dwelling call to mind *National Geographic*'s representational affinity with "life groups," living or replica ethnographic subjects shown performing ordinary tasks, in simulated native settings exhibited at natural history museums, world's fairs, and dioramas.[53] In this photograph, the focus is not so much on the verisimilitude of the sketch, but on the subject's psychological response to recognizing his likeness, as if never before having identified himself as an object. *National Geographic* images like this one, in which "natives" are "seeing themselves as others see them," have often been criticized for their perpetuation of imperialist attitudes, for implying the benighted, childlike status of colonized subjects.[54]

But this photograph is different. Instead of functioning as a "mirror" in which the subject acquires self-awareness, here it shows a subject seeing himself as an *object of representation*—a quite different experience. In the photograph of the African chieftain, the museum encounter itself is the object of exhibition, a gesture that both decontextualizes the chieftain and makes ethnographic representation and the ideological assumptions of museum exhibition the true objects of display.

With ethnographic photography's complicity in imperialist symbology rendered so visible, the image of the chieftain can now be understood to function as a "metapicture," what the art historian W. J. T. Mitchell characterizes as "[a]ny picture that is used to reflect on the nature of pictures" and whose purpose is "to explain what pictures are—to stage, as it were, the 'self-knowledge' of pictures."[55] Here, the representational media of painting, drawing, and photography nearly displace the chieftain as the true subjects of the photograph. The image not only comments on the relative position of art photography in relation to the period's other artistic forms in which the "primitive" functioned as a marker of avant-garde artistic sensibilities, but also exposes the imperialist ideologies implicit in both.

However artful the picture's transformation of the "type-photograph" into self-reflexive artistic portraiture may be, therefore, the doubling of representational genres ("primitive" illustration and "modern" photography) and the accompanying collapse of boundaries between artistic "portrait" and scientific "type" foreground the photograph's modes of production in unexpected ways. In staging the chieftain's dramatic encounter with his likeness as a symbolic form of self-knowledge, the photograph exemplifies the "two-fold structure" of ethnographic writing. The different kinds of representation (drawing/photography) exemplify anthropology's indebtedness to the scientific descriptive method, yet the descriptions themselves reach beyond to broader imaginative and symbolic cultural narratives. This "double attention to the descriptive surface and to more abstract, comparative, and explanatory levels of meaning," writes James Clifford, is what allows ethnographic narratives—and, by extension, *National Geographic* photographs—to impose "a common ground of understandable activity valid for both observer and observed, and by implication for all human groups."[56] In looking at his own likeness, the chieftain is doing what any other spectator does. In beholding artistic representations of ourselves, we not only scrutinize how accurately the representation reflects our perceived reality, but also become witnesses to how we are imagined in the eyes of others. The image is thus simultaneously "us" and "not-us" in that it may reflect accurately how someone else views us but not necessarily how we view ourselves. The photograph of the chieftain reveals the artistry behind ethnographic narratives and *National Geographic*'s "romance," one that allows the magazine simultaneously to offer itself as scientific realism and therapeutic aesthetic escape.

Placing the chieftain's photograph side by side with a 1922 photograph of a young black child dressed in worn overalls, titled "Not a Care in the World!" (fig. 11) illuminates yet another set of important cultural associations. While the title positions the child in a larger narrative about landscape and picturesque local color that elides a long history of racial and economic oppression, the photograph's representational systems serve as reminders of that history.

Nearly every detail in this photograph—from the child's tattered clothing to the holes in his shoes exposing his bare toes—contradicts the title. At a time when African Americans from the rural South were migrating by the thousands to the industrial capitals of the North, naming this photograph as one in a series of snapshots of American "scenery," and not humanity, functions as therapeutic distraction from the nation's growing racial unrest, evidenced by the resurgence of the Ku Klux Klan, the rise of eugenics, and bloody race riots in Chicago, Washington, and New York in 1919 during the "Red Summer."[57] This catalyzing period of African American civil rights history finds no place in the *National Geographic*'s photographs. Instead, the snapshot of the African American child is secured in a preexisting "local-color" narrative in which African Americans are part of the "scenery," reduced to the stereotype of grinning minstrels.

What *National Geographic* photographs and texts have in common

with local-color fiction, then, is a reliance upon the familiarizing agents of visual and verbal synecdoche that simultaneously produce an estranging distance between the reader and the ethnographic objects of contemplation. In a photograph, one person represents a whole group in the same way that a single individual in local-color fiction becomes representative of a larger regional constituency or racial group. Type photographs function psychologically to diminish the potential threat a particular group poses. In figure 3, the women portrayed as "local color" are not dangerous because they are so visibly marked by veils and water jugs as belonging "elsewhere," in a foreign country. Photographed in isolation, smiling, and in rags, the African American child similarly poses no visible threat to the status quo. How different from the caption "Swarm of Rhodesian Children" beneath a photograph in a February 1925 article.[58] Recalling Marlowe's vision of black workers swarming "like ants" in Joseph Conrad's *The Heart of Darkness*, the metaphor of the "swarm" also fuses insect behavior with local anxieties about racial conquest, exposing textual metonymy as yet another important narrative strategy by which *National Geographic* suffused racial and cultural attributes with iconic power. The nature of *National Geographic*'s "antimodernist" therapeutic role was to function much like a homeopathic remedy, to inject culture with savage contagion as inoculation against the racial menace of hybridity and the anarchic currents the hidden savage dangerously embodies.

Insects and Immigrants

Between 1900 and the start of the First World War, immigration to the United States reached unprecedented levels, intensifying anxieties about how different ethnicities and nationalities would blend with the predominantly "Anglo-Saxon" stock of Americans several times removed from their European origins. The stream of Eastern Europeans arriving in the nation's ports in the early decades of the twentieth century before the First World War have even been described as an instance of "reverse colonization."[59] Even as the magazine exposed its readers to the foreigners streaming into the nation's ports, while simultaneously acquainting immigrant "strangers" with American cultural values, its texts betray an equal desire to eradicate the threat of cultural difference. The conflation of immigrants with newly arrived foreign plants and insects in *National Geographic* offers perhaps the most explicit case study of how text and photograph function metonymically to reflect and refract prevailing cultural assumptions.

A central part of *National Geographic*'s educational mission thus involved educating Americans not only about the world's geography, but also about the nation's "racial geography." Former assistant commissioner of immigration Z. F. McSweeney, in his article "The Character of Our Immigration, Past and Present," expressed his fear that Mediterranean and Asian immigrants would fail to assimilate, either racially or culturally, to the nation's native Anglo-American stock. *National Geographic* contributors thus negotiated a shifting rhetoric of contagion or absorption. McSweeney vacillates between these two poles. As well as supplying a veritable taxonomy of the races entering American ports, with their supposed physical, moral, and intellectual strengths and weaknesses, McSweeney charges *National Geographic* with an explicit educative aim:

> [O]ur educational methods should include the study of racial geography to equip students who are being turned out of our colleges with a knowledge of the races that are annually coming into the American life, and especially with their economic, moral, and social effect on the community. The National Geographic Society can well initiate this

work by agitating for a more comprehensive and scientific study of racial geography in our various institutions of learning in the United States. (11)

Subsequent articles provided ethnic and cultural descriptions, including statistics and tables documenting the numbers of immigrants entering America by ethnicity and nationality. Additional articles featured photographs of representative types.

Knowledge of the nation's "racial geography" would fit hand in glove with the NGS's use of photographs to assimilate new Americans. Serving as a formal introduction of the new arrivals, articles such as "Some of Our Immigrants" (May 1907), "The Foreign-Born of the United States" (September 1914), "Our Foreign-Born Citizens" (February 1917), as well as others on eugenics, schooled American readers in the relative virtues and vices as well as the potential economic and social threat new immigrants posed. Verbal association with disease-carrying insect and plant pests transformed the word "immigrant" into an emblem of contagion. In *National Geographic,* visual and verbal metonymy established a way of picturing difference and educating Americans about the "monsters" in the nation's backyard.

By linking immigrants metonymically to blood, insect, and plant contagion, *National Geographic* tapped powerful national anxieties linking its economic health to the emergence of a nascent "American" race. Unlike synecdoche, which functions by abstraction, as in the case of ethnographic "type photographs" in which a constituent part or one group member represents the whole, metonymy operates through placement and proximity. Where seemingly unrelated ideas are joined by textual proximity, their repetition and recurrence within the same text supplies the necessary conceptual links.[60] Articles on immigration and articles on insects both emphasize the racial science that saw blood as a carrier of both culture and character, in language that scholars have described as "blood rhetoric."[61] In January 1908, Alexander Graham Bell wrote that "in the United States we have, in the new blood introduced from abroad, an important means of improvement that will act more quickly and that is eminently susceptible to control."[62]

Charles Lester Marlatt's "Why We Need a National Law to Prevent the Importation of Insect-Infested and Diseased Plants" (April 1911) anticipates anti-immigration advocate Robert De Courcy Ward's essay "Our Immigration Laws from the View Point of National Eugenics" (January

1912).[63] Photographic captions in Marlatt's essay use the term "immigrant" as a metaphor for parasitical contagion. Inspectors at "Horticultural 'Ellis Island,'" for example, check the "health" of "plant immigrants," while more than "10,000 naturalized plant citizens" from "every quarter of the world" await processing. Prohibitions against plant pests as "foreign plant enemies" retain and promote the psychological link between immigration and cultural and biological contagion.[64] Captions like these both magnify and minimize the dangers immigrants represented to a national imagination; on the one hand, immigrants were frequently and repeatedly associated with moral and physical blight and economic loss. On the other, the apparent ease with which insects are quarantined, expelled, or controlled also potentially diminished the psychological scale of the dangers new immigrants represented. Both representational modes reinforced the immigrant's association with unknown contagions, whether in foreign blood as a carrier of disease or in biological "germ" cells. Thus contributors' fears that "inferior blood" (i.e., "immigrant blood") may result in a "loss of jobs and degeneration of national racial characteristics" were nearly synonymous with ecological destruction and economic losses resulting from plant diseases and contagion.[65]

In subsequent articles, eugenic science builds on its romantic affinity with gothic literature as a popular genre thematizing moral and biological degeneracy and physical monstrosity. Opening "a door into a world as full of romance as the fairy tales of Grimm or Andersen" (575), David Fairchild's fanciful essay "Monsters of Our Backyards" (May 1913) reveals insect "monsters" "to the public as a showman might," in magnified photographs in which the appalling details of thorax, abdomen, and mandible are shown "on a level with the eye and not looking down on them as they are so often shown in text-books on entomology" (579). Magnified images of horseflies, grasshoppers, and crickets filled the pages of what became one of *National Geographic*'s most popular articles. Throughout the article, however, Fairchild tellingly associates common insects with foreign human threats. The domestic grasshopper he compares unfavorably with its kin the locust, "a creature quite as fascinating and actually more dangerous than the East African monsters of our school *Geographics*" (575). The question "What diseases may it bring into our houses?" that Fairchild asks about the German cockroach, an "importation from Europe" (587), is the same question implicit in immigration articles on human imports.

So popular was Fairchild's article that he and his wife worked with the NGS to publish a book on the subject. His subsequent *National Geographic* article, "Book of Monsters" (July 1914), reinforces the metaphorical connection between the biological germ cells of immigrants and insects as the carriers of disease. As with articles on immigrants in which the placement, proximity, and repetition of associated metaphors amplify their threat, a magnified photograph of a horsefly is accompanied by a caption that makes visible "the ghastly possibilities which lie in the piercing mouthparts of these flies. They suck the blood of those whose blood streams may be swarming with disease germs, and then fly directly to our houses and puncture our skins with a beak covered with these germs, which slip off into our veins" (90). Indeed, anticipating and forestalling the "ghastly possibilities" lurking within foreign genes laid the foundation for eugenicist social policies.

Both eugenics and romanticism express a profound longing for the perfect ideal. Such a longing was also reflected in *National Geographic* texts and photographs that functioned as object lessons in human efforts to control or to cultivate nature with "culture." As Fairchild writes of his magnified photographs of backyard insects, they enable the reader to "realize what vast and yet untouched fields of material value lie in the efforts man is making to outwit and circumvent, and even perhaps exterminate, such monsters as encroach upon his own environment."[66] Magnified images of backyard insects make readers see the previously unseen and make visible the "unconscious optics" of biological horror and future warfare.[67] Insects, hints Fairchild, present humans with an object lesson in human and racial supremacy, "because their own struggle for existence so often crosses ours, many of them are our enemies. Indeed, man's own real struggle for the supremacy of the world is his struggle to control these tiny monsters."[68] Immigration's potential threat to American labor and the nation's racial constitution become one with anxieties about white racial weakness that fueled racial and environmental "supremacy" in a social Darwinist narrative based on natural selection. Meanwhile, images of monsters with bloodsucking powers invoke a gothic imagination and the sensationalist print literature of the early nineteenth century, revealing the persistence of romance in *National Geographic* photographs and text. It does not take too dramatic a leap of the imagination to connect the two kinds of immigrants with efficacious social policies eliminating their threat. If insects and plant disease can be exterminated, so too can the immigrant population: through strict social hygiene involving education and absorption, exploitative labor and war.

More than any other magazine originating at the turn of the century, *National Geographic* gave vivid testimony to racial and cultural difference. Like Victorian natural history museums, *National Geographic* sheds light on the magazine's value as one among many visual systems inviting a more self-conscious recognition of the historic network of narratives—scientific, literary, and photographic—surrounding the politics of representation and visual display. By conceiving of geography broadly, as a means of documenting human communities, *National Geographic* had more in common with ethnography and local color than it did with conventional geography. In straddling the professional and amateur spheres, geography already had much in common with ethnography, since the first published accounts of the world's varieties of climate and land formations, as well as peoples, derived from the travelogues of amateurs, namely missionaries and early explorers. Geography and ethnography also shared much in terms of their epistemology, their eighteenth-century colonialist origins, and their representational realism.[69] Most of its ethnographic writing, like its photography, meticulously recorded the physical traits and cultural practices of the earth's peoples, reflecting the period's fascination with racial typology. Its attentiveness to speech patterns, belief systems, and the intricacies and idiosyncrasies of various human communities reveals *National Geographic*'s indebtedness to the representational strategies of local-color fiction. As it documented the nation's regional cultural diversity, the magazine also recorded its reigning cultural prejudices. More provincial concerns lurked beneath ostensibly international topics, exposing conscious and unconscious anxieties about the nation's changing racial and ethnic constitution and the United States' shifting position within a global community.

Tensions between scientific "type" and atmospheric "art" in *National Geographic* lent themselves to the construction of two very different, yet mutually constitutive "types": the ethnographic subject of the photograph and the photographer as the agent and chief architect of the photograph's content or meaning.

The Hunters Hunted: Stalking the *National Geographic* Photographer on Assignment

Alongside portraits of nude "savages" there is no more enduring icon in *National Geographic* than that of the intrepid photographer. While ethnographic photography had traditionally aimed at documenting ethnic and cultural difference, in this new dynamic the photographer becomes the object of the camera's lens when it targets the agents of Western technological modernity. Indeed, by 1910, snapshots of photographers on assignment constitute their own distinct genre in *National Geographic,* and, once again, the traditions of realism and romance interfuse. In these photographs, the landscape supplies the exotic backdrop for the photographer, who now usurps the place of the ethnographic subject to serve both as local color and as hero. Images of photographers still participate in a romantic "salvage" operation, only in this newer permutation, photography salvages the male body threatened by modern decadence.

The *National Geographic* photographer has been described as a twentieth-century adaptation of the eighteenth-century European male imperialist, what has been termed the "seeing man," a personification of the "imperial stance of possession through the act of witnessing." On its surface, the "seeing man's" act of looking appears innocuous and thus functions as one of imperialism's chief "strategies of innocence," masking its practices of conquest.[70] While the "seeing man" presents a useful archetype for the male imperialist explorer, it fails to capture *National Geographic's* exploitation of the photographer in the field as a modern "type" that in fact stages the production of type itself.

The *National Geographic* photographer was not just a "seeing man," he was a man *seen* by thousands of the magazine's member-readers. In such instances where the camera and photographer take center stage, I maintain, exposures of the technological sleight-of-hand behind the photograph further undermine the magazine's production of type as timeless essence by revealing the artifice behind the frontier mythology *National Geographic* sought to invoke. Although the spectacle of the photographer fearlessly conquering the dangers of precipice and volcano may have facilitated identification with his exploits, photographs in which the photographer and camera take center stage denaturalize the camera by calling attention to the technological artifice behind the institution's famous metaphor for photography as a transparent "window on the world."

In the early twentieth century, the vanishing frontiersman of the American West forsakes his gun and reemerges as the *National Geographic* photographer on assignment. Well before Susan Sontag identified the camera with violence through the "sublimation of the gun," *National Geographic* articles such as "One Season's Game-Bag with Camera" (1908) and "Hunting with the Lens" (1914) hailed it as an instrument of conservation in which "it is more glorious and profitable" to "shoot" animals "through a lens than through the bore of a gun."[71] "There are no game laws for those who hunt with a Kodak" affirmed an advertisement featured in *National Geographic*'s July 1909 issue. "No hunter can boast of so satisfactory a bag as falls to him who hunts with the clairvoyant eye of the camera," observed Maynard Owen Williams in 1921. "The focusing knob of a graflex is a more thrilling bit of mechanism than the trigger of a rifle." In this image of sublimated sexual desire, the gun has transmuted into the camera as the medium of voyeuristic pleasure. Natural conservation and cultural destruction unite through the *National Geographic* photographer who merged with icons of rugged individualism, such as Theodore Roosevelt, and the enduring mythology of the American West, immortalized by literary icons Natty Bumppo and Huck Finn. *National Geographic* has been dubbed the "Camelot of Kodachrome" and its photographers an eclectic band of "knights" errant.[72] Indeed, throughout its 120-year history, *National Geographic* portrayed the photographer as a latter-day pioneer, risking life and limb for the perfect photograph—an endeavor that participates in late-nineteenth-century narratives invoking the strenuous exploits of the "epic story" of American imperialist expansion.

The *National Geographic* photographer's historical association with what Theodore Roosevelt called the "strenuous life" embodies romantic transcendence and gritty realism. Roosevelt's 1899 address at Chicago's aristocratic, all-male Hamilton Club led the charge in an American manhood and a white racial supremacy founded on imperialism abroad and violence at home. In his four-volume *The Winning of the West* (1889–96), for example, Roosevelt urged his brethren to "retain the strength of their Indian-fighter ancestors" to combat decadence and overcivilization lest Americans be overtaken by a stouter race.[73] The NGS played a central role in supporting Roosevelt's quest to bolster American manhood, making him an honorary member on November 18, 1910. That same year, an excerpt of his *African Game Trails: An Account of the African Wanderings of an American Hunter Naturalist* (1910) appeared in the November issue; and the January 1911 issue contains a photo-essay entitled "Roosevelt's African Trophies" celebrating his successful acquisition of hundreds of animal hides for the Smithsonian Institute. Highlighting the self-serving nature of Roosevelt's policy, published photographs of his numerous trophies appear within a more conservation-minded article, "Protecting Our Forests from Fire," by James Wilson, U.S. secretary of agriculture. As Donna Haraway has famously shown, the taxonomic impulse of the nineteenth century, romantic preservation, also entailed catastrophic destruction. Recovering from his failed 1912 campaign, Roosevelt undertook an arduous journey through the Amazon along the River of Doubt—illustrated in picture biography that displays him in a "primitive dugout canoe." In describing this adventure as his "last chance to be a boy," it was clear that Roosevelt undertook the journey as a means of salvaging his youth.[74] It is clear, also, that *National Geographic*'s photographer, the perennial boy scout–adventurer-explorer-cowboy, is a figure for an American national childhood derived from the western frontier ethos.

From a cultural perspective, then, the photographer amid vanquished nature emulates what George Stocking and James Clifford have termed ethnography's "salvage" paradigm that reflects the early twentieth century's obsession with cataloguing racial and cultural difference and its nostalgia for a preindustrial past. The "salvage" narrative involves both preservation and destruction. The concern to document ethnography's "disappearing object," writes Clifford, is "'salvage' ethnography in its widest sense." It involves a rhetorical process by which the ethnographic "other is lost, in disintegrating time and space, but saved in the text."[75] In these decades, immigration, urbanization, and industrialization contributed to the magazine's alignment with "salvage ethnography," the ethnographic search for lost, forgotten, and primitive cultures before their demise. *National Geographic*'s display of "modern" photographic accomplishments and cultural changes was counterbalanced by a romantic desire to safeguard older national customs and traditions against encroaching modernity.[76] Equipped with the authenticating technology of the camera, the *National Geographic* photographer assumed this heroic role of witness and guide whose photographs not only salvaged a "lost" or "forgotten" Other, but recuperated the metaphorical "childhood" of the nation represented by its frontier legacy.

Like salvage ethnography, the nineteenth-century American landscape art that influenced *National Geographic*'s earliest photographs embodied a romantic desire to transform the memory of what was lost, or what existed only within the imagination—the vanishing Indian, an untouched American wilderness, the pastoral—into the physically tangible and presently available. Led by Thomas Cole, the painters of the Hudson River school in the mid-nineteenth century captured the revelations of a quickly vanishing American frontier on canvas. Often in such paintings the presence of a human figure records "a vulnerable present, offering images of a past we presently regret," reflecting the "salvage" ethos prevalent in ethnographic writing.[77] The solitary figure in a canoe that glides through nineteenth-century landscape paintings captures the longing for a harmonious reconciliation of civilization and nature that would soon become a recurrent theme in *National Geographic* photography.[78] The camera, as a figuration of modern technology, and the canoe, the embodiment of the primitive, inaugurate *National Geographic*'s dialectical fusion of realism and romance. Together, these icons thematize the modern conflict between preservation and possession.

These icons of rugged frontier independence and modern technology fuse in a photograph taken at Deerlake, Newfoundland, that appears in a 1908 essay by the flash-light photographer George Shiras, "One Season's Game-Bag with Camera." The photograph, "Deerlake, Sandy River District, Newfoundland" (fig. 12) invokes the familiar features of nineteenth-century landscape painting. As in such Hudson River school paintings as David Johnson's 1869 oil *View on the Androscoggin River, Maine,* mountains and trees surrounding the lake frame the figure and canoe, which appear as if part of the landscape itself. A crucial distinction, however, is that Shiras's photograph violates Robinson's cardinal rule of artistic unity by showing the camera hulking in the canoe's bow. The caption beckons readers to "note the camera" lest unwary readers mistake its bulk for fishing tackle (425). Another photograph dated 1893 appears earlier in the article and depicts a "boat rigged for night-hunting with cameras, showing flash-light apparatus and jack lamp" (421). Unlike other modern technology, such as trains, which become naturalized in nineteenth-century landscape painting, *National Geographic* resists naturalizing the camera as part of the landscape.[79] In so doing, *National Geographic* turns this departure from pictorialist unity into a new genre by making photographic technology and its alienation from the natural world the subject of the photograph.

The photographer's heroism in *National Geographic* would not have been possible without advancements in photographic and print technologies and the cultural celebration of the photojournalist as an icon of rugged individualism. Ungainly tripods gave way to lighter hand-held cameras, making it easier to clamber up a tree or to scale a mountain precipice. Furthermore, with the rise of half-tone print technology in the late nineteenth and early twentieth centuries, an entirely unprecedented means for disseminating information developed, and, along with it, a new breed of news reporter. The photojournalist inspired a mythology in which news chroniclers themselves became newsworthy. "The Perils of Photography," published in the *Nation* in 1907, and "The Swashbucklers of the Camera" appearing in *Collier's* in 1912, "acknowledged the manly,

Fig. 12 "Deerlake, Sandy River District, Newfoundland." (George Shiras/National Geographic Image Collection)

even heroic status of news photographers, who courted danger to record war, violence, and disaster." An adventurer who "had to be patient, thick skinned, indifferent to danger," the photojournalist sacrificed art for action.[80] Critics of photography saw photojournalists as those who merely recorded events rather than shaping an artistic vision and fretted over the loss of artistic originality. As the photograph assumed cultural dominance, it triggered a corresponding anxiety about diminishing human efficacy, which the photograph came to symbolize.[81] By training its lens on photographers who appeared "at home" in the natural environment, if not actively in control of it, *National Geographic* offered a ready salve to these anxieties. The "epic story" an image recorded of a photographer's work offered a refreshing antidote to modern decadence, while highlighting the photographer's conquest of adverse photographic conditions.

It was not enough that photographs were thought to tell a story, the "hunt" for the photograph was itself a story. Therefore, snapshots of photographers risking life and limb as in a 1912 photograph of the eruption of Taal Volcano titled "Scientists under Fire" (fig. 13) or in a 1914 photograph,

Fig. 13 "Scientists under Fire." (Dean Worcester/National Geographic Image Collection)

"How a Difficult Photograph Is Secured," featuring a photographer dangling from a precipice in the Grand Canyon.[82] The popular press emulated popular romance adventure in the figure of the newly heroic photographer. Although the camera made possible the domestic reader's gaze and its reconstitution of the male body, paradoxically, masculinity became simultaneously "more effective and more vulnerable for that dependence on the technologies the Anglo-Saxon warriors were meant to escape."[83] Amplifying the photographer's sexuality, the phallic camera caught on film also exposes the institution's historic dependence on the camera for constructing its self-aggrandizing narratives.

In contrast to the huntsman in the landscape, sustained efforts to photograph the camera fail to naturalize its appearance in the natural setting. When a camera enters the photographic frame, however, the artifice of the image is also underscored. Representations of *National Geographic* photographers in the midst of natural disaster, atop dangerous precipices, or secluded in untouched nature place them squarely in both the revelatory role of the landscape painter and the romantic role of the figure in the landscape. In images such as "Scientists under Fire," which depicts the photographer Charles Martin, one of the first full-time staff photographers in the "first generation" of *National Geographic* photographers, the camera functions much like the frontiersman's gun in that it enhances the heroism of the human figure.[84] But such photographs reveal not so much the romantic sublime of the natural landscape but the institution's attempts to invest sublimity in its visual technology and in its project of nationalist exploration and expansion. Snapshots of the photographer potentially undermine the reader's vicarious participation because they highlight the mediated nature of that experience.

While less threatening to wildlife than the gun, images of wildlife photographers on assignment in some ways function as allegorical enactments of imperial violence. In "Hunting Birds with a Camera" (August 1923; fig. 14), for instance, the presence of the camera displaces a heron chick from its nest. A photograph titled "Among the Skyscrapers of a Heron Village" bears the caption, "A nearly grown young bird in the foreground left the nest when the camera man sat down in it."[85] Underscoring the element of trespass, the caption exposes the violence implicit in an image likely intended to enliven a dry, conservation-minded article. The photograph was reproduced in Grosvenor's celebratory romp through NGS institutional history. This time, the caption reads: "A nearly fledged great blue heron chick surrenders its nest to the camera and cameraman near San Francisco Bay in 1917. Early wildlife photographers had to challenge the wild with equipment better suited to the studio."[86] Converting the wild to his own purposes, the photographer highlights his compositional ingenuity by transforming the bird's nest into a makeshift studio.

We see a similar transformation of nature into studio in a 1926 *National Geographic* photograph titled "A Tangle of Roots Converted into a Photographer's Darkroom" (fig. 15). The caption describes how "Santos, the motion-picture photographer, discovered this huge tree growing on the river bank, where water was handy. He saw its natural advantages and converted it into his 'laboratorio.'" The tree presents its "natural advantages" and, under the photographer's guiding hand, becomes nature's darkroom and the site of human cultural production.[87] Though part of a larger frontier narrative commemorating the NGS's pioneering role in wildlife photography, these photographs and their captions signal the implicit violence of the photographer's "occupation" of the natural setting. Chapter 5 takes up the photographer's trespass in the context of *National Geographic*'s "jungle housekeeping" genre.

Images in which the camera appears potentially disrupt the process

of audience identification with the camera in the phenomenon the film historian Christian Metz has termed "primary identification." Metz bases his theory on Lacan's paradigm of the "mirror stage" of infantile development, where the act of beholding one's reflection in a mirror, or "primary identification," marks a critical stage in the recognition of the self as an entity separate from others. Extending the analogy to the cinema, Metz views film as a succession of mirrors in which spectators identify with the camera as an agent of "all seeing" vision. Ellen Strain usefully describes primary identification as the internalization of the camera's extended powers of vision as a prosthetic "tool of muscular perception."[88] Where cameras break into the frame, however, seeing becomes self-reflexive. According to Metz, seeing itself involves a "double movement" of gazing outward upon physical objects whose images are in turn impressed upon

Fig. 15 "A Tangle of Roots Converted into a Photographer's Darkroom." (Albert Stevens/ National Geographic Image Collection)

the retina.[89] *National Geographic* snapshots of photographers on assignment potentially make this movement visible. Metz's formulation helps us understand *National Geographic*'s "double gesture" mentioned at the start of this chapter, of going out into the world to record images of exotic difference, while glancing backward at troubling images of difference at home. What images of photographers on assignment reveal is that the act of photography figures as the "occupation" of space, and that the "taking" of an image is itself a form of projection. It aims to fulfill a desire, whether unacknowledged or acknowledged, and thus to substantiate memory. By laying bare the institutional stage management of photographs, images of photographers caught in "the act" perform the modernist move of bringing these subtle machinations to mind. Such images expose the "unconscious optics" that Benjamin identified as a positive aftereffect of the destruction of artistic aura.

While *National Geographic* reproduces familiar iconic visual systems— from local-color markers of regional, cultural, and racial difference to aesthetic photographs that build on ethnographic and pictorial compositional conventions—any given issue also constitutes a unique arrangement or configuration of those systems. The tensions within and between these representational systems provide fertile ground for reading the magazine more critically, not just as an organ for nationalist and imperialist beliefs and policies, but as an institution that has, in turn, produced its own set of icons surviving in the popular imagination: the *National Geographic* photographer, popular images about the primitive, the savage, and, by contrast, the modern. In the early twentieth century, *National Geographic* was both a cultural product and a producer of culture. Moreover, it has much to tell us about how cultural institutions deploy familiar narratives and innovative aesthetic forms to achieve iconic force.

FRACTURING THE GLOBAL FAMILY ROMANCE

National Geographic, World War I, and Fascism

In the run-up to U.S. involvement in the First World War and the deployment of American troops in October 1917, *National Geographic*'s deepening internationalism often took the form—ultimately an iconic form—of photographs of families. Increasingly, ameliorative images of an extended global human family displaced biological language that in previous decades had linked cultural and racial difference to genetic contagion. Articles such as "Our Foreign-Born Citizens" (February 1917), along with the photo-essays "Little Citizens of the World" (February 1917) and "Madonnas of Many Lands" (June 1917), are a few examples of the many images of immigrant families, women with babes in arms, and, in particular, children of the world that celebrated national and global diversity during these years.

In taking this turn, *National Geographic* was tapping into, and adapting, a deeply rooted cultural tradition. The distillation of the nation's hopes and fears into iconic images of children dates back to the earliest days of the American republic. In the nineteenth century, ideas connecting the child to national democratic ideals found expression through a robust culture of information. Images of healthy youth, cherubic infants, and frolicking country lads and lasses circulated widely: in genre paintings, and in illustrations and photographs in classroom primers, child-rearing manuals, and the popular press. Not only did such pictures visually symbolize the nation's prosperity, but the figure of the child as "world evangelizer," spreading the blessings of the American system, provided an innocent gloss to the nation's twofold domestic and global imperial interests.[1]

Images of families and children are powerful precisely because they link private emotion to public interest. The emotional power of seeing children derives, in large measure, from the powerful biological and social bonds they invoke, for not only do they give the individual parents a kind of genetic immortality, they are also carriers of a national culture for future generations. At the same time, a child's inherent vulnerability can trigger an instinctive protectiveness on the part of adults and call forth a sense a civic responsibility regarding the proper rearing of the nation's young citizens. Crucially, this civic imperative for adults to shelter a child's innocence, to preserve its safety, and therefore to safeguard a cultural legacy for the members of a larger community or national "family," helps rationalize the apparently irrational: personal sacrifice in a time of war.

From this perspective, *National Geographic*'s familial photographs on the eve of U.S. entry into the First World War served a twofold purpose: They could stir nationalist loyalties and transnational sympathies alike, as Allied nations saw themselves as members of an extended global family united against a common enemy. In June 1918, for example, U.S. Secretary of State Robert Lansing invoked the globe's "wretched throngs of unhappy women and children" in the cause against "Prussianism," a menacing will to "world domination" thought to originate in a German racial "mind." In an accompanying photograph, a soldier clutches his bayonet while bidding his wife and infant farewell, and the caption, as though to amplify Lansing's case against Germany, proclaims, "He goes forth to fight for the safety and happiness of future generations."[2] Familial images like this worked to cultivate cosmopolitan sympathies and international loyalties—based on the assumption of shared democratic, or national, ideals.

In *National Geographic,* the concept of family both includes and excludes, thereby embodying the period's "paradox of American nationalism" in which people sought "national unity through fraternity *and* through hatred, developing modes of sympathy as well as repression."[3] The magazine's photographs of families and children were not mere catalysts for consent around national ideals and cultural myths, but made visible consent's darker side in the "political socialization" of the nation's youth through iconic symbols. In the same way that learning to "read" images as iconic signs requires instruction in repeated acts of looking and assigning meaning, political socialization similarly involves the steady accumulation and organization of attitudes toward one's national political culture.[4] As we will see, chilling examples of political socialization resurfaced after the war in *National Geographic*'s profascist articles of the 1920s and 1930s, featuring photographs of Hitler Youth and gun-toting, boy Blackshirts of Mussolini's fascist regime.

Indeed, in the wake of the "Prussianism" it decried during the First Word War, *National Geographic* went on to ignore more pernicious forms of global domination in the form of fascism. While fascist Italy and Nazi Germany steadily built up their industrial military might throughout the 1920s and 1930s, *National Geographic*'s seventeen articles on Germany and thirty-three on Italy presented bucolic countrysides, picturesque castles and medieval villages, dramatic landscapes, historic monuments, and popular vacation spots. When Mussolini's troops marched on Rome on October 29, 1922, *National Geographic* published "The Island of Sardinia and Its People" (January 1923); when Hitler became Germany's chancellor in 1933, it published "Freiburg—Gateway to the Black Forest" (August 1933); when Mussolini's army swept through Ethiopia on October 3, 1935, while planes overhead spewed mustard gas throughout the seven-month invasion, *National Geographic* published "Horace—Classic Poet of the Countryside" (December 1935); when Mussolini signed his "Pact of Blood" with Hitler in 1939, it published "Italy's Monuments Tell Rome's Magnificence" (March 1940). If ever there was a moment for *National Geographic* to warn of "Germany's dream of world domination," as it did in June 1918, it was after Hitler's remilitarization of Germany in 1936. Instead, the magazine's tacit support of fascism peaked in December 1937 with "Changing Berlin," by Douglas Chandler, an American Nazi propagandist later convicted of treason.

How can we reconcile *National Geographic*'s repudiation of Germany and its expansionist "Prussianism" during the First World War with its seeming endorsement of German and Italian fascism—a movement committed to romantic notions of familial national identity and racial destiny—in the run-up to the Second World War? While the nativist and anti-Semitic sympathies of the magazine's editor-in-chief, Gilbert H. Grosvenor, partially account for its hospitality to fascist countries, fully addressing this question requires setting *National Geographic*'s familial images against the backdrop of global fascism, a broader cultural climate in which the solidarity of a national "family" excluded outsiders, even when those "outsiders" shared the same geographic or national space.

This chapter explores how *National Geographic*'s iconicity as an educational institution, as expressed in its ubiquitous images of the family, and especially children, helps to illuminate the twentieth century's defining cultural conflicts between individual identity and group identification within an emerging global public sphere. In *National Geographic*, "family" became a visual master trope that mediated tensions between inclusive cosmopolitanism and exclusionary nativism, national identification and global affiliation. In what follows, I trace how disagreements between nativists, like Grosvenor, and advocates of a "cosmopolitan spirit" during the First World War reveal an underlying culture of dissent most vividly expressed by *National Geographic*'s critical readers. Readers did not march in lockstep to Grosvenor's conservative politics, but instead reflected the nation's complex attitudes toward the war and the radically heightened fears of internationalism that followed in its wake. Furthermore, *National Geographic*'s coverage of the war and its aftermath foregrounds the complexities of fascism—and their latent forms in the United States—in relation to global complex connectivity.

The War Within: Cosmopolitanism versus Nativism

With the onset of the First World War, lingering "Anglo-Saxon" nativist sentiment in the late nineteenth century mutated into the assimilationist rhetoric of "100 percent Americanism," while a cadre of progressive intellectuals, including the pragmatist philosopher and progressive educator John Dewey, the Jewish intellectual Horace Kallen, and the social critic Randolph Bourne, among others, embraced cosmopolitan cultural diversity as a weapon against regional, socioeconomic, and global divisiveness.[5] In the years just before and during the war, the United States experienced a dramatic reconfiguration of its racial demographic across geographic lines, as immigrants and agrarian blacks flocked by the thousands to urban industrial centers. The years 1899 to 1914 also saw a dramatic rise in immigration from southern and central Europe. By the time the United States officially joined the Allied cause in April 1917, some 4,662,000 of its immigrant citizens originated from "enemy" soil.[6] Against that backdrop, liberal progressives increasingly turned their attention to education as an ameliorative measure against economic and racial factionalism at home and abroad.

"It is not enough to teach the horrors of war and to avoid everything which would stimulate international jealousy and animosity," argued Dewey in *Democracy and Education* (1916). "The emphasis must be put upon whatever binds people together in cooperative human pursuits and results, apart from geographical limitations" (76). The First World War, and the debate it sparked among intellectuals, dramatized the potential of global interconnectedness to transform traditional ideas of nationhood, citizenship, and cultural allegiance. In the war years, *National Geographic* reflected this "cosmopolitan spirit" by negotiating America's divided loyalties in images of cosmopolitan diversity at home and abroad.

On the eve of war in Europe, many *National Geographic* readers identified with its cosmopolitanism. As Myra Hedges of Philadelphia quite bluntly put it, in August 1914, "I have so thoroughly enjoyed each number as it came to me, and I am beginning to feel like a cosmopolitan." This was so much the case that some *National Geographic* readers suggested renaming the magazine the "International Geographic" to convey more accurately its global scope.[7] Notwithstanding its founders' earlier emphasis on cultivating national civic identity, an unanticipated consequence of *National Geographic*'s global images was to heighten its readers' international sensibilities.

National Geographic's February 1917 issue, "Our Foreign-Born Citizens," called forth this "cosmopolitan spirit" to challenge a congressional bill mandating literacy tests for new immigrants. Celebrating immigrant contributions to national progress, the issue featured eighteen photographs of both "typical" immigrant families from Scotland and Scandinavia and the "new" immigrants from Italy, Russia, and India, who represented the country's cultural diversity. Ten years after the magazine's contributors warned of immigrant blood contamination, the magazine now celebrated assimilation. A caption under a photograph titled "Serbian Gypsies," for example, declared: "Ethnological measurements show that even the very bones of the immigrant's body are warped into an American type in his children and his children's children. What could be more eloquent than this of the success of the process of Americanization as the generations rise and pass!" (128). Here, the caption suggests that the new environment and the mingling of peoples produce a more evolved "American type." Besides familiarizing readers with the human varieties blended in the American "melting pot," however, photographs of immigrant families also recalled its readers to an earlier developmental stage before civilization's fall from an imagined state of innocence.

In a number of articles, in fact, *National Geographic* invited its readers to imagine the human family before its differentiation, its fragmentation, into a multiplicity of cultures and conflicts. In "Little Citizens of the

World" (February 1917), for instance, fifteen snapshots of children conjure up a precultural or prelapsarian condition that contrasts with the present state of the world. From Sweden to Japan, North and South America to the Philippines and the Middle East, the globe's children are shown at work and at play, expressing a complex array of emotions, from curiosity and skepticism to smiling pleasure. Each photo expresses a romantic nostalgia for childhood as a precultural state of innocence, however tenuous. The first of these images, suggestively titled "The Apple of Discord," shows a small boy gazing at an apple in his hand. The next shows an impoverished Mexican child under a giant saguaro cactus; its wistful title, "Child of Sorrow and Woe," invokes Blakean innocence and experience. Whereas progressive educators of the 1880s and 1890s had sought to guide small minds through successive stages of development from savagery and barbarism to civilization, this photo-essay reclaims a romantic understanding of childhood as a haven from civilization's ravages. At the same time, the figure of the Mexican child, figured as a "waif," sounds a warning of its fragility and, indirectly, of Germany's threat to global democracy.[8]

Given the United States' long history of enlisting children to support its most cherished beliefs regarding individual liberty and collective responsibility, it is perhaps not surprising that children in *National Geographic* served as uniquely powerful icons of an extended global family.[9] In an era when the formerly bright lines between "home" and "abroad," the "foreign" and the "familiar," grew increasingly blurry, images of childhood and of harmonious family life promised psychological security in the midst of international turmoil. If imagined communities cohere, in part, around shared sentiment, then *National Geographic's* photographs of the essential human qualities of families—their happinesses, hardships, and sufferings—could be understood to mark the beginnings of an emerging global sentiment.[10]

The global ethnographic variety portrayed in *National Geographic,* and the opportunities it presented for the reader's vicarious global travel, in many ways reflected Dewey's ideal for geographic education. "Geography is a topic that originally appeals to imagination—even to the romantic imagination," wrote Dewey in accord with the longings of the magazine's earliest founders and *Geographic* readers. "The variety of peoples and environments, their contrast with familiar scenes," remove the mind from "the monotony of the customary," argued Dewey; "local or home geography" provides "an intellectual starting point for moving out into the unknown." By exposing its readers to "the large world beyond," *National*

Geographic fostered, at least in principle, what Dewey's protégé, the social critic Randolph Bourne, would call the "cosmopolitan spirit," an ideal of intercultural contact and understanding based on sympathetic identification with foreign peoples and nations.[11] Throughout the war, readers identified with what they saw as the magazine's positive internationalism in a world increasingly divided into factions.

In this way, the magazine negotiated the psychological stresses of complex connectivity by supplying the visual counterpart to the "rhetoric of variety" prevalent in the 1880s and into the twentieth century. This "rhetoric of variety" portrayed "modern America not as a place of social and labor unrest, a republic divided by class, race, and regional factions, but instead as a land of spatial and material abundance."[12] In *National Geographic,* iconic images of the family and children both celebrated human variety and imagined its containment through assimilation. The magazine's preoccupation with racial and ethnic "types" helped to canonize visual markers of difference, which could symbolize cosmopolitan variety, while simultaneously reinscribing the line between Anglo-Saxon "natives" and the as-yet-unassimilated foreign masses.

Throughout the First World War, the *National Geographic* magazine reflected these national tensions between cosmopolitan diversity and "Anglo-Saxon" nativism. Its photographs of families at first followed Grosvenor's 1915 editorial principle of nonpartisan "kindliness," an editorial stance befitting the nation's initial neutrality toward the European conflict.[13] Soon after, however, the national mood shifted in response to the sinking of the Lusitania, Mexico's threatened revolt, and Germany's growing interest in Central and South America. A wave of anti-German sentiment swept the nation, and public opinion turned against its 2.3 million German Americans.[14]

With U.S. troops on French soil in October 1917, *National Geographic* began to ignore its nonpartisan editorial mandate by publishing articles referring pejoratively to "boches" (French slang comparing Germans to a head of cabbage), and what contributor Harriet Chalmers Adams called the "maniacal Hun." To boost troop morale, U.S. Secretary of War William Howard Taft cheered the Allies in "hunting the Hun" over the Atlantic. Even Grosvenor's father, Edwin, a history professor at Amherst, lent a hand to "Hunnism" in his December 1918 article, "The Races of Europe," in which he colorfully described the "horror" with which Romans and Teutons regarded the ancient Huns. Of the Germans themselves, he wrote, "Because of the enormities of the past four and a half years, this group cannot be trusted until they have shown repentance not of a few days or months, but by a generation or more of decent action."[15]

Not all readers, however, took that view. In response to Grosvenor's account of "blood-thirsty" Germanic tribes, one reader wrote, "after reading the description of the Land and people I sprung from (having been born and raised in the small town of Berlin) I had to look in the mirror to see if I could find traces of my *barbaric* origin." By the war's end, more readers had grown weary of the magazine's persistent "hymns of hate."[16] While these comments reflect the internationalist "cosmopolitan spirit" of *National Geographic*'s members, both the nation and the magazine were divided between those who embraced America's growing cultural pluralism and those who clung to "100 percent Americanism" modeled on Anglo-Saxon nativism.

Amidst this clash of interests and motives, *National Geographic* drew upon icons like the national flag to stir nationalist loyalties while also appealing to global idealism. Flags, wrote Grosvenor, have "deep and noble significance far removed from their use in leading men to battle. In reality flags are bulwarks of idealism" (281). That idealism, he went on to suggest, linked individual patriotism with broader communitarian, perhaps even global, impulses. The NGS even stopped its presses to raise money for the Red Cross with its "Flag Number" (October 1917) featuring 1,917 world flags "in their accurate colors and design." Here was a perfect example of the magazine's unique blend of nationalism and cosmopolitanism; each flag symbolized a particular national identity, yet together they seemed to stand for the collective interests of the global family.

Still, the American flag's power as an emblem of the militaristic protection of national sovereignty and American cultural ideals took center stage. That power, moreover, was heightened by the presence of children, the building blocks of a larger national "family," as in the studio portrait "Flag-Makers," which depicts a young girl sitting in a chair mending an American flag (fig. 16), while a boy beside her threads a needle.[17] Reminiscent of Norman Rockwell's then-popular cover illustrations of children for the *Saturday Evening Post,* the hazy, backlit image also recalls the early American notion of republican motherhood in such homespun anecdotes as Betsy Ross's making of the first American flag during the Revolutionary War.[18] Underscoring the iconicity of the flag as a near-sacred emblem of national identity, the caption both invokes the late-nineteenth- and early-twentieth-century "culture of character" and positions *National Geographic* as the nation's educator.[19] "They are the flag-makers of the future," the caption declares, "for the flag represents just the character and ideals of American citizens." The caption also draws on nationalist narratives identifying children's health with the nation's health by appealing to adult readers' civic duties in the "care and development of the children's minds and bodies," which "must not be neglected in the stress of war" (474). Here, two fair-skinned American youths are presented for the nation's adult and young readers alike as an object lesson in patriotism and national character: industry, thrift, and hard work are shown in the service of raising, quite literally, the national standard.

The magazine's progressive educational aims, centered as they were on public education and civic responsibility, were highlighted during the war years. Yet some readers objected to the magazine fueling exclusionary "Hunnism" at home. Between 1914 and 1918, by far the loudest outcry and steepest drop in membership came from "hyphenated" Americans who found the magazine's description of Germans as a race of bloodthirsty "Huns" at odds with its spirit of internationalism. The *National Geographic*'s coverage was so unabashedly partisan that some angry readers declared it "a common British war-sheet." Even "war is not a reason for science to become partisan," wrote a doctor from New York. Others questioned whether it was "geographical knowledge" or "personal knowledge" that prompted the magazine "to call the Belgians or some other races, Huns" and chided the magazine for sowing "the seed of hate between races in our beloved America." As a result, many withdrew their membership in the NGS. "I believed when I joined your club that I was associating myself with a scientific body which had an international patriotism and that calm poise which would hold it secure against the howling of the mob," one reader remarked. "Nor can we as a nation wash our hands in innocence with a holier-than-Thou mien," wrote a pastor in Wisconsin, "for we not only helped to prolong the terrible carnage in Europe by furnishing the Allies with enormous amounts of ammunition, but we must also confess with shame that there are plenty of species of Hunnism in our own country."[20]

The pastor's objection to a more broadly chauvinistic American "Hunnism" reflected a fear in some quarters of the steady erosion of First Amendment freedoms within a climate of intensifying coercion. Most notably, Woodrow Wilson issued a series of executive orders curtailing freedom of speech, while the Espionage Act of 1917 and the Sedition Act of 1918 banned pro-German speech, or, conversely, speech against Great

Fig. 16 "Flag-Makers." (Edwin Jackson/National Geographic Image Collection)

Britain or its allies. In April 1917, Wilson established the Committee on Public Information, headed by the journalist George Creel, to spread prowar propaganda. He also sanctioned the American Protective League of 250,000 quasi-official officers to police anti-American activities.[21] Numerous photographs in *National Geographic* published in the war years were credited to the Committee on Public Information, including two of American soldiers performing drills in Lansing's article on "Prussianism." The magazine's embrace of a national prowar consensus needs to be read in light of such broader efforts to institutionalize consent. These efforts were complicated by the magazine's internationalism, and were resisted by some readers, yet they form an essential part of the story of *National Geographic*'s complex reaction to the cataclysm of world war.

"Hunnism" at Home: Haitian Savages and English Allies

National Geographic's coverage of the U.S. occupation of Haiti in 1915 vividly illustrates the nation's own expansionist "Hunnism" and the limits of the magazine's progressive internationalism. The U.S. occupation of Haiti following the Haitian government's overthrow and execution of President Vilbrun Guillaume Sam in 1915, rather than restoring democracy to a nation that had struggled for independence since the eighteenth century, showed that U.S. policy in the region had moved into the realm of military law. And the coverage of these events in the press and in *National Geographic* tended to position Haiti as outside the "civilized" community of nations. By assuming the task of determining a nation's ideological and blood "kinship" with other nations, the *National Geographic* positioned itself as arbiter of those standards for membership in a global family of democratic nations.

As early as 1908, with Rear Admiral Colby M. Chester's article "Haiti: A Degenerating Island. The Story of Its Past Grandeur and Present Decay" (March 1908), the image of Haiti as a fallen Eden presaged later justifications for U.S. military intervention. Evoking Christopher Columbus's image of Hispaniola as the "Garden of Eden," where "all go naked, men and women, just as their mothers bring them forth," Chester chronicles the island's unfortunate fall and expulsion from domestic paradise. "Since [Columbus's] time a sad change has gradually crept over the island," he writes, as the Haitians have reverted to "barbarous religious customs handed down from their African ancestors" (214). Chester's narrative of a backward people unable to govern themselves echoed an all-too-familiar refrain that, a few years earlier, had sanctioned U.S. colonialism in the Philippines after the Spanish-American War.[22] With the onset of World War I, then, as the Germans stirred up anti-American sentiment in Central and South America, this same rhetoric justified U.S. military occupation.

Following the U.S. military takeover of Haiti on July 28, 1915, *National Geographic*'s emphasis on Haitian savagery intensified. The unattributed article "Wards of the United States," subtitled "Notes on What Our Country Is Doing for Santo Domingo, Nicaragua, and Haiti" (August 1916), portrayed the United States as a benevolent patron ministering to its Haitian children by providing loans to pay debts and encouraging economic stability, in an effort to restore these countries to paradisiacal innocence. Rather than participants in a collective human family, the descendents of the Haitian Adam and Eve are portrayed as degenerate offspring unfit to survive in a global community without the intervention of kindly American overlordship.

The reality, as reported in the *Nation* and elsewhere, was that Uncle Sam's policies were destroying Haitian families. The four-part exposé "Self-Determining Haiti" by the African American social activist James Weldon Johnson, for example, testified to the atrocities and denial of civil liberties committed in the name of humanitarian uplift. Under U.S. military governance, a nation that had been independent for more than a century was now ruled by martial law. Its press had been censored, its constitution emended to allow foreign purchase of land, its legislature dismantled, and its judicial system replaced by a military court. In order to build a highway to transport military equipment and officers from Port-au-Prince to Cape Haitien, the occupation revived the long-defunct *corvée*, or "road law," requiring all Haitians to provide several hours of service in the repair of local public roads or pay a fee. Under the pretense of the *corvée*, the occupation forcibly took Haitian men from their families "to toil for months in far sections of the country." Those who refused were "beaten into submission" or shot if they tried to escape. Others who fled to nearby mountains provided further pretense for the U.S. military to hunt down the supposed "bandits" and rebels. Within five years after U.S. occupation, three thousand Haitian men, women, and children had been killed, far outnumbering the handful of American military casualties.[23]

Despite the publicizing of such atrocities, another unattributed *National Geographic* article, "Haiti and Its Regeneration by the United States" (December 1920), continued to disparage Haitian culture. Describing the nation as a "carnival of barbarism," it went on to characterize Haiti's inhabitants as practitioners of "cannibalism and the black rites of voodoo" and the "sacrifice of children and of animals to the mumbo jumbos of the local wizards" (500). To their credit, discerning *National Geographic* readers recognized the piece for what it was: a blatant attempt to "whitewash" the U.S. occupation, which had received negative press in the wake of atrocities committed by U.S. Marines. In one case, an outraged Wisconsin doctor who had received an unsatisfactory response to his complaint from the magazine's assistant editor, John Oliver La Gorce, forwarded the letter to the *Nation*, which published its own outraged rejoinder to the magazine's "imperialist propaganda."[24] As this episode suggests, *National Geographic*'s readership continued to offer astute commentary on the nation's "Hunnism" and its expression in the magazine.

While metaphors of a fallen Eden worked to deny Haitians membership in a global family and to justify U.S. military occupation, metaphors
of blood kinship with the English served, conversely, to strengthen America's frayed colonial ties. In an address to Congress days before the U.S.
officially joined the cause of the Allies in the First World War, Mississippi
senator John Sharp Williams appealed to shared ethnicity and shared republican values to encourage popular support for America's entry into
the war. As a Southern Democrat, Williams boldly declared his sympathy
with the Allies on the nativist basis of a common Anglo-Saxon heritage:
"I love my plantation better than any other plantation, my country better than any other country, my State better than any other State in the
Union, and my country better than any other country in the world, and
my race—the English-speaking race—better than any other race." Calling upon Americans' "natural sympathy" with the English, the address
proclaimed Anglo-Saxon racial inheritance and British colonialism the
origins of the nation's republican ideals.[25]

Again, however, *National Geographic* readers proved a tricky lot. Boil-
ing with anticolonialist rage against England and her allies, some of them
urged the magazine to publish "what Britain has done to Ireland, India,
South Africa, and to her women and workingmen, who are now bearing
the brunt of the war." Others invoked the nation's "traditional" enmity to
England to declare Williams's speech "un-American and un-patriotic if
not worse."[26] In a polyglot, multiethnic America, what it meant to be an
"American" had not yet been determined, and as *National Geographic*'s
war coverage attempted to consolidate Allied consensus, it drew forth
dissenting notions of "Americanness" from its readers.

Although Williams's remarks drew fire from readers, when the United
States declared war on Germany one month later, *National Geographic* endorsed Williams's Anglo-Saxonism, featuring an address from President
Woodrow Wilson, "Do Your Bit for America," and "A Tribute to America"
by former British prime minister Herbert Henry Asquith, whose gratitude to "our kinsmen in America" renewed England's "fealty and devotion"
to the United States (295). The March 1917 issue thus brought before Americans' eyes chilling images of trench warfare and bold sacrifice and rousing
articles on Russia's revolution and its (short-lived) promise for democracy.

Over the next two years, *National Geographic* recorded the emotional
toll of the Great War, its high price in human and economic sacrifice, and
a generation's disillusionment. *National Geographic* readers likewise reflected the sharply divided mood of a country torn between older, nativist

loyalties urging the assimilation of America's new arrivals, and the feelings of recent immigrants who retained deep sympathies with their countries of origin. Still others who had welcomed the magazine as a haven from politics found themselves weary of war coverage. "Won't you please stop filling up your magazine with war stuff?" wrote Mrs. C. R. Daniels of Massachusetts. "All we see anywhere and everywhere, in newspapers, magazines and all manner of periodicals is war, war, war. Everybody is on the verge of a nervous breakdown with all this war business." Or as A. E. Breen of Mt. Morris, New York, wrote on May 7, 1917, "I believed when I joined your club that I was associating myself with a scientific body which had an international patriotism and that calm poise which would hold it secure against the howling of the mob." Still other readers based their appreciation of the magazine's war reportage on cosmopolitan grounds. As if echoing the words of Dewey, a reader from Texas gave his "hearty approval" of the "patriotic contents" of *National Geographic*'s recent issues: "To my mind this work is directly the business especially of our Society . . . not lands but people are of prime importance. Only when we come to actually know each other can there be permanent peace."[27] Readers' letters revealed the stirrings of cosmopolitan sympathies that events following the Bolshevik uprising later undermined.

How well the citizens of different countries could truly know one another, or understand each other's hopes and aspirations, became a matter of profound disillusionment in the violent aftermath of the Russian Revolution, which the *National Geographic* covered as part of its general reporting on World War I. At first, the fall of the Russian monarchy in February 1917 seemed to herald the triumph of democracy over social oppression. The war, seemingly, was no longer about ethnic-nationalist clashes in a Europe that, in Bourne's view, had failed to realize the "cosmopolitan spirit," but became, in the words of *National Geographic* contributor Stanley Washburn, a "war for world democracy and the cause of humanity against the German Government." For Washburn, the "establishment of the democratic idea, based on morals, ethics, equity, and justice, which must come from this war, is worth, not a million or ten million casualties, but fifty million, if from this struggle there emerge an enduring conception as to the fundamental basis on which society, progress, and civilization must rest in perpetuity."[28] Though it focused on Germany as scapegoat, his address, which grounded its conception of democracy on "morals, ethics, equity, and justice," nonetheless strikingly evokes the contemporary concepts of "rule of law, political equality, democratic politics, [and] social justice" that social theorists have identified as the basis for a global cosmopolitan social democracy.[29]

This vision of global democracy, however, was soon darkened by a protectionist nationalism that developed in response to the Bolshevik seizure of power in October 1917. In the May 1917 issue of *National Geographic,* former U.S. president William Howard Taft had portrayed the ideological divide between democracy and communism as an unbridgeable chasm, maintaining that "we have arrayed on the one side the democracies of the world against the military autocracies on the other." That same month, another contributor invoked the iconic vulnerability of the child by describing democracy as a "waif left to die unless we, as trustees, accept the task of rescuing it."[30] The term "waif" was particularly fitting, conjuring the fragility of the orphan at a time when 6 million children had lost parents as a consequence of the Great War.[31] The terms of sympathy had shifted from international understanding to an increasingly defensive sense of nationalistic mission embodied in the emotionally charged imagery of vulnerable childhood in the figure of democracy as a "waif." The undeniable turn of Russia toward authoritarianism, together with the looming specter of international Bolshevism, later fueled widespread agitation in the United States against Wilson's vision of collective world governance in the League of Nations. Indeed, many feared that communism had its own ambitions of creating an international family, on its own terms, through a unification of the peoples of the earth under its banner. The evolution of Western nationalism and isolationism in the early twentieth century went forward, in no small part, precisely because of the presence of this rival global vision.

In that climate, a generalized fear of the masses, particularly the lower classes, and of international movements in general, spawned a collective attentiveness among U.S. educators, politicians, and magazine editors to the vital importance of visual media for shaping mass perception.[32] New geopolitical battle lines had been drawn, and the struggle was on for the loyalties of "the people"—between the totalizing ideology of communism and the more ethnic-based and soil-based nationalisms of the West, with the media as central players or pawns.

Marshalling the Armies of Democracy: "Pictorial Geography," Education, and Assimilation

National Geographic emerged with a heightened profile during the First World War because it not only educated readers on the geopolitical boundaries marking the European conflict, but also documented the psychological boundaries between nations and "races" perceived as hereditary enemies and rivals. If the "modern form" of the *National Geographic* was born in the crucible of the Spanish-American War in 1898, then its educational mission and iconic stature achieved full flowering after the First World War.[33] Education, assimilation, and military conscription fit hand in glove with the magazine's own political commitments to the Allied forces.[34]

Following the war, *National Geographic* reclaimed its international image through its "Pictorial Geography" series of geographic flashcards for elementary schools in 1919. The brainchild of Jessie L. Burrall, an educator from St. Cloud Minnesota, who collaborated with Grosvenor to produce the series, "Pictorial Geography" focused on children as its predominant audience. The series highlighted the nation's cultural diversity as well as that of the globe's geographic regions. At the same time, it symbolically linked childhood to militaristic nationalism in the face of external threats to democracy, rising fears of communism, and the psychological trauma of war.

A trial run of pictorial geography's socializing function took place at U.S. military training camps for foreign-born soldiers. "Bringing the World to Our Foreign-Language Soldiers" (August 1918) featured a U.S. military camp in California that used *National Geographic* to help forge a "family" from the nation's recent immigrants. Indeed, the magazine's role in assimilating the foreign-born to military command is revealed in one photograph that shows a khaki-clad officer standing over the foreign soldiers, one booted foot planted firmly on a chair and one hand on his hip in a posture of authority reinforced by the conspicuous display of a *National Geographic* magazine in his hand, its trademark gilded cover visible to the reader (fig. 17).[35] Situating the magazine's gilded frame within the camera's frame, the article deliberately reinforces the magazine's iconicity as the nation's educator and as a bridge between cultural differences in the "new" and "old" worlds disordered and rearranged in its pages.

Both the image and the article reveal the persistent tensions between the magazine's implicit cultural pluralism and its overt assimilationist nationalism. In one sense, the military training camp sought not only to educate foreign-born soldiers to fight but also to develop in them "that intangible something" that "took from the classes the taint of the 'Mex' and the 'Wop' and the 'Squarehead' and made them all plain fellow-men—Americans. Is it not, after all, a little strange to speak of *foreigners* in the

Fig. 17 "Bringing the World to Our Foreign-Language Soldiers." (Christina Krysto/National Geographic Image Collection)

American Army?"[36] Throughout the article, dialect and broken English communicate the immigrants' cultural distinctiveness and variety—yet they speak within an assimilating context of developing a shared military language of national allegiance and personal sacrifice. As with the image of the military commander holding the magazine aloft, here *National Geographic* serves as the nation's educator, as a visible embodiment of the political and cultural ideals believed to transcend language, race, and birth. It was the embrace of those abstract ideals—all offered under the sign of Americanism—that allowed the magazine to navigate (not always successfully) between a narrow ethnoculturalism on the one hand and a debilitating neutrality on the other.

Following its precursor in the military training camp, "Pictorial Geography" offered the magazine a means of salvaging the internationalism that had been tarnished by its readers' denunciations of "Hunnism." Prior to its public launching of the series, *National Geographic* published an address by Secretary of the Interior Franklin Lane, an NGS board member, that in many ways reflected the cosmopolitan principles Burrall and Grosvenor sought for the series. In "What Is It to Be an American?" (April 1919), Lane proclaimed the United States a cosmopolitan nation in which "blood alone does not control the destiny of man," but "out of his environment, his education, the food that he eats, the neighbors that he has, the work that he does, there can be a formed and realized spirit, an ideal which will master his blood. In this sense we are all internationalists" (352). Lane's international vision amplified the nation's cultural and racial cosmopolitanism, a vision of community in which soldiers from many nations who had fought side by side now shared the common language of democracy.

In the "realized spirit" of an "ideal," Lane argued that in spite of—or perhaps because of—Americans' various cultural differences, they could be united. Like Dewey and Bourne, Lane sought "a catholic and sympathetic spirit" (352) to bring together Americans of all nations and races. For Lane, education was the linchpin in this formula. Advocating civic responsibility through education—and, more importantly, through understanding the plight of the foreign-born in America, he observed: "We ourselves, have failed to see America through the eyes of those who have come to us. We have failed to realize why it was that they came here and what they sought. We have failed to understand their definition of liberty" (352). If "Hunnism" could be stripped of its racial quotient to delineate a system of values antithetical to democracy, then Lane would go on to redefine "Americanism," not as Anglo-Saxon or nationalistic, but in terms of shared aspirations and international sensibilities.

Lane's urgent appeal for national literacy took a big step forward with the collaboration of Grosvenor and Burrall, who suggested that they produce a "pictorial geography" series of unbound *National Geographic* photographs for the nation's educators. Within a year of their initial February 1914 correspondence, Grosvenor hired Burrall as "literary assistant" to the NGS, so he could oversee the series' development and promote his editorial principles of kindliness and aesthetic timelessness.[37] In keeping with its global focus, the series appealed to children's curiosity about cultural varieties both within the United States and in the world at large.

The series could not entirely rid itself of nativist racial attitudes, but it was remarkably complex in its portrayal of national and global diversity. Some of its picture cards reproduced the clichés of hereditarian and evolutionary discourse. A picture card showing Philippine tribesmen scaling a greased palm tree, for instance, condescendingly compared the agility of "our brown cousins" to that of "monkeys." Other cards showed the institutional processes of education and assimilation at work as Native American children relinquished native customs in order to attend government schools "for lessons in writing and arithmetic." Yet others were quite progressive, introducing children to the complexities of such matters as global economics and labor relations. The picture card "Transplanting Rice," for instance, describes the "Grueling 10-hour work day" of Philippine laborers and asks children to consider, "Have you ever weeded a flower bed or a garden? How did your back feel? Think of working this way all day. Yet these men work rapidly and steadily ten hours a day for a few cents or a share of the rice."[38] Questions that call a child's attention to global economic disparities not only reflect the spirit of progressive education but also offer a refreshing counterpoint to Grosvenor's editorial mandate to avoid criticism or controversy.

In fact, this discordant array of images and attitudes in the series hints at Burrall's broader hope to promote dialogue over Grosvenor's efforts to force consensus through a bland aestheticism. When Grosvenor charged that the questions Burrall devised for the series were too advanced for young pupils, for example, she remarked that children's minds "will not be confined to the obvious." Well-chosen questions, she reasoned, would allow "each member of the class . . . to come to a slightly different conclusion," and promote "lively discussion, which makes a study of the picture and the print beneath it well worth while."[39] Although "Pictorial Geography" was too costly for financially strapped educators and school districts to survive into the next decade, Burrall's focus on lively dissent anticipates progressive educators' investment in cultivating a civic-minded readership equipped with the critical reasoning skills to combat stereotypes.

In her article "Sight-Seeing in Schools" (1919), Burrall voiced the hope that pictorial geography would promote the cosmopolitan spirit of global humanitarianism. Although the article, likely heavily edited by Grosvenor, represented children militaristically as "a mighty army mobilized for service and for life" (489), its sympathies were unmistakably internationalist. Taking up the social documentary impulse of Jacob Riis and Lewis Hine, Burrall argued that photography could promote peaceful global coexistence through education. "The sympathetic understanding of world peoples, which is the only possible foundation for permanent world peace," wrote Burrall, "is fostered through a wide knowledge of pictures" (408). Moreover, Burrall concluded, pictorial geography will inspire children to "feel that they are part of a great world family" and that they are "no different from French or Russian or Australian" (497). In order to broadcast this global vision beyond the schoolroom, *National Geographic* turned its attention to the nation's print media. With financial assistance from the National Educational Association, the NGS published its "Geographic Bulletins" in national newspapers and as pamphlets for educators and students.[40]

Regardless of the magazine's overt aesthetics, in its "Geographic Bulletins," as with its "Pictorial Geography" series, the boundary between cosmopolitan and nationalist attitudes persistently shifted. Among its first bulletins was an editorial by a school superintendant to the board of education urging curricular reform in response to world events. He maintained that students must have an "intelligent interpretation of 'history in the making,'" so "that they may have the broad sympathies for foreign folk that must be predicted as the basis of a league of nations or its equivalent." Weeks later, a bulletin titled "Ants—and Bolshevism" argued that one had only to "peer into an ant-hill to see why the communistic state is not adapted to man." Globalization's continued growing pains were evident in such bulletins as "Preserving a 'White Australia'" and "Mexico, a Modern Babel."[41] *National Geographic* reflected the instability of the international community as lines of national and cultural affiliation were continually redrawn.

Notwithstanding its problematic "Hunnism" during the First World War, *National Geographic* had emerged as a recognized cultural commodity widely believed to foster international goodwill and an appreciation of the extended human family—a belief reflected in NGS's growing international membership. After 1919, the utopian image of an "International Geographic," however, increasingly catalyzed fears, in both the United States and Europe, associating internationalism with communist "Bolshevism." Wrote one reader, "I think it should be strictly National. Your National Society may claim an International scope and such a criticism be [*sic*] inconsistent."[42] Although the magazine advanced cultural pluralism as a kind of marketplace of values that could harmoniously, if competitively, coexist, it frequently framed its cosmopolitanism in nationalist and nativist terms—an internal tension that aptly expressed the similar conflicts of allegiance felt by many during an era of global travel and global war.

Fascism and the Family Frame

As faith in the prospects of international democracy waned, the year 1919 also saw a decline in the status of national symbols, whose ubiquity as war propaganda had led to widespread disillusionment. The immediate postwar period also witnessed a dramatic shift among Western democracies away from international sympathy toward nationalist protectionism, in response to the rise of global communism on the left and, somewhat later, reactionary fascism on the right. In the United States, to prevent a reprise of the Bolshevik revolution, the Committee on Public Information helped spread the misinformation that the Bolsheviks were in league with the Germans. Demobilization had left thousands of former soldiers unemployed, and in January 1919 riots broke out among thirty-five thousand garment workers, first in New York and then in metropolises across the Eastern Seaboard.[43] During the "Red Scare," communism continued to be fought along nativist lines in a nation that saw immigrant mobs as a radicalizing element that threatened the status quo.

Such was the cultural climate in which Grosvenor and his assistant editor John Oliver La Gorce allowed *National Geographic* to publish articles celebrating the anticommunist rhetoric of fascist dictatorships. An Anglophile at heart, Grosvenor, who in 1917 had acclaimed the "British race" for its "inventive genius," by 1921 feared that Wilson's doctrine of "self-determination" would destroy the British empire and justify Southern secession and the formation of a separate "black republic" within the United States.[44] While the magazine's visual variety often expressed a cultural pluralist worldview, its notion of an idealized, racially pure Anglo-Saxon family resonated with the romantic sensibilities that fueled the European fascist movements of the 1920s and 1930s. Vacillating between these two ideological poles, *National Geographic* embodied a struggle between the pragmatist model of a "usable past," as in Lane's celebration of cultural intermixture, and the fantasy of a mythic past in which national identity was unitary and uncomplicated.

The word "fascism" is itself a notoriously problematic term that prohibits sweeping generalizations. It may be more appropriate, therefore, to refer to "fascisms" specific to particular nations, and to acknowledge the different forms it has taken in Italy, Germany, and Spain, along with copycat movements in France, Romania, Hungary, and elsewhere.[45] Still, we can identify a number of recurring themes or patterns that give the term weight and stability: the intensification of group solidarity as a result of social and economic crisis; the fear of internal or external threats; the coercive use of force to produce consent; the assertion of biological, cultural, or hereditary supremacy to justify violence against those outside the group. There are also less visible traits, or, as Hannah Arendt has put it, more "banal" practices, of fascism: propaganda and the censorship of the press; the erosion of parliamentary procedures and representative government; the concentration of executive powers in a messianic paternal figure.[46] As I have suggested, some of these fascist elements of propaganda, censorship, and rising nativism were latent or partly visible in the United States just before and during the onset of the First World War.[47]

With their investment in a romanticized past and their desire for a powerful ruler who can return the nation to a bygone splendor, fascistic or quasi-fascistic nationalist movements might be said to follow the psychological narrative of the Freudian "family romance" in their unfolding. Most pointedly, the childhood fantasy of substituting culturally or economically aristocratic parents for those of more humble origins corresponds to the psychology that fueled fascist movements. Beginning with the fantasy of an exalted or mythic national past, fascism replicates the terms of the Freudian "family romance," in which the child's desire to replace "the real father by a superior one" can be expressed nationalistically as well. Under a powerful new leader, or national father, the nation likewise expresses a "longing for the happy, vanished days" in a mythic national history.[48] This longing characteristically expresses itself as a romantic aesthetic that salvages mythic national ideals from regional local-color or "folk" traditions and beliefs.

Of course, the psychic wellsprings of fascism were not at first understood by the American press, which tended to portray Hitler, in particular, not as the grand patriarch of an "Aryan race," but as a buffoon of sorts, at least in his early years. Beginning with his October 1923 failed "Munich Putsch" and arrest for sedition, Hitler's activities were covered regularly by *National Geographic*'s contemporaries: the *Literary Digest, Current History,* the *Review of Reviews,* the *Living Age,* the *Nation,* and *Reader's Digest.* Although some early U.S. reportage made it clear, to watchful eyes, that Hitler sought nothing less than the overthrow of the Weimar government and the reunification of Germany, coverage was often dismissive of him. *The Literary Digest* in 1923 called him an "excited and muddle-brained Bohemian" who was "devoid of solid convictions and incapable of a definite line of action" and compared him to Mussolini as a master of "opera effects." *Current History* in November 1923 similarly characterized Hitler as a member of the "smaller middle class" with "little education." His party consisted of nothing but "featherbrained, unbalanced types" such as "students, clerks, mechanics" and "plain hoodlums." *Reader's Digest* concluded that a "great majority of the people will never support such patent foolishness as Hitlerism."[49] His humble origins, along with the general political disarray in Germany, were widely taken as evidence that even if some misguided Germans embraced Hitler, he would have difficulty commanding a national following.

Against that background, *National Geographic*'s favorable coverage of fascist Germany and Italy has often been attributed to the conservative politics of Grosvenor himself. On Christmas Eve of 1918, for instance, Grosvenor wrote a lengthy diatribe to his father, expressing his outrage at a front-page newspaper photograph showing Woodrow Wilson with George Creel, chief of Wilson's propaganda machine, the Committee on Public Information. Grosvenor's letter accused Creel of "anti-British feeling," and in a burst of crude anti-Semitism, wrongly concluded that Creel was Jewish. "How I hate that race," Grosvenor wrote; "they are responsible for all the Bolshevik's [*sic*] propaganda everywhere and the Bolshevik horrors." Grosvenor's bigotry here typified the period of "anti-Semitic nationalism" that followed the First World War, as "the Jew" became an international "symbol of foreign radicalism" and a scapegoat for those fearful of Bolshevism.[50]

But simply condemning *National Geographic* for condoning fascism, with the benefit of 20/20 historical hindsight, can obscure some of the more interesting dynamics taking place. While articles featuring favorite vacation spots in Germany and Italy willfully ignored these countries' political ambitions, by the early 1930s this attitude was not particularly unusual. Conservatives like Grosvenor saw fascism as a legitimate counterforce to socialism and international communism, and even mainstream observers expressed admiration for the leadership of Hitler and Mussolini.[51] In 1932, on the eve of his election as chancellor, *Time* magazine referred to Hitler as "Handsome Adolf," and President Franklin Roosevelt saw Mussolini as an ally for European peace. Many, in fact, regarded Mussolini's leadership as a positive stage toward expanded liberalism; none other than Winston Churchill called Mussolini "the greatest living legislator" in 1933. A year later, Mussolini appeared to be playing the role of "good European citizen" by upholding Austrian independence in the aftermath of a failed July 1934 coup led by Austrian Nazis. And even popular culture took notice. Lyrics from Cole Porter's song "You're the Top" (from the 1934 Broadway musical *Anything Goes*) suggested just how pervasive was the "cult of Mussolini" internationally: "You're the top! / You're the great Houdini! / You're the top! / You're Mussolini!"[52]

If *National Geographic*'s account of "Hunnism" in Europe had disrupted its narrative of the international family by revealing the magazine's nationalist colors during the outbreak of the First World War, the magazine's disavowal of all things political made possible the publication of several articles that, on the surface, suggest sympathies with emergent fascist regimes in Italy and Germany. However, the articles present contradictions that allow them to be read against the grain of their overt celebration of fascism. On the one hand, these articles enlist visual and textual local color as a means of promoting romantic "folk" culture and national civic pride. On the other hand, they make visible fascist systems of cultural production and industrial rationalism. Ultimately, they help to expose fascistic strategies for politically socializing a country's youth and for suppressing dissent.

By exposing the romantic attractions of local color, Lincoln Eyre's "Renascent Germany" (1928) reveals the fascist aesthetic behind state-sponsored programs to produce loyal German youth and catalyze civic loyalties around older national traditions paradoxically threatened—and maintained—by global modernity. The state's efforts to promote the physical and psychological unification of "the masses" takes center stage in photographs of children congregated in sports fields and at political rallies (652). Snapshots depicting children dressed in peasant costume assure readers that children are at once the future of a modern, organized Germany and the carriers of a vanishing culture; as one caption laments, "Many once well-known German peasant costumes are doomed to disappear" (656). Indeed, in this modern Germany, photographs of people in peasant costume amid rural settings outnumber images of industry and modernization. Despite the article's celebration of German modernization, then, its photographs and captions reveal an anxiety over the loss of local particularity in the midst of growing systematization and cultural homogenization.

Throughout Eyre's article, the longing for an exalted national past conjoins local color with imperial militarism to reveal the seeds of fascism already latent in the fledgling German republic. A country strangely devoid of local color, according to Eyre, "[t]he Republic, like most democracies, has nothing to offer the tourist gaze comparable to the splendor of Imperial spectacles" (645). Drab democracies, Eyre suggests, lack the grandeur of empire. When President von Hindenburg received the Afghan king, Eyre writes, "only the dazzling uniforms of the monarch and his suite and a few score yards of bunting relieved the drabness of Reichswehr uniforms and frock coats of republicanism" (645). Eyre's article, like others in

National Geographic, reveals a more dangerous form of local color, militaristic or otherwise, in the form of reverence for a mythical national past and a universal conformity to its ideals.

While local color fulfills Eyre's desire for the particular and the picturesque, the underlying movement toward fascism—as the mobilization of the nation's youth reveals—is one of economic and social amalgamation. Eyre chronicles this shift from private to nationalized ownership by observing a generalized "unification movement" in both the "German mind" and its corresponding political structures. The nationalization of railroads, for instance, as well as the application of "standardization and so-called 'rationalization'" to all facets of economic production, for Eyre, were evidence of Germany's efforts to keep pace with global modernity (667).[53] The sense of motion here is important, for we might argue that the seeds of fascism manifest themselves in both the psychological and physical movement of the masses, united by collective worship of the "folk." Where Dewey and Bourne would associate mobility and migration with the cosmopolitan spirit of cultural pluralism, in Eyre's representation of Germany a local-color aesthetic orchestrates the movement along strictly nationalist lines. And, as German history illustrates, the symbol of modern industrial mobility—the railroad—would later take on much more sinister meaning in the transport of Jews, Catholics, homosexuals, and political dissenters to labor camps.

The fascistic aesthetics fusing the tensions between the folk belief in an exalted past and the routinization of modern economics—from the goose step and the "Sieg Heil" salute to the ubiquitous swastika—become increasingly prominent in *National Geographic* articles after 1928. In Eyre's "Renascent Germany," published just five years before Hitler's appointment as vice chancellor, we find a single photograph of the swastika-bearing National Socialist Party during a parade at Nuremberg. By comparison, in "Changing Berlin" (February 1937) by Douglas Chandler, a Nazi propagandist later convicted of treason for radio broadcasts promoting Hitler's regime,[54] there are no fewer than ten photographs depicting dozens of swastikas displayed prominently on banners and flags at Nazi rallies. Images of Hitler Youth, of Third Reich banners lining Berlin's streets, and of surging crowds awaiting Hitler's address all vividly presage the outbreak of the Second World War.

Just as "Renascent Germany" blended Germany's new modernity with the nostalgia of local color, so too does "Changing Berlin" establish the "civic religion" of National Socialism through its depiction of Old World ties to the earth, the folk, and a cult of youth.[55] The very first snapshot invokes the "revival of an old folk custom" in the "May Day masses" who "jam the Berlin Lustgarten to hear Adolf Hitler speak" (132). The article is resplendent with photographs of "the masses," none of which are more compelling than those of children, and their captions invoke the state's paternal obligations to "develop boys and girls in body and mind, and thus insure a sturdy race to defend Germany in the Future" (140). Promoting a "sympathy" of common interests, one caption actually likens Hitler Youth to the Boy Scouts of America (158). Chandler portrays a nation bustling with growth and progress, mobilized and inspired by the physical strength of the young and fortified by ancient and exalted ties to the soil.

If it did not indicate Grosvenor's outright sympathy with Hitler's regime, "Changing Berlin" at least signaled the editorial leadership's tacit acceptance of Chandler's position. The specter of communism, particularly as imagined by the patrician class to which Grosvenor belonged, fueled Grosvenor's own Anglo-Saxon nativism and accounts for—but certainly does not excuse—his enthusiastic endorsement of Hitler in a May 12, 1933, memo to assistant editor John Oliver La Gorce. "I hope I shall live to see Hitler unite all Germans of Germany and Austria into one powerful country," he wrote, encouraging La Gorce to publish an account of the Nazi regime.[56] Chandler, who had traveled widely, and who had met La Gorce at a dinner party, supplied the opportunity. Despite numerous indicators of Chandler's admiration for Hitler and the Nazi regime, La Gorce published four additional stories by Chandler on Belgium, the Baltics, Turkey, and Yugoslavia in the following two years.[57]

The magazine's uncritical portrayal of Nazi Germany's consolidation of power nonetheless exposed the darker side of consent, in visual propaganda and in the transformation of classrooms into sites for political indoctrination. Hitler's portrait hung in every public classroom; in parochial schools, his visage appeared beside the crucifix. Lessons in race and eugenics schooled students in how to detect Jews by visible signs. Nazi education stripped the idea of childhood of all sentiment and trained students to be fierce, brutal, and, above all, indifferent to suffering and pain. Furthermore, cultural pluralism did not exist; "un-German" books were burned, and jazz and American music, in particular, were denounced as subversive.[58]

Where local color in *National Geographic* generally associated the United States' strength with its diversity—however stereotyped and problematic—fascistic aesthetics promoted the mythic "folk" of the fatherland to the exclusion of all others. The differing uses of local color by fascistic and democratic nations, then, represent one way of understanding complex cultural responses to internationalization in the early twentieth century. In both cases, however, it was the youth of a nation who were imbued with the iconic force of its reigning mythologies, who were deployed to organize public emotion around shared values, and who were imagined as the carriers of a unique national culture and political system.

Appearing only a month after Chandler's article, John Patric's "Imperial Rome Reborn" (March 1937) reveals fascist Italy's similarity to Nazi Germany in its use of local color to downplay fascism's threat to Western democracy. The "large mole" on Mussolini's graying temple, for instance, which "added homely character to his nearly bald head," undermines his well-crafted image as Italy's imposing patriarch (269). Then, in an image vaguely reminiscent of the grizzled Liberian quoted by Edgar Allen Forbes in his 1910 article (see chapter 3), Patric portrays Mussolini as a kind of modern minstrel. Mussolini "smiled often, rolling his eyes so much" that Patric's "strongest memory" was the "continual sight of their whites" (269). Despite Mussolini's commitment to Italy's modernization, Il Duce appears as just one of Patric's many "local-color" characters who refuse modernity, including country women now living in the drained Littoral who pump water by hand and use outdoor ovens, and a "wrinkled old violinist" who plays for pleasure rather than for "the battered coppers" (271).[59] Indeed, the article's resistance to global complex connectivity is such that its face appears only in the diminutive form of Mickey Mouse, an American import, decorating a bill of fare, and the popularity of modern cinema in Rome. Finding familiar remnants of "home" while abroad, Patric draws upon a local-color aesthetic in ways that soften Italy's fascist identity.

Images of children participating in state-sponsored programs, however, offer a chilling counterpoint to local color. Photographs featuring a line of young fascists in knee breeches and gas masks or as a phalanx, chins upthrust, marching with guns produce photographic discord against other images of smiling young women in provincial costume gathered to celebrate the annual grape harvest. "Weird visitors from another world?" asks the title of a photograph of boys in gas masks standing at attention (fig. 18).[60] The title's answer, "No; schoolboys preparing for war," neatly summarizes the agents of social control: state-sponsored

Fig. 18 "Weird Visitors from Another World?" (© Bettman/Corbis)

education, media propaganda, and ritualized drills that encourage youth to identify with a powerful leader. "Drilling with gas masks and miniature rifles," the caption reads, "they stand as rigidly erect as Roman legionaries. Italian youngsters don uniforms at six and receive real weapons in their 18th year on the traditional anniversary of Rome's birth, April 21" (280). The point Patric's article does not make, however, is that such images might highlight for American readers parallel institutions for the political socialization of their own children through various forms of civic public performance: in the Pledge of Allegiance, in national holidays and parades, and in public school events in which students act out revered national narratives.

Moving back and forth between local-color depictions of Italy's humbler citizens and the industrial modernism upon which the fascist regime depended, Patric's article exposes the contradictions within the fascist family romance. Rome, which Patric describes as a "haven for many an alien," actually proves the opposite. For all of Italy's seeming friendliness, the author finds himself taken to a police station for questioning after taking photographs of a shepherd in front of a modern high-rise; another time he is awakened at his hotel for questioning (308). Similarly, Patric's description of a child depositing a toy tank atop a heap of scrap munitions, or of a kiosk where husbands and wives exchange gold wedding bands for the iron forged rings of militarism and martial law, render these visual tokens of the family as ironic, unstable, and perhaps even complicit symbols of belonging and kinship (319, 325). As a result, the article whose overt emphasis is on the supposed universality of certain transcendent familial human behaviors, such as marrying or playing with toys, ends up calling into question the possibility of an international membership based on shared democratic values.

What is fascinating about the images of children in *National Geographic*'s articles on Nazi Germany and fascist Italy is that, as emblems of collective national endeavor, they are so devoid of emotion. In that sense, they lack the emotive force of iconic images to bond audiences and mobilize action.[61] Whatever emotion a viewer sees in these photographs likely derives from their startling discord with sentimental narratives regarding childhood vulnerability and innocence. Whether of German youth taking physical exercise on a field or of Italian "boy Blackshirts" stoically marching in imitation of Mussolini, fascist photographs of children are impersonal, as if to highlight a central strategy of fascist youth indoctrination: the state's deliberate alienation of children from familial social networks in order to force identification with the state as a powerful surrogate "father."[62] However unwittingly, *National Geographic* photographs of children mobilized for war reveal these dynamics at work. In the process, they also suggest how propagandistic photographs of children function differently from traditionally iconic photographs by stripping the child of its power to tap civic emotion. In so doing, such images actually have the potential to undermine fascistic aesthetic strategies for consolidating consent.

Readers' divergent reactions to the articles on Germany and Italy reveal this potential. A few expressed relief at finding "such a fair and sympathetic article about Germany" to counter the "distorted view" and "propagandized material" that had been perpetuated by the press.[63] Yet far more readers responded angrily, and their letters attest to the sharp tension between fascistic local color grounded in the romance of the "folk" and *National Geographic*'s visual cosmopolitanism. Many dropped their membership to signal how widely the magazine had veered from its readers' more internationalist sympathies. A doctor from Newark declared, "A government . . . that fills concentration camps with decent men, that perpetrates inhuman acts, that reverts back to barbarism and savagery, surely does not deserve any commendation." Out of "love for my own country," he cancelled his "subscription," a choice of words that was significant, since "membership" had long been held to represent shared goals and values among *National Geographic* readers.[64]

Readers' letters condemning *National Geographic*'s treatment of fascism dramatize the larger failure of fascist aesthetic principles—and nationalist propaganda more generally. The obsessive reproduction of national myths centered on the folk, chauvinistic nationalism, and a great leader arguably contributed, in the end, to fascism's undoing. As Tracy H. Koon has shown in her study of the political socialization of Italian fascist youth, "The divergence between observable fact and familiar rhetoric created at a certain point in many a cognitive dissonance: the more often the myths were repeated, the less credible they became. The sense of incongruity among the young grew as the subjective orientation toward the system instilled by the socialization process received less and less validation from their actual experience of the world."[65] That "sense of incongruity" helps to explain why some Hitler Youth, weary of conformity to Nazism's bankrupt ideology, went on to form an underground resistance movement.

In the United States, meanwhile, progressive educators were training students in resistant reading practices, cultivating their ability to discern gaps between "observable fact and familiar rhetoric." This educational movement arose partly in response to the demonstrated power of fascist aesthetics, but it took on a larger significance in the context of the United States' own political rhetoric and media-saturated culture of consumerism. Transferring Americans' pleasure in vicarious travel to the more searching intellectual exploration available through critical thinking was the next step for progressive educators invested in combating coercive media at home. Despite widespread fears of international communism, progressive educators and intellectuals continued their "plea for [a] world culture" in which "all men as individuals and as races may share equitably."[66]

The Rise of the Critical Reader

Widespread media propaganda during the First World War had revitalized progressive educators' spirit of reform. In the 1930s, these educators responded to the rise of fascist propaganda by encouraging strategies of critical media consumption. There was one thing upon which educators agreed: that the strength of a democracy depended on the strength of its citizens' critical thought, their ability to distinguish between truth and propaganda, and their capacity for reasoned and thoughtful debate. The conflict between individual freedom and social responsibility was resolved in the concept of the "critical reader": the "individual citizen" capable of critical and unemotional examination of the "social and political issues which confront him daily," and who, after "weighing carefully the best available evidence, exerts his influence toward the goal which he believes is best for the population as a whole and for himself as an individual."[67] Accordingly, throughout the 1930s and 1940s, educators' concerns over the "social, political, and economic illiteracy of students" intensified, sparking numerous initiatives to strengthen students' critical reading skills, particularly the ability to detect media bias.

By the mid–1940s, educators saw the role of English instruction as one of educating a citizenry literate in the important social and political issues of the day and equipped to read print media with a discerning eye. In addition to local and national newspapers, magazines such as the *Saturday Evening Post, Life, Time, Collier's,* the *Nation,* the *New Republic, Newsweek,* and the *American Mercury* were studied for biases and political viewpoints. Educators identified five principle objectives of cultural literacy necessary to an informed democratic citizenry: maintaining "interest in the affairs of life, learning to distinguish between fact and propaganda, establishing the habit of critical reading, developing the sense of social responsibility, and developing individualism in a social setting." Chief among the desired outcomes were the cosmopolitan value of "open-minded study" and "recognition of the need to solve our problems co-operatively" as well as a recognition that truth is subject to change and not "absolute."[68]

It is a remarkable fact of *National Geographic*'s history that individual readers frequently expressed greater internationalist sympathies than did the magazine itself. As we have seen, during the First World War in particular, its cosmopolitan spirit was put to the test, as an entire generation's ideals were challenged by new visual and print technologies for mobilizing mob violence and warfare on an unprecedented scale. No clear consensus emerged among readers or within the magazine itself regarding how to conceive of America, whether as a "novel international nation," as Randolph Bourne put it, or as a nationalist "melting pot," where immigrants would conform, in almost assembly-line fashion, to the racial and cultural standards of their adopted country.[69] The decades of vacillation between national sympathies and a desire for broader international contact and understanding do reveal, however, a dramatic shift in attitudes toward complex connectivity. In their rejection of the magazine's "Hunnism," *National Geographic*'s readership expressed an emerging transnational view of identity, one that was not limited by the geopolitical borders of their native land.

What we have seen is how the fascist obsession with family represents a kind of malignant hyperextension of the discourse of family that *National Geographic* deployed, for the most part unself-consciously. The concept of family is necessarily predicated on a principle of exclusion, in that some people are members of the family while others are not, but it is also a concept that incorporates the differences between biological/literal and metaphorical/ideational families. "Family," as biologized in the discourse of fascism, consists in the literal transferral of culture through the blood. This discourse arose, ironically, or perhaps appropriately, at the very moment when the contingencies of nation and race were foregrounded by accelerated international population flows, including dramatically increased emigration to the United States. The widespread migration of people across borders unavoidably complicated the question of national affiliation, underscoring the difference between nationality as a birthright and nationality as a choice.

In the United States, the exigencies of war made it possible to overlook the ethnic background or "blood-and-culture" identity of immigrants (most of whom, during the First World War, came from "enemy" countries), and to postulate national belonging as a voluntary act of allegiance to shared democratic values and ideals.

Before the term "global citizen" entered twenty-first-century discourse, *National Geographic* readers expressed an emergent identification with an international community, the result, in part, of seeing themselves as "members" of an international scientific body. This willingness to identify with others beyond the nation's borders offers a unique perspective on competing national and international allegiances at a time of growing internationalism. The various reader criticisms of *National Geographic*'s response to the First World War and the rise of communism and European fascism express a schism in American democratic culture between individual autonomy and inclusive membership in an increasingly complex global culture.

The highly charged emotional content of cultural icons like *National Geographic* is what makes them so valuable to liberal-democratic culture.

For Hariman and Lucaites, icons not only present a public revelation of the ideals and aspirations consolidating collective identification, but also expose the underlying tensions within civic life. The conflict, they argue, is between the doctrines of liberalism based on individual freedom and self-determination and those based on democratic collective governance, which requires adherence to written laws and unwritten social rules of membership in a broader political body. The conflicting ideals of cultural pluralism and national patriotism unite, for example, in a *National Geographic* photograph of foreign-born soldiers reading the magazine to acquire literacy necessary for war. Such images are powerful in their ability to mobilize public consent around ideas of citizenship and civic virtue. In this way, iconic photographs provide visual scripts for individuals to perform similar acts of civic virtue, and they provide a means of negotiating the complexities of national public discourse.

By making the conflict between national and international identification visible, as in the case of the jarring images of Nazi and fascist symbols, *National Geographic* could be said to have revitalized liberal-democratic culture by disturbing its readers' democratic sensibilities and inviting their dissent. Letters from *National Geographic* readers foregrounded what features of liberal democracy were problematic, calling attention to how individual differences of race, class, or national origin complicated national membership and became a basis for exclusion from, rather than participation in, a national citizenry.

5

JUNGLE HOUSEKEEPING

Globalization, Domesticity, and Performing
the "Primitive" in *National Geographic*

Well into the twentieth century, the primitive jungle, the naked savage, and the lone explorer were potent icons of escapist adventure.
In this regard, "Cairo to Cape Town, Overland," subtitled "An Adven-
turous Journey of 135 Days, Made by an American Man and His Wife,
through the Length of the African Continent" (February 1925) by Felix
Shay is vintage *National Geographic,* but with a twist. While Shay's narrative incorporated Western imperialism's most sensational icons—from
throbbing tom-toms and nude black bodies dancing around a "lurid central fire" to a wild-game safari—his wife, Porter, took center stage as an
intrepid sharpshooter. After Felix Shay misses a zebra, he confesses: "I
have not the stomach of a hunter. I hate to kill things." Porter, by contrast,
spotting a herd of kongoni, "sat down like a professional, leveled her gun
on her knee, and promptly knocked over a large male." So self-assured
is Porter, remarks her husband, that she "explained to me the defect of
my stance, and how my gun should not have wiggle-waggled." A moment
later, the dead zebra's discovery redeems him from Porter's devastating
hint at sexual impotence and restores the "natural" sexual order. Felix
had not missed his mark after all, and he ensures his wife cannot get the
verbal upper hand. "Quietly, when the White Hunter was not listening, I
mentioned that pertinent phrase, 'Woman's place is in the home.'"[1]

Felix and Porter Shay's rollicking adventure inaugurated a popular
National Geographic theme in which the marital bond, the family, and
the collective travails of "keeping house" in various out-of-the-way jungle locales appeared with such frequency as to constitute its own "jungle
housekeeping" genre. Written mostly—but not exclusively—by women,

these narratives address the common problems of adapting traditional American recipes to unfamiliar local foods and training native servants to adopt Western housekeeping standards and techniques. Encounters with aboriginal bodies tattooed, pierced, and painted, as well as exposure to new cultural practices and domestic arrangements, reveal the contributors' growing intimacy with unfamiliar cultures and their longing for Eden—a return to a simpler past.

Post–World War I disillusionment with all things "civilized" and a nostalgia to return to the primal scene of human origins remote from technological modernity hint at one reason for the remarkable proliferation of "jungle housekeeping" articles in *National Geographic.* By presenting the search for, in the words of contributor Phoebe Binney Harnden in 1924, "tranquility" that is "untouched either by modern hurry and bustle or the equally hurrying and bustling modern tourist," the genre exhibits the "romantic primitivism" typical of anthropological writing of the 1920s.[2]

The jungle housekeeping genre, however, encompasses a broad array of motives, domestic arrangements, and remote settings in response to modernity. Husband-wife adventurers took to the air to celebrate human technological conquest over nature; they set sail on ocean byways for the sheer "fun of the thing" or to experience "that feeling of sovereign freedom";[3] women tagged along with their businessman husbands to exploit the jungle's natural resources or assisted their scientist husbands in the field; tourist couples sought novel places from which to escape modernity's frenetic pace; families lit out for the globe's unexplored territories in order to pass on the "heritage" of their pioneer ancestors.[4]

Disenchantment with civilization, then, only partially accounts for the jungle housekeeping phenomenon. A genre that spanned the primitivist artistic vogue of the 1920s to the Cold War era of the 1950s, jungle housekeeping portrayed both the lure of the exotic as a form of escape and broader historical and cultural shifts in gender roles, psychological responses to globalization, and complex reactions to economic pressures at home. *National Geographic* articles like "Mrs. Robinson Crusoe in Ecuador," wrote Mrs. W. R. Poulterer, of Audubon, New Jersey, "certainly help to dispel the depression hangover."[5] The aftermath of the First World War, the U.S. policy of geopolitical isolation, and the Great Depression all gave new significance to the domestic home front. Jungle housekeeping played off the increased focus on domesticity by transporting home themes into exotic environments.

Primitivism, in the context of *National Geographic*'s "jungle housekeeping" genre, signals something more than the commonplace icons of imperial nostalgia, such as ecstatic rituals, exotic costumes, and bodily markings. While it reveals an underlying dissatisfaction with technological modernity by taking refuge in older, preindustrial forms of survival and homemaking, it also signals a desire, however problematic it may be, to embrace cultural differences not as mere spectacle but as a means of revitalizing a connection with the past, whether it be an imagined ancient ancestry or a historical past more alive to nature and humankind's harmonious dwelling within it.

The jungle housekeeping genre in *National Geographic*, then, did not merely reproduce the familiar primitivist tropes of imperial nostalgia, but also exposed its representations to critique. Despite its complicity with Western imperialism, *National Geographic*'s jungle housekeeping genre exemplifies in a particularly telling way attributes of "primitivist performance," where adventuring couples act out the gendered imperialistic conventions of primitivism in ways that disclose their origins in a broader network of institutional and cultural "scripts." By recognizing "performance" as behavior not exclusive to the theatrical stage, but part of daily life as we "act out" the various cultural roles we inhabit, we begin to see the ways in which behaviors are not intrinsic or "natural," but rather are the by-products of a complex history of "imitative practices."[6]

From an anthropological perspective, the term "performance" denotes acts that are not only "framed in a special way," and "put on display"—as if framed by *National Geographic*'s yellow border—but also are subject to critical evaluation.[7] Once we understand Felix Shay's remark, "Woman's place is in the home," as a cultural "frame," or containment strategy, that affirms his supremacy within a masculine domain that Porter threatens, we recognize the African safari as a staging ground for gendered performances. With additional probing, other cultural frames emerge: the tom-toms and dancing "natives" in Shay's account reflect the vogue of commercially successful travel films, H. Rider Haggard's pulp adventures, and Edgar Rice Burroughs's famed *Tarzan* series. We see how Shay's 1925 narrative betrays his anxiety about the new cultural ideal of the "companionate marriage" based on shared interests, "mutual affection, sexual attraction, and equal rights," at a time when such professional partnerships as the piloting duo of Charles and Anne Morrow Lindbergh and the sensational ethnographic filmmakers Martin and Osa Johnson entered the national spotlight.[8] Moreover, by observing the many negotiated performances among contributors, the institution, and its readers, we become more aware of the machinery operating behind the magazine's manufacture of consent. Not all readers cherished the magazine's nostalgia for an imperial world order.

Performance in this sense offers a basis for cultural critique irrespective of the intentions of the players.[9] Jungle housekeeping juxtaposes three kinds of primitivist performance: those of explorer couples grappling with the uncertainties and ambiguities of changing gender roles in remote jungle outposts; those of women narrators commenting on their makeshift domestic arrangements; and those of scientist-explorers and *National Geographic* photographers working in improvised laboratories or preparing film in mobile jungle darkrooms for the ultimate benefit of NGS members. While the trespass on and occupation of exotic space are inherent aspects of jungle housekeeping, they also reveal the technological processes by which science inhabits and domesticates the wild. The adaptive processes of domestic improvisation similarly result in cross-cultural exchange that yields unexpected moments of self-reflection and transformation. In this sense, jungle housekeeping highlights the potential of performance to place both the performers and their audience in "the role of the other" and to view themselves from an otherwise unfamiliar perspective.[10] In other words, the contributors' cultural dislocation necessitates a corresponding psychological reorientation: the adoption of an "Other" point of view that approaches cultural relativism, a willingness to evaluate cultures on their own terms rather than from a Western bias.[11]

In much broader terms, by showing its contributors adapting to unfamiliar customs in improvised domestic arrangements, "jungle housekeeping" dramatizes the psychological and historical pressures shaping an emerging global consciousness. A consistent theme of jungle housekeeping narratives is the "*disturbing* of intimacy—the outer world penetrating the inner" that sociologists attribute to globalization.[12] In that context, "jungle housekeeping" reflected its contributors' and readers' desires to come to terms with a shifting geopolitical climate and to engage with globalization's deepening complexities at a safe remove.

Performing Eden: "Romantic Primitivism" and Ethnographic Time Travel

The remarkable proliferation of jungle housekeeping articles in *National Geographic* beginning in the 1920s coincides with the rapid industrialization of the American home following the First World War and its transformation from a space of production to one of consumption. By the 1920s, the American home was increasingly regulated by business-minded efficiency. Advertisers turned desire into need, as images of abundance flooded magazine advertising space.[13] Reading a January 1927 issue of *National Geographic* by the light of an electric lamp, for instance, readers encountered gleaming Lincolns, Packards, and Buicks. "How many homes are interested in General Motors?" asked an ad, which answered, "As many homes, in total, as in Detroit, a city of 1,242,000." An ad for Hoover vacuum cleaners exhorted housewives, "Can there be a question of *how* clean a rug ought to be—particularly when that rug is your baby's play-place?"; "Look for the red and white label," urged Campbell's soup. The middle-class domestic homescape as reflected by *National Geographic* advertising was electrified, mobile, hygienic, and contained.

In the magazine's advertising pages, technological modernity and its touristic means of escape competed for readers' attention. With increased leisure, *National Geographic* families were invited to "Play outdoors NOW in warm sunny Tucson," tour Egypt and the Mediterranean on Cunard cruise lines, or "Follow the Birds to the Southland" on the Louisville and Nashville Railroad. So charmed was Mrs. Evelyn M. Mance of Chelmsford, England, by the magazine's advertising that she wrote, we "thoroughly enjoy every page, even to the advertising, some of which make us long to start off on a world tour."[14] Radio, telephone, automobile, train, and ocean liner represent the literal figurations of global connectivity, of crossing geographic borders and shrinking geographic distance and of swift movement into futurity.

If globalization brought forth an accelerated sense of futurity in *National Geographic*'s advertising pages, the jungle housekeeping genre worked in the other direction to hasten movement into the past. What unites all the articles in *National Geographic*'s jungle housekeeping genre is travel back in time. That is, literal geographic travel allows for figurative or imaginary travel to human family origins, the origin of the species, in pretechnological time. Capturing jungle housekeeping's prevailing mood of Edenic solitude, contributor Virginia Hamilton writes, "We were alone in a green world of pure primitive living."[15] Traveling with her biologist husband in Columbia in 1948, Nancy Bell Fairchild Bates recorded a utopian paradise: "one is in a new green world" that is "remote from the world of current history."[16] Trading electric stoves for open charcoal fires and indoor plumbing for outdoor streams, the couple imagines the jungle

as exempt from historical pressures and cultural change. In the couples'
attempts to reproduce this popular imperialist script, however, its impossibly mythic dimensions break the surface. Paradoxically, as we shall
see, it is this same imaginative backward glance that makes the jungle
housekeeping genre a powerful vehicle for reorienting Western cultural
assumptions.

As geographic spaces deemed outside time and outside history, the air,
the sea, the mountain pass, the jungle, the savannah, and the desert embody the atemporal framework typical of early ethnographic writing, in
which adjectives like "savage," "primitive," and "stone age" translate cultural difference into temporal distance emptied of cultural and historical detail.[17] With their emphasis on solitude and timeless vastness, jungle
housekeeping articles attempt a radical break with the technological time-
space of modernity exemplified in *National Geographic*'s advertising. Jungle housekeeping narratives thus derive their romantic primitivism from
"anachronistic space," in which the cultural imperialist explorer's progress
through geographic space is figured as atavistic time travel to an ances-
tral, primitive past. Whether one calls it "anachronistic space," "distanced
immersion," or a denial of "coevalness"—that Westerners and non-Westerners share the same historical time space—representations of the jungle
as a site untouched by technological modernity and historical change is a
narrative-framing strategy whose artifice the jungle housekeeping genre
makes visible.[18]

As a case in point, Gladys Day's 1932 account of her and her husband's
flight across Europe and Asia in their home-built plane, the *Errant*, shows
technology as a mere prop against a dramatic jungle backdrop upon
which the imperial performance of "first contact" is staged.[19] As the Days
are en route to Asia, engine trouble forces them to make an emergency
landing on an uninhabited beach in Borneo. "Ahead of us was the sea,
behind us the dripping, tangled undergrowth of jungle," writes Day. The
sea's sweeping expanse on one side and the jungle's tangled undergrowth
on the other frame the plane as a mechanism of Western technology and
historical change. In this way, the beach itself forms the stage upon which
Day replays the trademark moves of Western travel writing dating to the
eighteenth century. As if on cue, "dark-brown men wearing loin cloths"
emerge. "We were in no position to fight," Day writes, and introduces her
husband as the narrative hero: "Charles Healy [Day] stepped out, raising
his hand. The savages took this as a friendly gesture and swarmed about
the plane" (670). Thus rescued from certain cannibalism, Day provides all

the standard primitivist tropes her *National Geographic* readers would expect. Women, "bare-breasted" or clothed in "brilliant loongees," wearing "brilliant flowers" in their hair and "huge gold earrings" (672) in their ears, supply the color and bare breasts missing in the article's photographs.

The Days' encounter with "the natives" marks a crucial point in the narrative, where the plane—as an emblem of technological modernity and its unexpected breakdown—allows the couple to greet the jungle's inhabitants in the gleaming splendor of New World conquistadores. "Women and men formed a strange, colorful group around the crippled plane," wrote Day, "a mechanism of the West which had suddenly come to rest in a part of the world where machinery is unknown" (672). This mythology of the jungle as "anachronistic space" free from technology unravels a few paragraphs later, however, when the tribal headman escorts the Days into the jungle's interior to a neighboring village, where, reports Day, another headman "led us behind one of the dwellings, and there, to our amazement, was a ramshackle, but nevertheless real, automobile" (673). The automobile's sudden and unexpected appearance in the jungle reveals Day's previous depiction of the jungle as a pretechnological Eden to be a failed containment strategy. A photograph showing the repaired engine ferried in a canoe piloted by tribesmen further underscores the point that historical, technological, and cultural change has indeed entered the jungle.

As well as troubling the conventional separation of nature from culture, jungle housekeeping narratives are punctured throughout by a historical violence that disrupts the imperialist trope of primitive jungle timelessness. After making the requisite tourist's pilgrimage to India's famed Taj Mahal, Day and her husband visit hospital wards in Calcutta, which she found "depressing past belief" (665). During their return journey to the United States, Chinese officials detain the Days in the aftermath of Japanese invasion. Day witnesses student demonstrations and, from the safe distance of the plane, views the "sleek Japanese gunboats" dotting China's coast (686). Sweeping geopolitical changes are not so easily glossed over in jungle housekeeping narratives. Despite Day's efforts to recoup a pretechnological past, her narrative records the destructiveness of imperialism and the birth pangs of a new global order.

Despite their nostalgia for the premodern, what jungle housekeeping narratives foreground, then, is the impossibility of escaping technology and its inevitable encroachment on spaces previously deemed remote from modernity. This time travel does allow, however, for glimpses of a nascent cultural relativism in the form of a growing self-awareness and a recognition of imperialism's failures. The couples are "doing primitiv-ism" in a way that echoes its basic tenets going all the way back to the eighteenth century, but there is a distinctly modern cultural sensibility at work—one more casual, more playful, more humorous, and, in some ways, more self-aware of their presence in the global mediascape. Jungle housekeeping's quest for Edenic solitude expresses the nation's political isolationism at the very moment when modern transport and commu-nication networks belied the so-called "remoteness" of distant cultures. Nonetheless, by continually reminding readers of modernity's encroach-ment on the previously remote and unexplored regions of the world, *National Geographic*'s jungle housekeeping contributors ushered their readers into a global era.

Little House in the Jungle

In addition to the jungle itself as a space of isolation and retreat, one of the most enduring icons evoked in jungle housekeeping articles was that of the Western frontier and the pioneering fortitude of American settlers who endured wilderness hardships. Jungle housekeeping's iconic eigh-teenth- and nineteenth-century precursors of strenuous existence, such as *Robinson Crusoe* (1719) and *The Swiss Family Robinson* (1879) had par-ticular resonance for *National Geographic* readers of the 1930s caught in the economic crisis of the Great Depression.[20] References to makeshift and improvised jungle homes appeared in *National Geographic*'s pages when Americans lived similarly precarious existences. The frontier mo-tif recalled readers to the ways of their pioneering ancestors as couples indirectly provided Americans at home lessons on not just how to make do—how to survive on local resources and endure geographic disloca-tion and cultural isolation—but how to grapple with increasing global interconnectedness.

As an effort to contain global complexity, invocations of the "wild West" and all it has represented culturally—self-reliance, innovation, and masculine enterprise—attempt to salvage an American identity mytho-logically grounded in the frontier. While jungle housekeeping narratives adhere to the frontier's adventure motif of self-reliance, they persistently reveal how the adventuring families were, in fact, entirely dependent upon local labor in ways that call attention to the narratives' underlying element of performance. In their performances of the frontier script, the couples unwittingly destabilize the mythology upon which imperial nar-ratives are based. These narrative contradictions between independence and dependence, isolation and cultural contact, help to expose not only the historical and cultural expectations shaping gender conventions but their underlying imperial power structures.

Mrs. William H. Hoover, in "Keeping House for the Shepherds of the Sun" (April 1930), presents a narrative riddled with just such contradictions. With her eighteen-month-old daughter, Hoover accompanied her scientist husband and his colleague on an NGS and Smithsonian Institution–sponsored expedition to Keetmanshoop—"a small Western town of the cattle- or sheep-ranching country at home" (486)—in South Africa, to set up a solar-radiation observatory. Hoover's narrative exploits the region's geographic isolation and hardship to place her family in the mythology of the western frontier. For three years, the family lived in a government-built corrugated iron house atop a "lonely volcanic mountain that rises from an arid plain" (483). Their struggle to keep a cow to supply the baby's milk, the "menfolk's" ingenuity in rigging a makeshift icebox from a refrigerator freezing unit ordered from the United States, and Hoover's efforts to provide her family with "enough vitamins" from tinned goods, dried beans, peas, and squashes (495) replay the conventions of pioneering hardihood.

While these demonstrations of male and female domestic prowess reinforce conventional gender behaviors within a genre that has typically been dominated by eccentrics, the couple's dependence on local labor to construct their gender identities within the context of the frontier mythology are exposed as performances in which locals are the chief props.[21] Her narrative of frontier primitivism begins to break down when readers discover that the "small Western town" boasted sixty miles of telephone line, and numerous newspapers and radio broadcasts connecting them to the world outside. Nine hundred "whites" lived in a district with a variety of stores, four tennis courts, and six churches. Each household had at least one servant, she notes (486). Taken together, these details call attention to the manufactured aspects of Hoover's frontier narrative. While touching the surface details of pioneering fortitude, Hoover's hardships extended to managing obstinate servants, skipping rope to keep in shape, and substituting evaporated milk, gelatin, or flour for the whipped cream and marshmallows in American recipes (502, 495). She left the most arduous domestic tasks to their African servants, and her husband had only to clap his hands and call out "Boy!" to have several appear "as if by magic" (657).

Hoover's narrative highlights the ways in which the reliance on native labor cannot be contained within the boundaries of the frontier narrative. As a result, jungle housekeeping's frontier primitivism must be restaged and enacted in front of the camera. An episode involving a leopard's untimely invasion of the chicken coop and Mr. Hoover's revenge wonderfully calls attention to this prevailing pattern in jungle housekeeping narratives. Hoover describes how her husband and his partner in the scientific expedition take up guns instead of telescopes. Enlisting the help of Cornelius and Autumn Teapot, their household servants and animal trackers, the men corner the offending leopard at its den. Mr. Hoover emerges from the scene heroic, having shot the leopard in the back and eye just before it attacked his colleague. The men return in triumph with a seven-foot-long female leopard slung on a pole, "tawny and lithe, so perfectly suited to its environment that we felt the least bit sad," wrote Hoover (504). The hunt itself was a quick affair, taking just two hours, yet, as Hoover's narrative reveals, it is built up into a saga of male prowess.

But it does not end there. Hoover's recording of the heroic aftermath takes on a comic tone that serves as an ironic commentary on the men's efforts to replay frontier heroism. "Such excitement!" writes Hoover. "Mr. Hoover posed as the mighty hunter; Mr. Greeley posed; they posed together; we posed the natives; then the whole family posed." In addition to giving Autumn Teapot and Cornelius "strict instructions" not to skin the leopard until he developed the film at the observatory darkroom, Mr. Hoover "wasn't satisfied with the background, so we had to pose all over again" (504). The facing page shows a photograph of Mr. Hoover and his colleague in the foreground holding the slain leopard (fig. 19).[22] The photograph's every element is calculated to secure Mr. Hoover's prowess and his superior relation to the Hottentot tribesmen in his employ. As if to diminish their role as guides, Cornelius and Autumn Teapot stand just behind and on either side of the men. West Africa's inhospitable desert mountainscape looms as the iconic frontier backdrop, heightening our sense of frontier hardship and isolation. Hoover's humorous repetition of the word "pose," however, acknowledges her husband's efforts to restage the masculine heroics associated with the iconic frontier.

Perhaps it is the recognition by the women who write jungle housekeeping narratives that they are writing for popular entertainment that prompts their ironic commentary on the ways in which the couple's wilderness antics burlesque the imperial project as represented in popular culture. In "Mrs. Robinson Crusoe in Ecuador" (February 1934), Mrs. Richard C. Gill observes: "After all, was it the early, and doubtless furtive,

Fig. 19 "The Chicken Thief That Became a Fur Rug." (William Hoover/National Geographic Image Collection)

reading on Dick's part of too many paper-bound dime novels? Or was it in reality a sincere desire to create a permanent expeditionary base on the edge of the Amazon Valley, from which point he could do that ethnologic work among the Indians which had been his ambition for so long? I suspected a good measure of both influences" (134). With this comment, Gill acknowledges the "dime novel" origins of their so-called "real pioneering" efforts.

As the article's title invoking the marooned Robinson Crusoe indicates, Gill's narrative mythologizes the couple's attempts to realize a "baronial wilderness life" (135) in remote Ecuador. She describes temporarily living in an abandoned home infested with cockroaches; her efforts to educate Zoila, her Ecuadoran housekeeper and cook; and the chaotic aftermath when a roaming bull breaks into their kitchen, scattering the "golf clubs and balls" they brought with them for their future putting green and destroying Zoila's "favorite red dress" (138). Their "chairs and tables were, in the main, improvised from gasoline boxes" and "5-gallon kerosene cans" were used for dishpans, water buckets, dustpans, and for heating water (138–39). These comic images of frontier disorder and improvisation, however, are thrown into relief by photographs that show the Gills "at home in the wilderness" (fig. 20) and their newly built home's spacious living room with handmade wicker furniture, gleaming wood floors, framed paintings, and dining room replete with a china hutch—all made by locals.[23] As Mrs. Gill notes, "we are really an isolated bit of the United States," as global communication networks keep them occupied reading the two American daily newspapers and "constantly in touch with the outside world" by telephone (152). A short-wave radio similarly provides a "link with a world that had seemed so remote," as they listen to an address by President Hoover and a Broadway melody (145, 156). Despite the essay's title, the cockroaches, gasoline tins, and general chaos are all window dressing for a tale of the global export of American middle-class living standards.

As the Gills' case suggests, jungle housekeeping contributors of the 1930s lived more comfortably than the locals in their employ—and fared much better than the hardest-hit Americans during the Great Depression. The peregrinations of explorer couples among unfamiliar and exotic lands in no way rivaled the migratory and makeshift existence of the nation's most destitute who lived in "Hoovervilles," tents and tin-roofed shantytowns on the periphery of cities, or, in extreme cases, dwelt in caves or even sewer pipes.[24] Although the magazine appealed to a broad readership that crossed class lines, its advertising circulars boasted of having a larger share of the nation's most affluent, those who, as a 1930 circular put it, "live above the fear line."[25] A 1936 National Geographic advertising circular reported that "15 out of every 100 National Geographic families will build or buy homes averaging 7.1 rooms each," underscoring the wealth of the magazine's "first million" readers.[26] To National Geographic readers, the Gills' efforts to build up a "baronial wilderness" in Ecuador likely reinforced the prevailing hope that Americans at home would not only endure economic depression but come through on the other side better poised to realize the "American dream" of success.

Despite the magazine's homage to its "first million" affluent readers, economic hardship hit many National Geographic readers who parted with their magazine memberships with reluctance. Still, even when the Depression was at its bleakest, in 1932, when unemployment peaked at 11.5 million and deprived 34 million families of the earnings of their breadwinners, National Geographic's readers clung to their memberships.[27] "Times are tough, but some families can't afford to omit the Geographic; mine is one" wrote W. F. Schrader, of Fort Wayne, Indiana. Mrs. O. D. Nelson of Greensboro, North Carolina, wrote, "we would feel that we had

Fig. 20 "At Home in the Wilderness." (Richard Gill/National Geographic Image Collection)

lost a valued friend if we ceased our subscription." While many Americans were doing without food, others could not do without, as one reader put it, the "food for the mind" they found in *National Geographic*.[28]

By foregrounding the cultural and technological forces of globalization, the jungle housekeeping genre far exceeded *National Geographic* founders' modest goal of "geographic diffusion." In a larger sense, the magazine was a powerful vehicle for cultural diffusion, particularly through the example of explorer couples whose antics in the globe's remote outposts exposed the layers of institutional and personal performance. At the height of the Great Depression, the romantic primitivism that distinguished jungle housekeeping articles of the 1920s gave way to a more ironic sensibility in which contributors were aware of their own actions as somehow falling short of popular imperial narratives, and, moreover, that the imperial narratives were no longer worthy of emulation.

Reading against the Imperial Grain

While a more sophisticated historical hindsight makes the jungle house-keeping genre's imperialist attitudes readily visible, *National Geographic*'s earliest readers were similarly alert to the kinds of imperial performance taking place in the magazine. Readers were particularly disgusted by captions that denigrated the magazine's ethnographic subjects. An October 1929 caption, "in the Nazir's eyes, these girls are beautiful," came under attack.[29] G. R. Carlin of Halifax, England, wrote, "I suppose it is meant to be slightly humorous and that one should think, with a laugh, well it is only the Nazir that thinks so. This may be a small matter, but it illustrates the tone and mentality of the whole magazine."[30] The liberties *National Geographic* photographic editors took with captioning that trivialized and degraded its human subjects was typical of sensational ethnographic films in which captions were used for humorous effect or exploited their native subjects as sight gags. Captioning in Martin and Osa Johnson's 1928 film *Simba,* for instance, referred to African women in native costumes as "black flappers."[31] So familiar were *National Geographic*'s readers with the commercially successful vaudeville trade in magic lantern slides and silent films capitalizing on primitive stereotypes that they often questioned the veracity of its contributors' photographs.

Even as early as 1925, when the Shays' "From Cairo to Cape Town" appeared in *National Geographic,* angry readers expressed dismay at photographs they felt were literally and figuratively recycled from American popular culture. Miss Rose Scorgie of Richmond, Virginia, who identified herself as formerly of South Africa, complained that "all articles, even the pictures shown at the Moving Picture Houses, persistently show only the 'wild and wooly' side" of South Africa and that Mr. Shay "gives no adequate description, or a sufficient number of typical photographs to show that South Africa is a progressive, enlightened, civilized part of the world." Other readers observed that the article reproduced photographs that appeared in another magazine the previous month. "Am I to assume," quipped one reader, "that the [African] women in the first picture mentioned did not move from February to March and that the characters mentioned in the second picture only moved slightly during the month?" A letter that serves as a scathing indictment of what has been termed *National Geographic*'s narrative of "place-bound cultural timelessness," it demonstrates how the photographic recycling of images undermined the realism they were intended to authenticate.[32] Wrote another reader: "In this wonderful age I realize it is possible to make good African pictures in these United States, with the help of a 'movie' studio. Also it is very possible for a writer with a fertile imagination to string a very good African yarn, all from one of our big office buildings in a city of the United States, so tell me, are things as they seem?"[33] This reader keenly comments on how scripted images on film impacted how readers responded to photographs. If events could be staged on screen, then why not in a photograph? The reader's question, "are things as they seem?" not only hints at the photograph's demise as a reliable index of an existing reality "out there," but suggests that photographic authority could no longer sanction racist cultural beliefs or imperialist social policies.

On this count, the most damning recognition of the article's artifice comes from an African American NGS member acutely offended by "the performance of Mr. Shay and his wife." G. Savels of Alameda, California, commented ironically, "I made that trip and more twenty years ago when I was a young unsophisticated 'negro' boy." He continued, "Europe may have civilization, but I found in the thirty-five years I lived in Africa more culture than I ever found in Europe or America. I hope that you will not leave the record of the *Geographic* so incomplete as to take an unsophisticated 'white' man's judgment on Africa."[34] Like the other readers' letters, G. Savels's criticisms reveal how ethnographic photographs, like their film counterparts, were scripted to reproduce common assumptions about the "primitive" in relation to the "civilized." What jungle housekeeping narratives make visible, then, is how the process of scripting the Other photographically or textually also implicitly produces a alternate script: a script that reveals the cultural assumptions observers bring to their representations of the Other. This act of looking at oneself from the outside and coming to terms with the cultural assumptions that govern vision has been termed a "third eye" that promotes a more critical reception of ethnographic visual and written "texts."[35]

The isolation of women jungle housekeeping narrators from the official public realms of imperial administration enables them to achieve this "third eye" perspective on themselves, their culture, and its assumptions concerning gender and cultural difference. In so doing, they recall such female travel writers as Mary Kingsley, whose 1897 *Travels in West Africa* similarly deploys the familiar imagery of masculine imperial exploits in such a way that she masters imperialism's narrative forms precisely by parodying its conventions.[36] Self-deprecation and humor in women's travel writing, it has been argued, critiques imperialism "from its margins"; at the same time, these same strategies can be seen as ingenious efforts to salvage Western "innocence" in the face of the most egregious imperial violence and exploitation.[37]

Though they are imperfect exemplars of anti-imperialism, *National Geographic*'s female contributors to the jungle housekeeping genre are unique in both their acknowledgment of the popular cultural origins of imperial performance and their candid recognition of imperial power structures. "No white man does manual labor," observes Mrs. Hoover. "Every white man is a master, and it is a true saying that heads as well as feet swell in South West Africa" (486). Hoover's comment, "the natives here are strictly controlled" (498), records imperialism's complex history and notes its traces in the German songs sung by her servants. Similarly, Ruth Q. McBride's "Keeping House on the Congo" (November 1937) documents the lingering artifacts of the slave trade in the Belgian Congo's architecture and jungle landscape. The buildings are "long and low," she writes, with "small barred windows up near the roof. Here and there are iron rings still in the walls, the slave chains of these former warehouses for their unfortunate cargoes" (644). In the Congo's interior she observes imperial policies that continue to enslave the Congo, as "native prisoners chained together sawed crude planks from logs used in building the cottages" (645) for colonial administrators. The women writers' candid acknowledgment of imperial power gestures toward a cross-cultural sympathy. In this way, jungle housekeeping narratives bear witness to global interdependences and the social and economic injustices visible in the lingering imperial economic power structures that exploit native labor.

National Geographic's management of its contributors' commentaries through its editorial policy of nonpartisanship did not prevent images of imperial exploitation and the corresponding failure of its enterprise from bubbling to the surface. Even within the magazine's homage to popular versions of "the primitive" as exhibited in sensational ethnographic films *Grass* (1925) and *Chang* (1927) by Merian C. Cooper and Ernest B. Schoedsack, contributors exhibit a refreshingly ironic stance toward imperialism's complicity with the commodified exotic of tourism and popular fiction. On his 1928 ornithological expedition to the island port of Juan Fernandez, the fabled domicile of Robinson Crusoe 365 miles west of Valparaiso, Chile, the ornithologist Waldo L. Schmitt noted a rag-tag pair of "island idlers" garbed as "Crusoe and Friday" who entertained tourists for tips. Schmitt wryly gives readers a chronology of conquest from pirates on the high seas and scientific exploration to global tourism:

"Pirates, whalers, sailors, scientists, tourists—that is the sequence in pacific conquest. Darwin on the *Beagle*; Moseley on the *Challenger*; Americans on the *Albatross*; and the deep-sea workers dragging the ocean's bottom, hunting the best place to lay cables." "Later," he observed, "ukuleles, hula skirts, Kanaka songs, and South Sea scenes for motion-picture melodramas" completed "the romantic Pacific picture."[38] Although it falls outside the "jungle housekeeping" narrative genre, Schmitt's account is worth noting because of its self-awareness regarding the history of performances underlying the metaphors of imperial conquest.

As we have seen, jungle housekeeping articles are riddled by persistent and illuminating cultural paradoxes. First, in the couples' efforts, in a contributor's words, to escape "beyond the reach of mechanized civilization," they depended upon the very technologies from which they sought escape.[39] Second, by repudiating the literal, technological manifestations of global interconnectedness, such articles construct a myth of solitude, even as they show the couples' dependency on local domestic help. Further, the mythic nature of their solitude is revealed as newspaper, radio, and telephone collapse the temporal distance, and historical distinction, between remote jungle settings and modern cities. Finally, the contributors to *National Geographic*'s jungle housekeeping genre claimed a more authentic relation to nature through a Thoreauvian effort to simplify and pare down to the essentials for living, yet they did so because they had the economic means to do so. "Really, the game of Crusoe or Swiss Family Robinson is the pursuit of the rich or the moderately wealthy," remarked a contributor in 1938.[40] Only the wealthy could afford the elaborate props— a jungle estate and servants—to make them look like pioneers.

Cultural Assimilation and Gender Critique

In the jungle housekeeping genre the remote jungle frontier was a staging ground for traditional masculine and feminine domestic feats and changing gender roles. In Martin and Osa Johnson's 1928 film *Simba*, for example, Osa fashioned a rolling pin from a wine bottle in order to make a celebratory pie after a successful hunt. But she was also a known "crack shot" who once rescued her husband from a charging elephant, and reviewers lauded her as an "an element of striking contrast" in the couple's popular films.[41] Though intended as novel entertainment, the examples of Osa Johnson and Porter Shay nonetheless showcased the ways in which traditional boundaries between the sexes were increasingly unstable.

As proof of the ensuing cultural unease, Ernest Hemingway envisioned a more sinister denouement to the Shays' African safari in which women like Porter (she who killed a "large male") would take revenge. Several "large males" die at the hands of women in Hemingway's African fiction. In "The Short Happy Life of Francis Macomber" (1936), after having an affair with their White Hunter guide, a wife shoots and kills her husband, and in "The Snows of Kilimanjaro" (1936), a wife allows her husband's gangrenous leg to doom him to a slow, painful death. In each story, the male and female roles are reversed: woman is predator while man is prey, an example of the "predatory wife" who appeared in popular fiction after women's suffrage.[42] Meditations on failure, these stories complicate the nineteenth-century romance adventure model built upon masculine heroics and the strenuous life, as much as they do the later ideal of "companionate marriage" and successful male-female collaboration. In marked contrast to romance fiction of the 1880s in which "woman's act of witness" is what "validates the hero's virility," *National Geographic*'s jungle housekeeping genre both reflected and reconfigured popular notions regarding race, gender, and the exotic.[43]

Gender, then, is a complicating factor in the escape-to-Eden fantasy. A common thread within *National Geographic*'s jungle housekeeping genre is the frontier fortitude exhibited by women giving birth or caring for children while traveling abroad with their husbands. The Norwegian novelist Erling Tambs sailed the high seas with a pregnant wife who raised their son on the yacht they inhabited for two years (December 1931). Nancy Bell Fairchild Bates bore a daughter in a remote Andean village while helping her husband with his scientific research (August 1948). Edith Bray Siemel, who married a Latvian jaguar hunter, bore three children in the seven years they dwelt in the Brazilian rain forest (November 1952). An image of female fortitude, childbirth and child rearing in primitive settings reasserts the magazine's aesthetic of timelessness and stability against cultural change and global upheaval.

But readers should not conclude too hastily that the jungle housekeeping genre affirmed Felix Shay's 1925 remark, "Woman's place is in the home," for it also featured women who were handy with guns. On Afghanistan's remote Wakhan corridor, Jean Shor takes up arms to defend their camp against wolves (November 1950).[44] On her first jungle hunt, Edith Siemel kills a puma (November 1952). As recounted by her husband, Sasha: "She raised her gun, held it steady an instant, and fired. The mountain lion rolled off the branch, dead before it hit the ground.

I looked at Edith. She was calmly reloading. The jungle, I decided, had found a new 'white hunter.'"[45]

As the examples of frontier fortitude illustrate, though the women in jungle housekeeping occupied positions outside the colonial administrative order, they remained within its patriarchal system. As has been observed in colonial British women's travel narratives, this relative position of powerlessness helped establish more sympathetic bonds between women and the inhabitants of colonized countries.[46] As mediators of cross-cultural contact between Westerners and locals through shared survival and household management, communal celebrations of marriage, birth, and death, the female narrators of jungle housekeeping narratives impose a familiar Western domestic cultural frame on unfamiliar global locales. In this way, the jungle housekeeping genre seems, on the one hand, to reinforce a gendered "innocent eye" in which domesticity, sentiment, and cultural difference sanction imperial domination.[47] On the other hand, jungle housekeeping narratives also call attention to the less visible and historically overlooked "domains of the intimate," the more subtle ways in which U.S. imperial power has constituted itself.[48] The women narrators of *National Geographic*'s jungle housekeeping expose the "politics of sympathy" underlying the magazine's educative mission and its complicity with U.S. imperialism.[49]

There are several ways in which jungle housekeeping narratives are refreshingly transgressive. Transporting the conjugal relationship to the jungle, its contributors do not just call into question conventional Western gender roles and power arrangements. In their emphasis on the gendered dimensions of colonial power, in their willing witness to represent divergent cultural attitudes toward marriage and gender roles, and in their exposure of the interpersonal backdrop to scientific objectivity, they represent a critique of imperialism from within the magazine's anachronistic narrative of frontier heroism. In so doing, they illustrate the potential of the global mediascape to forge more self-aware forms of engagement with cultural difference.

While the spectacle of women fashioning middle-class domesticity in unlikely settings was indeed a novelty, the jungle housekeeping genre also showed women sharing their husbands' scientific labors and, as *National Geographic* contributors, enjoying a level of professional status.[50] The candid insights of *National Geographic*'s jungle housekeeping contributors had important ethnographic antecedents. Women anthropologists such as Margaret Mead, who achieved renown for her landmark *Coming of Age in Samoa* (1928), and Ruth Benedict, whose *Patterns of Culture* (1934) was a best seller, established a popular audience for serious ethnography. These students of Columbia University's leading anthropologist, Franz Boas, were in the vanguard of professionally trained ethnographers in the 1920s whose observations of cultures from the field challenged the scientific racism promoted by eighteenth- and nineteenth-century armchair ethnographers. Despite retaining traces of the "romantic primitivism" that pervaded the earlier variety, this new field research based on the ideals of cultural relativism—of examining cultures on their own terms—and of participant observation established a more contextual approach to representing cultural differences. It also established anthropology as a powerful force for cultural critique.[51]

Though written by self-styled "amateurs," *National Geographic*'s jungle housekeeping genre provided candid insights on gendered imperial power and cultural differences; it also introduced a critical perspective on Western cultural assumptions. Eleanor De Chételat's "My Domestic Life in French Guinea," subtitled "An American Woman Accompanies Her Husband, a Swiss Geologist, on His Explorations in a Little-Known Region" (June 1935), makes keen observations regarding gendered colonial and tribal power structures. Villages, she notes, are ruled by chiefs, who are in turn "under the control of a local French administrator" (695). As an outsider, she captures the subtle ways in which the colonized are forced to submit to Western sexual politics. As part of the Armistice Day festivities to which local chieftains are invited, "four white men of the European population" preside as judges of a "beauty contest" among Fulah women (696). At the same time, De Chételat also exposes their resistance to Western gender conventions. When she played records for villagers in the evenings, Mangalai, an African military guard who learned to foxtrot while serving on the Western Front during the First World War, "grabbed one of the girls around the waist in an attempt to demonstrate the manner in which the white man dances, but after a second she broke away, screaming and laughing, shocked at this 'indecent' European custom" (720). In showing the local rejection of "indecent" Western courtship behaviors likely taken for granted by *National Geographic* readers, De Chételat reverses the terms of cultural observation to expose Western customs to an outside perspective. By highlighting how other Africans mock the military officer's Western dancing as "indecent," De Chételat's narrative undermines the "innocence of whiteness" typified in women's travel writing.[52]

Rather than foreground her own domestic circumstances, De Chételat's narrative stands apart for its self-conscious "ethnological investigations" (729) of African gender roles in Kioniagul, in French Guinea's interior. A woman, De Chételat observes, is forbidden to marry until "she has proved her fertility by bearing at least one child. In the intervening years, after the initiation of the youths and the excision of the girls, until their marriage, promiscuity is looked upon as obligatory" and marriage is consequently delayed (729). In the detached tone of the scientist, De Chételat denaturalizes the conventions of Western marriage while also noting cultural rituals, such as female circumcision ("excision"), "for the purpose of teaching the male how to keep woman in her place" (729). Though De Chételat's narrative does not achieve anthropologist Ruth Benedict's dramatic "juxtaposition of the all-too-familiar and the wildly exotic in such a way that they change places," her frank discussion of female sexuality reflects an unexpected candor in women's travel writing.[53]

National Geographic articles on "keeping house" in exotic places reveal varying degrees of identification and cross-cultural interaction between the women and the foreign places and peoples with whom they share their domestic lives. They document a shift in perceiving cultural differences from conventionally imperialist portrayals of savage and benighted children of nature to a recognition and appreciation of cultural differences as a necessary means of survival within a specific environment. Women writing about their growing understanding of a previously unknown culture embody a cultural relativism, in which borrowing from local cultural practices signals their adaptation to unfamiliar environments rather than their reproduction of stereotypes regarding a culture's place in an evolutionary hierarchy. The women's emphasis on their own assimilation to the culture in which they find themselves also indicates a notable educational shift in the magazine. Instead of escape and imaginative transport through aestheticized images of cultural difference, as seen in chapter 3, *National Geographic*'s jungle housekeeping contributors invited readers to reflect critically on Western privilege and power.

Articles in which the women reconsider their cultural assumptions stand strikingly apart from those of earlier contributors to the genre. Marion Stirling's "Jungle Housekeeping for a Geographic Expedition" (September 1941) and Virginia Hamilton's "Keeping House in Borneo"

(September 1945) show the authors' increasing identification with the local inhabitants. In both Hamilton's and Stirling's narratives, the preparation and eating of native foods presents an alternate allegory to that of Eden, one that vividly conveys *National Geographic*'s role as an agent of cultural diffusion as each woman literally digests and assimilates the new culture. Stirling acquired a taste for the spicy empanadas and *gordas* she learned to cook in Venezuela. Hamilton came to enjoy tortoise eggs, "stink" beans, and the pungent durians beloved by Indonesians.[54] In this way, culture was implicitly presented not as static but as fluid, a negotiated process rather than a product of cultural contact in which Western culture bestows enlightenment values and modern technology on childlike natives. Both women consciously adopt local survival strategies that shine a light on Western culture from their newly adopted other-cultural perspective.

While in Veracruz with her archaeologist husband, Stirling forges relationships with local inhabitants on an equal footing and develops greater self-awareness regarding American wastefulness. Writes Stirling: "I soon learned the value of tin cans, boxes, bottles, magazines, illustrated pages from newspapers, bits of colored ribbon, tin foil, and postcards. We saved them all and apportioned them" (319). Stirling's sensitivity to the deprivations the Venezuelans endured daily—"Any native family is lucky to own one blanket for the use of the entire household"—invites a similar sensitivity in her readers (320). "The natives never wasted anything," wrote Stirling. "When we left, one man asked permission to cut down the palm tree to which our pistol target was nailed so he might extract the lead bullets imbedded in the trunk" (319). In contrast to previous jungle housekeeping articles that describe local inhabitants as simple and childlike, Stirling's emphasis on the Veracruzanos' thrift and hard work instructs readers in more economizing ways.[55]

The geographic shift in domestic localities that jungle housekeeping narrators undergo correspondingly requires increasing self-consciousness. Movement from place to place involves a "domestic seriality" in which having repeatedly to re-create home spaces invites a kind of self-aware reordering of relations between domestic locales.[56] This conception of serial domesticity is crucial for acknowledging the growing cultural relativism that occurs in jungle housekeeping articles. Until she lived in Borneo, Hamilton writes, "I didn't realize how many things I could do without. . . . There you don't just go out and buy a dress if you think you need it" (324). Similarly, for Stirling, the Venezuelans provide a lesson in economy and thrift, inviting her to reflect on American wastefulness. She returns from Venezuela to Washington, D.C., with the memory of her Veracruzano home so vivid that, "For a long time after we arrived home, I had a guilty feeling every time I threw away a tin can, especially a valuable one with a lid" (319). In the jungle housekeeping genre, geographic dislocation supplies a shift in context that instills a heightened degree of awareness of the imperial economics and power dynamics of globalization.

Admitting the imperialist motives for traveling to Borneo, Hamilton writes: "It was oil which brought my husband and me to the island. It was oil which kept us moving, pushing ever farther inland" (293). Like Stirling, Hamilton also assimilates to Indonesian custom by adopting local survival tactics, but her dawning cultural relativism appears in more explicitly pedantic terms. She writes, "One should not judge the natives by our standards before learning to understand their own Mohammedan religion and age-old customs" that set "rigid, high standards, but these standards do not always coincide with our own" (301). By acknowledging, in her own words, that "color and creed" are not an accurate basis for judging "whether a person is noble or ignoble" (301), Hamilton acknowledges cultural differences in a way that departs from the language of benighted "savages" and "children." Here, global interconnectedness is not feared, but embraced, not as a cultural commodity, but on a footing that, however problematic—both Stirling and Hamilton refer to their hosts as "the natives"—seeks more egalitarian forms.

In keeping with this backward glance at Western culture through "Other" eyes, we see female jungle housekeeping narrators representing local women's critique of Western women's domestic lives. Hamilton's domestic help discarded the American washboard because they were "disgusted with the inefficiency of such civilized nonsense."[57] Another contributor described a mother's pride in her daughter's resilience after the daughter had given birth. The elder "mother's smile held a hint of condescension, as she proudly replied, 'Ah, you Americans, in truth you must lie abed with much pain, and have the doctor. But not my Graciella. For her the making of a baby is so simple as to make bread.'"[58] From the perspective of the elder Venezuelan mother, not only her American visitor but also Western medicine become distinctly unwelcome "Others."

This encounter suggests how jungle housekeeping narratives also implicitly critique the masculine scientific enterprise represented by *National Geographic* from within the genre itself. In a domestic setting where personal and professional roles coexist, the kitchen and the laboratory are sites where both the exotic and science are processed and assimilated. In "Keeping House for a Biologist in Columbia" (1948), Nancy Bell Fairchild Bates, who assisted her husband with his study of yellow fever, exposes the interpersonal and subjective dynamics of cross-cultural exchange that underwrite official science. The sounds of children playing, writes Bates, and their appearance "in various stages of undress do not enhance the dignity of a research institution" (268). Bates and her husband shared a bustling family compound with Columbian employees, laboratory equipment and specimens, and live animals for testing in the remote Columbian village of Villavicencio. Bates's narrative is remarkable for both its critique of the impersonal conventions of scientific writing and its embrace of the extended cross-cultural "household" whose figurative "hearth" is the scientific laboratory.

Typically gendered sites of female and male endeavor, the kitchen and the laboratory respectively, are shown throughout Bates's narrative as having indistinct and permeable borders. She describes her laboratory work in terms of routine domestic tasks: "It looks very simple and reads like a recipe: Put a little ether in a big glass jar, remove six small mice from their box with pincers and place them in the jar, stir well, and remove each mouse as he goes to sleep" (270). Reducing scientific activity to a "recipe," Bates not only caricatures her own gender-assigned domestic performances against the more "profound" efforts of scientific progress (251), but makes science itself a more hospitable and familiar place for women. Furthermore, in showing the boundary between official science and domestic activity as indistinct, Bates reveals the messy, personal contexts typically concealed in "objective" scientific writing.

Bates rejects the distancing metaphors that endow science with its objective posture in order to expose the makeshift, improvisational qualities of scientific endeavor. Casual observations, like the fact that monkeys appear in places with the highest incidence of yellow fever, have to be couched in "objective" terms and "well peppered with 'it would seem' and 'in all probability'" (260). Underscoring the validity of the personal and subjective, Bates concludes her essay with an ironic commentary on the masculine domain of science: "These observations I should never dare to write up seriously, having read too much about 'anecdotal natural history'; so until I master the true style of complete objectivity, i.e., 'the animal oriented itself with respect to the banana and took a bite,' science must wait" (274). Mimicking the "true style of complete objectivity," Bates provides a more personal glimpse of the interpersonal contexts surrounding her husband's research. Though Bates refers throughout her narrative to her husband as "the Boss," the appellation takes an ironic form because Bates humorously highlights how her husband's science is exercised in the midst of domestic chaos. In so doing, she calls into question the objectivity that has historically constituted *National Geographic*'s ethnographic authority.

Bates's article shows how, by the 1940s and 1950s, the jungle housekeeping genre exhibited a subtle change in which the jungle is no Eden, but a place of struggle, hardship, and cross-cultural contact that yields unexpected friendships and, in some ways, a more self-aware critique of gender roles as well as Western privilege and scientific endeavor. These later jungle housekeeping narratives show families embracing cultural relativism, as they adopt local customs and food sources. In these decades marking the Cold War era, the jungle housekeeping genre intensified as a vehicle for global interconnectedness and cultural diversity to penetrate and fracture the self-contained domain of the modern American home.

Intruders Abroad: The *National Geographic* Photographer on Assignment

As a modern-day peddler of the world's discordant visual wares, the *National Geographic* photographer was, like the narrators of jungle housekeeping, an agent of cultural diffusion. Images of photographers on assignment share the jungle housekeeping genre's potential for dramatically upsetting *National Geographic*'s institutional performance of Western imperial supremacy.

I return to the *National Geographic* photographer on assignment in order to show how such photographs complicate the magazine's production of cultural icons. In the 1940s and 1950s, photographs that document the photographer's tools and labor form a photographic genre in *National Geographic*, described in chapter 3 as "self-documentary" photographs whose composition and captioning call attention to the processes of photographic production. Snapshots of the 1940s and 1950s sanction the nation's history as explorers and colonizers at the same time that they portray America as a pioneer of technology and world exploration. The readings of *National Geographic* photographs reproduced in editor Gilbert H. Grosvenor's institutional histories, published in 1936 and 1957, explore the contradictions within *National Geographic*'s documentation of its photographers on assignment. Though meant to highlight the photographer's ingenuity, the magazine's self-conscious "institutional gaze" reveals *National Geographic* photographers as not always in control of their environments, estranged from their contexts, and clumsily out of place as they pursue their quarry. The same images contain an element of trespass: the American photographer in pursuit of photographs exposes the institution's self-promotional tactics, and perhaps, therefore, the potential artifice of the imperialist narratives embedded in the photographs themselves.

Improvisation and performance connects jungle housekeeping's ethnographic representation to images of photographers on assignment. As recapitulations of a masculine frontier ethos, both jungle housekeeping articles and photographers in the field highlight the processes by which science and art facilitated the magazine's own imperial performances. While the camera's sympathetic magic surrounds the photographer in a heroic aura, photographs where cameras break into the frame highlight the artifice behind *National Geographic*'s performance of imperial mastery. Like the jungle housekeeping articles that trade on popularized icons of the "primitive," self-documentary photographs expose their fictive underpinnings. Snapshots of *National Geographic* photographers are a form of institutional performance, whereby the photographer exemplifies the artifice of performance itself, of being "'on' or doing something 'for the camera'" in order to fulfill the magazine's imperial script.[59]

A photograph taken just after World War II that appeared in Grosvenor's 1957 institutional history underscores its stagecraft even as the magazine attempts to document the photographer's prowess (fig. 21). In this image, Volkmar Wentzel, a NGS staff photographer who spent two years traveling in India and Pakistan, stands atop what the caption describes as a "war-surplus ambulance that he converted into a mobile hotel and photographic darkroom" (138). The caption thus frames Wentzel as an imperial adventurer, capable of mastering any situation. Bundi's "massive gate" frames the photographer, dwarfing him beneath the towering architecture. Our eyes are drawn upward in a movement that calls attention to his height relative to that of the crowd. Wentzel's dominant posture, echoed by the archway of the gate itself, presents the illusion of magnified height, as though the gates of civilization and the photographed subject were complicit in orchestrating the shot. Here, the institution documents a scene in which the photographer literally takes center stage. His glance, directed away from the camera and toward the crowd, lends the photograph the appearance of a candid shot.

Fig. 21 *NGM* photographer Volkmar Wentzel on top of a World War II surplus ambulance. (Volkmar K. Wentzel/National Geographic Image Collection)

However, the photograph betrays its self-promotional purposes, directing the reader to its theatricality and away from the "reality" the photograph seeks to represent. The caption heightens the artifice, describing Wentzel's travels as a round of encounters with friendly "Maharajas" who "entertained him with tiger hunts, elephant fights, and polo matches" (138). Here, the Maharajas are portrayed as darker-skinned Europeans, whose possible threat is neutralized by their shared enjoyment of polo matches. Yet the photograph's suggested dynamic of imperial aggression is ambiguous. On the one hand, Wentzel appears the aggressor; he stands assertively and holds his camera like a weapon directed at the crowd; on the other hand, the crowd outnumbers him, and his look is one of anxious confusion.

Though our gaze is focused on the photographer, several people in the crowd cast quizzical glances toward the "other" camera—the one trained on Wentzel. These glances highlight the staged aspect of the institution's documentation of its own history. It is realism of this kind that unwittingly fractures the romanticized gaze the NGS turns on its photographers. The crowd has drawn apart so that the transcendent institutional camera can document the photographer on location. The crowd's scattered glances—some directed at Wentzel, and others directed to the camera aimed by another photographer "offstage"—function as the photograph's "punctum"—that partially concealed element in a photograph that wields unexpected psychological power.[60] In the case of *National Geographic*'s self-documentary images, the punctum also undoes the photograph's realism.

The punctum evades the intentions of the photographer, and for that reason captivates the viewer. Indeed, its power comes precisely from the fact that it is an element serendipitously caught. "Serendipity," in fact, is the word *National Geographic* photographers use to describe the unexpected convergence of chance elements involved in capturing an image.[61] The "serendipity" of the punctum, however, has nothing to do with these factors. Its powers transcend those of the ordered, contrived composition. In every case, the punctum reaches beyond the frame of the photograph and points to a context outside the documentary moment. If the photograph of Wentzel attempts to document what the magazine's earliest photographers falsely portrayed as a "collaboration" between the photographer and his subjects, then the photograph shows how it is a forced one, indicated by the ambulance's blocking of the street and the parting of the crowd.[62] The only collaboration taking place in this photograph is between the photographer and the institution itself.

Frequently, the accompanying captions highlight the makeshift qualities of the equipment or photographic lab. Many such photographs describe how the camera or special lenses were engineered in a "*National Geographic* Laboratory" before being tested and modified in the field. A series of dislocations by which the scientist transfers "himself and his laboratory into the midst of a world untouched by laboratory science" reverses the order of what constitutes the inside of the lab and the outside world, and rearranges the social order to conform to the standards of measurement in the laboratory.[63] The same strategy is involved in *National Geographic*'s relocation of the institution vis-à-vis improvised photographic studios in the field. And yet the camera's very presence in the field belies the institution's efforts to claim nature as a space free from technology. Such images destabilize the nature/culture divide that has constituted conventional ethnography, highlighting the history of photographic representation in attempting to assert a definitive boundary between the two.

In these efforts at "self-documentary," the magazine's images of photographers on assignment resemble experimental forms of modern cinema, as for instance in Marxist cinematographer Dziga Vertov's *A Man with a Movie Camera* (1929). Moving with the camera across various spaces and locales, weaving in and among the moving crowd, Vertov made visible for his viewers the processes by which cinematic "reality" is constructed as an invitation to cultivating a "more sophisticated and critical attitude" toward the medium.[64] Anticipating more self-conscious ethnographic film techniques, Vertov's film also "delights in the camera's own self-consciousness, its reflexivity as an integral part of its discovery of the world."[65] Jungle housekeeping articles and self-documentary photographs can achieve potentially similar effects. By training a lens on the visual and textual processes of scientific production, they make readers more aware of the performative aspects of so-called scientific forms of representation, such as *National Geographic* photography.

The same holds true in a 1954 photograph from Thomas E. Gilliard's "New Guinea's Rare Birds and Stone Age Men" (April 1953). The photograph of two cameramen suspended thirty feet atop a bamboo "tree house" while photographing the New Guinea bird of paradise (fig. 22), also reproduced for Grosvenor's institutional history, attempts to portray

Western modernity by focusing on the technological superiority of the equipment. The men, one squinting into the viewfinder of a telescopic lens, the other using an equipment case as a stool, are shown as adepts in making the natural world conform to their needs. From the photographers' transcendent position in a makeshift tree house–cum–photographic studio, the technological and modern usurp the natural and "real" as photographic subjects. The photographers and their equipment, "special cameras with long lenses and high-speed electronic flash"—not the birds, which are excluded from view—are shown as the subjects of the photograph. Yet this photograph also calls attention to the technological and institutional contexts outside its frame. The caption reminds us, for example, that in a previous expedition, one of the featured photographers made "the first jungle use of the remarkable speedlight spotlight" developed in a NGS photographic laboratory.[66] Both caption and photograph conjure *National Geographic*'s institutional presence by affirming the technological ingenuity of its agents.

Though the institutional gaze invites a "candid" glimpse of the photographers in their habitat, the potential for readers to resist the institutional gaze occurs when we realize just how out of place these men are, as both wear polished loafers and oxford shirts with button-down collars. Like a Freudian slip, the punctum of the photograph evades the photographer's control even as it reveals the intentions of its maker. The early twentieth century's sharpest critic of mechanical reproduction, Walter Benjamin, writes that the photograph substitutes "unconsciously penetrated space" for an artistic space "consciously explored by man."[67] His anxiety about the photograph is that it often reveals far more than spectators bargained for. Unbeknownst to its agents of mechanical reproduction, the photograph is as likely to disclose, as it is to conceal, the photographer's conscious or unconscious motives. While attempting to appear spontaneous and candid, self-documentary photographs are as carefully orchestrated as the compositions of photographic pictorialism. On the one hand, snapshots of photographers on assignment invite spectators' identification with the photographer as the heroic protagonist of *National Geographic*'s imperial epic. On the other hand, by documenting the visible tensions between staged image and candid snapshot that shatter *National Geographic*'s illusion of improvisational realism, such photographs also trouble that identification.

As has been acknowledged, technology is not always within the control of its operators; what seems at first outside the photographic frame—the

Fig. 22 "Cameramen Build a Tree House." (E. Gilliard/National Geographic Image Collection)

cultural institutions, internalized cultural narratives, unconscious motives that direct vision, or a culture's internal political and cultural strife—often intrudes upon the composition. By calling attention to composition and point of view as manipulating factors that direct our vision, reflexive and self-documentary photographs momentarily disrupt the surface realism that the photograph portrays. Because it exploits the "unconscious optics" within photographs that reinforce conventional cultural practices and beliefs, the *National Geographic* might be understood to promote a passive "political spectatorship" over "active citizenship."[68] The self-documentary photograph, however, opens a space for active resistance because it exposes and makes conscious the technological machinery within the photograph and the cultural narratives behind the lens. Such photographs pierce readers, momentarily shattering the sense of the real that the photograph seeks to evoke. The resulting cognitive dissonance creates an opportunity for reimagining national selfhood—and one's membership within a larger global community—apart from the institutions that attempt to shape it.

The Suburb and the Veil: Cold War Containment and the Nuclear Family Abroad

This chapter closes by way of a thematic coda in which the middle-class suburb and Middle Eastern veil are explored as charged icons of cultural, political, and economic containment. Though not part of the equatorial zones typical of "jungle housekeeping," the domestically focused articles on American families in the Middle East in this period share the jungle housekeeping genre's concerns with domestic and cross-cultural adaptation and improvisation. While its contributors similarly sought an Edenic sanctuary in the Orientalist timelessness the West has traditionally associated with Islamic cultures, internal political change and historical violence rupture its contributors' efforts to contain global interconnectedness.[69]

Historians have shown that the isolation of the American family corresponded to the nation's Cold War strategy of communist containment, reflecting a pervasive ideology in which the domestic sphere became a refuge against global conflict. The home bomb shelter modeled on the well-provisioned "Grandma's Pantry" and preparedness campaigns educated women on improvising utensils and shelters from the ruins of atomic warfare.[70] Survivalism and domestic refuge became part of a new Cold War rhetoric in the magazine.[71] In this era of the bomb, *National Geographic* softened the threat of atomic energy in such articles as "Man's New Servant, the Friendly Atom" (January 1954) and "You and the Obedient Atom" (September 1958).[72] Just as domestic servitude in colonialist discourse neutralized the threat of unruly savage bodies, "containment" and control of both "commies" and "nukes" were watchwords in a world grown increasingly interdependent.

The American suburb and the Middle Eastern veil are icons charged with containment symbolism. While commodities crossed national borders and images of economic globalization penetrated the intimate domestic spaces with increasing frequency, American women in the 1950s confined themselves to monochromatic "cookie-cutter"–style houses in suburbs, like those of Levittown. Despite the seeming sprawl of suburbs, the single-family home, with its uniform, single-level floor plan, is a vivid emblem of containment, for it further isolated women by prohibiting extended family living arrangements or exposure to the messy, diverse bustle of city living. Middle Eastern women behind veils or sequestered in family compounds seemed to endure similarly cloistered lives. Yet their domestic lives, as portrayed by *National Geographic*'s contributors, offer a unique counterpoint to those of Western women in the Cold War era.

Historically, imperialist discourse has shrouded the Arab world and Middle East in a mysterious "Orientalist" veil of Western construction. *National Geographic* has been shown to reproduce Orientalist stereotypes of the Middle East as a region of oppressed women and violent men, a cultural zone trapped in a time warp taking visitors back centuries to biblical history. This assessment yields only a partial truth. Women contributors' observations of Afghan men as devoted husbands and nurturing fathers stands strikingly apart from portraits of "violent, dagger-wielding" men seen to typify *National Geographic*'s "one-size-fits-all racism."[73] Given jungle housekeeping's emphasis on the domestic as a space for cross-cultural commerce, what is more fascinating is how the image of a Middle Eastern extended family network reveals how comparatively trapped and isolated Western women, "emancipated" from labor by modern amenities, in fact were.

The wife of a Quaker missionary who lived in Afghanistan and Iran with her husband and two children in the late 1940s, Rebecca Cresson portrayed the Middle East as too impossibly diverse to uphold Orientalist stereotypes. Far from homogeneous, the city centers themselves are cosmopolitan. In Iran, the children at her husband's school spoke four or five different languages and represented a variety of cultural backgrounds. "Within a few moments one day," wrote Mrs. Cresson, "I heard Hebrew, Russian, Armenian, Persian, and English as I passed a handful of boys practicing on the basketball court."[74] In Afghanistan, Cresson describes the knee-length *chaderi* veil dispassionately, as a matter of cultural fact, rather than as a symbol of mystery, intrigue, or oppression.[75]

In contrast to the Cressons, who embody a typical American nuclear family, with an older daughter and younger son, in Afghanistan women and men are shown supported by an extended family network. Because of the extended family of one of Oswald Cresson's pupils, the Cressons traveled throughout Afghanistan hosted by his student's distant cousins and uncles. Upon the death of a neighbor's invalid wife, the Cressons observed the sorrow of the bereaved husband and listened as the extended family gathered at the husband's home and mourned for days. "We truly sorrowed with the bereaved husband," writes Cresson, "for he seemed devoted to his wife, an invalid for several years" (423). While Cresson presents the usual array of failed servants and semi-primitive conditions that characterize jungle housekeeping narratives, readers also get a snapshot of a diverse culture, one in which men and women participate equally in the nurturance of children: "it is common to meet them walking the street, child in arms, or to see a shopkeeper tending his child as well as his store" (427). From Cresson's perspective, hospitality and filial devotion characterize the Afghani people, rather than intrigue and violence. This is not to say, however, that she reverts to eighteenth-century idealizations that sanction imperial takeover. Instead, Cresson records a culture in the midst of upheaval and struggle for independence from economic and political colonization.

Between the 1940s and 1950s, the Middle East was a geographic space of concerted European and American interest. In 1939, the British had already begun drilling for oil in Iraq. Particularly as the processes of decolonization began to unfold in British-run India and in the French-occupied nations of Morocco, Algeria, Lebanon, and Syria; and as the United States and Soviet Union competed for global supremacy, the Middle East became an especially charged and contested space in global politics.[76] In "We Lived in Turbulent Tehran" (November 1953), Cresson records her family's two-year stay in Iran during this moment of political upheaval, revealing the nation's resistance to Western economic imperialism and the transformations of globalization.

The article vacillates between embracing global cosmopolitan interconnectedness and longing for Persian cultural traditions to provide sanctuary from political tumult. Premier Mohammed Mossadegh had seized the Iranian oil fields; workers stripped gas pumps of the "British Petrol" insignia. Throughout their stay, the Cressons were "conscious at all times of martial law and curfew" (719). Riots at the university and parliament between communist youth groups and "ultra-nationalists" resulted in violent outbreaks of "acid throwing and stoning of military vehicles" (719). Frequent police raids on a nearby communist "Peace House," writes Cresson, "kept us constantly aware of the activities of Soviet agents in this buffer land" (719). Save for a stray bullet that grazed her son's head as he ran through their garden, Cresson maintains that the family was sheltered from the violence and there were relatively few interruptions to domestic routines.

This insistence on the domestic as a haven from the political was in keeping with the United States' own domestic ideology of containment. Where bomb shelters and suburban isolation in America embodied a repressive domestic ideology, Cresson takes refuge in cultural artifacts of an earlier, premodern Persian culture. Here, the fantasy of discovering ancient customs in the midst of global transformation is figured by the family's quest for the "real flavor of old Persia"(718) as they travel to Iran's oldest city. Cresson's purchases of handcrafted silver jewelry "from the days when designs were simpler and more attractive, less doctored to meet the presumed tastes of travelers from other lands" (713) reflect a similar desire to escape globalization.

Even as the Cressons seek cultural purity and authenticity, the Iranians themselves embrace the trappings of Western culture. She notes that many are foregoing clothing tailored by hand for "ready-made clothing" that does not fit as well but is describable for its "Western touch" (713). Other evidence of global economic connectedness includes the invasion of Western terms and icons into the local vernacular. Children call the local popsicle man the "Alaska man," and popular food resembling yogurt called "mast" is brand-named "Mickey mast"(713), a testament to the globalization of Walt Disney's popular mascot.[77] Where political unrest and proliferating American images presage economic globalization, Cresson portrayed the domestic realm as a space free from historical forces: "In truth our lives were relatively cloistered behind the walls of our compound; the political disturbances had little direct effect on us" (720). Not unlike families in America, the Cressons embrace the protection of the home, as the domestic order salvages traditions under threat of modern globalization.

The jungle housekeeping genre was both reactionary and progressive. In performing the primitive, the women writing jungle housekeeping accounts reproduced the narrative contours of National Geographic's romance of the exotic—the colorful local customs and regional peculiarities, the telltale monuments, landmarks, and cultural differences that form the imagescape of an "American iconographic" vision of the globe. In their assimilation to cultural differences, however, jungle housekeeping contributors also disrupted the magazine's visual narrative containment by showing the ruptures of historical violence and global transformation. Through their outsider status and acknowledgment that Western cultural practices are neither universal, nor even universally desirable, contributors provided readers with a glimpse of global cultural knowledge as one of negotiated "relations"—of ideas, customs, and beliefs—that, as a consequence of global economic and human migrations, are no longer "foreign" but "shared."[78] Such relational knowledge confronts the masterful performances of an ersatz cosmopolitanism with discordant, disjunctive,

Fig. 23 "After Nine Years with the Stirlings, Your Society's Flag Shows Wear and Tear." (Richard Hewitt Stewart/National Geographic Image Collection)

and often contradictory appeals to cultures as vehicles for both the transformation of societies and the diffusion of their traditions across national borders.

Despite *National Geographic* attempts to impose an older order on an increasingly interconnected world and affirm older values, evidence of dramatic cultural change continually broke the magazine's placid surface. A 1948 photograph of the Stirlings at the headquarters for an archaeological expedition has husband and wife posed in front of an NGS flag showing signs of "wear and tear" (fig. 23).[79] With closer scrutiny, the photograph's affirmation of a traditional gendered global order breaks down. Photographers positioned a thin and stooped Mr. Stirling on the topmost step to affirm visually his dominance over his much taller wife. Panamanian children playing in the background complete the familial scene, but their indifference to the camera calls attention to the outsider status of the white nuclear family on display. By the late 1940s, in addition to the NGS flag, the magazine's imperial formulas were also showing signs of wear and tear.

In the era of Cold War containment, the magazine could boast of its 2 million readers, but it was no longer the nation's leading photographic magazine. In 1956, *Life*'s 5.8 million subscribers were double those of *National Geographic*.[80] *National Geographic*'s failed attempts to impose its editorial ideals of a placid timelessness and permanence in the face of global cultural change and historical violence did not escape its readers' notice. "Perhaps it is only sentiment that prompted my decision [to renew her membership]," wrote Mrs. Claire Ashkin of Pittsburgh, Pennsylvania, in 1951. A woman who credited *National Geographic*'s "stimulating articles" with inspiring her pursuit of a career in biology and geography, Ashkin found the magazine's tone "disturbing" and complained of its avoidance of controversy and its tendency to "talk down" to readers.[81] A general consensus was forming among readers that the magazine no longer kept pace with the times. *National Geographic*'s denial of global complexity became by the 1940s, a theme ripe for parody in popular adaptations of *National Geographic*'s imperial performances, as the book's concluding chapter on "camp" adaptations of the magazine illustrates.

6

NATIONAL GEOGRAPHIC'S ROMANCE IN RUINS

From the Catastrophic Sublime to Camp

National Geographic's evolution from scientific journal to popular icon was in large measure a result of the romantic stereotypes it perpetuated. But iconic status had its downside. If in 1896 the magazine's photographs of the exotic and little-known parts of the world made *National Geographic* a novelty, by the late 1920s the magazine's conventions seemed predictable, clichéd. From exotic images of the Far East to local-color regionalism, *National Geographic*'s formula had grown downright tiresome for some American readers. With "articles on Chickens, very familiar States, wild flowers, and etc., it certainly is losing its interest," wrote a reader. "Why not let the poultry journals handle this subject?" protested another. A third agreed that *National Geographic* had "gone down with the chickens."[1] If these readers were bored by local color, others were equally weary of foreign spectacle. "Too much Asiatic stuff entirely," sniffed one reader. "We are surfeited with it." Then followed an eloquent tirade on just how fatigued this member had grown with its more exotic fare:

> We are fed-up with Holy City pictures, with camels, with the great unwashed swarms of peoples, their turbans, their market-places, their squatting in the sunshine to have their pictures taken, their temples, their mosques and shrines and homes and clothes and pies and vehicles. We are tired of Chinamen and Mongols and Hindu snake-charmers and drear, Biblical landscapes that give no ray of hope to one who likes a dollar limit game once in a while. In fact we are weary of everything Asiatic, for a time at least; the great unwashed have

lost their appeal. Turn 'em over to the Salvation Army and the Near East Relief and you give us another Cruise of the Dream Ship, or the Big Trees of California, or another article like the recent one about Maryland, or fishing off Catalina Island; anything modern with pretty pictures where we do not have to think of all the dirt and smells that must accompany these Asiatic and wonder how in Sam Hill we would ever get a bath if we were foolish enough to go a-visiting there. No more Mount of Olives, please, and no more Jerusalem, or Algeria, or Egypt, or China. Let the desert sands blow where they listeth and the camel graze, if he can find anything, but Rabbi, sheik and priest we have seen aplenty and want to forget—in their native habitat anyway.[2]

The pleasure this reader takes in caricaturing the magazine's clichéd portraits of the Orient is in keeping with the many parodies of *National Geographic* then entering the mainstream media. Popular media satirized what one reader termed its "chamber of commerce style" of focusing on America's homelier attributes and pastimes—including reading *National Geographic*—on the one hand, and exotic spectacle on the other, what I term the "catastrophic sublime," an epic narrative that dramatizes the heroic conquest of nature and the indigenous groups who dwell within it.[3]

While *National Geographic* readers watched their magazine devolve into self-parody, popular appropriations of its trademark aesthetics acknowledged the iconic status the magazine had achieved. As Robert Hariman and John Louis Lucaites have shown, popular appropriation of iconic images is the most tangible sign of their iconicity. Adaptations of iconic images, like the flag-raising at Iwo Jima, they observe, are "strategic improvisations" that both reflect social norms and perform "satiric mimicry" to challenge its conventions.[4] Humorous adaptations of an iconic image in political cartoons and other popular media comment critically on the present historical moment's failure to fulfill the civic and cultural ideals represented in the original image. Such images become expressive of a broad "range of attitudes" toward national interests, particular social groups, and ideas circulating in public discourse more generally.[5]

Certainly, *National Geographic*'s iconic place in the popular imagination derived from its historic association with photographs of the exotic thought to express its readers' cosmopolitanism and highbrow aspirations. Cartoon spoofs of *National Geographic*'s trademark motifs similarly exhibit public disenchantment with its readership's pretensions as well as its outdated portrayals of so-called "primitive" cultures. In this spirit, *National Geographic* spoofs take spectators behind the scenes and, winking at its audience, show what is "really" happening on assignment. In some, African women change from modern Western attire into grass skirts to appease the backward aesthetics of the *National Geographic* photographer. Or, instead of mastering their environment, *National Geographic*'s hunters with the lens are held hostage by natives or presented to the gods for sacrifice. Salvaged from the ruins of the magazine's former grandeur, such images disclose the performative aspects of cultural diffusion. They also bring to the surface public dissent regarding the magazine's imperial romance.

The many parodies and adaptations to which *National Geographic* has given rise play variations on a camp theme: performance, or the visual management of what Susan Sontag in her "Notes on Camp" (1964) has called "Being-as-Playing-a-Role."[6] In the years since Sontag's landmark essay, "camp" has typically been associated with a queer aesthetic arising from the transgressive theatricality of drag and its exploitation of gender codes.[7] Here, I treat camp as comparable to salvage ethnography, the romantic pursuit of a "vanishing primitive" culture in order to preserve it from extinction.[8] Camp performs a similar cultural rescue mission. Camp is a kind of performance that salvages the ruins of a popular cultural past and, in so doing, reveals the preexisting cultural scripts mobilizing attitudes and behaviors that seem "natural" on the surface. In this salvage mission, as another critic suggests, "Camp irreverently retrieves not only that which had been excluded from the serious high-cultural 'tradition', but also the more unsalvageable material that has been picked over and found wanting by purveyors of the 'antique.'"[9] Camp functions like ethnographic salvage, but its reclamations are ironic ones, for camp reads against the grain of the culture industry in ways that revitalize culture through humorous critique. In this regard, camp has special relevance for the study of imperialism and visual culture, particularly in humorous parodies of the *National Geographic* photographer as a masculine archetype.

The imperial markers of primitivism belong to a canon of camp artifacts that includes zebra stripes, grass skirts, pith helmets, and *King Kong*.[10] If Sontag's example of "naïve camp"—performances that are unaware of their susceptibility to camp treatment—is the "Art Nouveau craftsman who makes a lamp with a snake coiled around it," and who says "in all earnestness: Voila! The Orient!" then *National Geographic*'s pantheon of exotic women and photographer-explorers seems to proclaim with equal earnestness, "Voila! Adventure!"[11] As an aesthetic that exaggerates the representational terms by which cultural insiders and outsiders are determined, camp inscribes the limits of membership. In the case of *National Geographic,* its sweeping educational mission, its exotic ethnographic content, and its membership concept had come to seem all too grandiose and shopworn to popular audiences. Camp highlights the failure of audiences to identify with the magazine's imperialist narratives. Where appropriations of iconic images such as Joe Rosenthal's Iwo Jima flag raising or Dorothea Lange's "Migrant Mother" are expressions of civic identity, parodic adaptations of *National Geographic's* iconic photographers and nude women reveal a public suspicion of NGS membership as a marker of "high middlebrow" cultural status.[12]

In what follows, I treat camp as a form of ethnographic performance that makes popular culture available for more critical consumption. In parodies of *National Geographic,* for example, camp turns its ironic gaze on the magazine's icons of masculinity: the swashbuckling lone adventurer and the photographer who stalks his ethnographic prey. Such images critique the hypermasculinity of the *National Geographic* photographer and the phallic camera as his masculine prosthesis. *National Geographic's* transformation into camp not only indicates its iconic status, but also reveals camp's value as ethnographic critique in contesting publicly the magazine's imperial vision of national global dominance and criticizing implicitly those who share its worldview.

The Catastrophic Sublime as Naïve Camp

The photographic spectacle of ethnographic difference made *National Geographic* a ready object of camp ridicule. In its early decades, *National Geographic* fulfilled Sontag's criteria for "pure camp," that is, the cultural artifact that is naïve, or unself-conscious about its own potential for humorous exploitation. For pure camp, writes Sontag, the "essential element" is "a seriousness that fails."[13] Camp thus finds its fulfillment in irony, the attitudinal gap between a cultural artifact's lofty aims and its lighthearted reception.

Camp parodies of *National Geographic* target the photographer's heroic role in what Grosvenor called the "epic story" of human geography. The magazine's hero required an equally heroic backdrop: spectacular mountain ranges, cataclysmic volcanoes, treacherous earthquakes, and tempestuous seas—in other words, the eighteenth century's natural "sublime," an aesthetic quality of overpowering vastness and indifference to human endeavor that induced dread and awe in spectators.[14] Nature and racial difference were visually keyed to the same threatening psychological registers. In *National Geographic* and other media trading on the exotic, sublime terror was transferred to dramatic racial and cultural difference—dark-skinned nudes or customs that appear strange and fantastic to Western eyes.

National Geographic's availability as camp arises from its images of photographers performing on the world's stage as they confront danger, whether posed by natural disaster or primitive tribes. In what I term the "catastrophic sublime," the spectacle of the photographer risking life and limb for his art provides its audience with both psychological tension and its release. The catastrophic sublime in *National Geographic* provides a dramatic backdrop to the photographer as he performs the role of the hero-adventurer in the magazine's imperial romance.

Nowhere is the catastrophic sublime registered more forcefully than in the magazine's coverage of natural disaster.[15] One of the magazine's earliest examples of the photographer confronting the catastrophic sublime appears in a 1912 article on the eruption of the Taal Volcano on January 31, 1911, in the Philippines in which "in the twinkling of an eye some 1,400 human beings had perished." Photographs show a jumble of charred bodies and scattered limbs, eerily dusted with ash. The caption under one stunning shot of photographer Charles Martin poised with camera amid the blast commended him as "one of the few competent observers who witnessed the eruption at short range."[16] The caption's high seriousness in presenting the photographer's triumph over the natural sublime seems to affirm both his role as eyewitness and photography's burden of truth. Camp adaptations of this motif, however, reveal how that heroism has been stage-managed, a central theme of parodic representations of popular culture. For Martin's heroism has been presented for *display* by yet another photographer offstage, highlighting the potential of such photographs to expose the institutional machinery at work.

As previous chapters illustrate, *National Geographic*'s photographers on assignment constituted a genre unto themselves. These images proclaim his heroic masculinity, but crucially underscore its offstage orchestration. As with the romance fiction of the 1890s, *National Geographic* snapshots of its photographers on assignment exploit "[t]he fantasy of turning gunfire into the flash of a photograph." They salvage masculine identity "threatened by the violent, inscrutable political affiliations of the imperial battlefield."[17] Yet, by turning the gaze from exotic women to the male photographer-explorer, these images invert the object of the gaze. They place the photographer in a role typically occupied by women. The erotic pleasure of visual spectacle has historically been experienced vicariously by a heterosexual male gaze, which places the image of woman at its center.[18] By placing the male photographer in a position typically occupied by females, the image underscores the photographer's vulnerability, both to disaster and to the viewer's critical eye as potential camp.

Camp images of *National Geographic* exploit this vulnerability in order to undercut the magazine's attempts to suffuse the photographer with a heroic aura. In each, the ethnographic subject usurps the photographer's power as imperialist agent in a gesture that both acknowledges and ridicules the *National Geographic*'s imperialist worldview. Cartoons that upend or reverse conventional power relations between the explorer-photographer and his "savage" subjects avenge his trespass on the cultures he documents. Several, for example, show the magazine's photographers trussed and carted off by natives, or offered as a "sacrifice" to primitive gods. A July 12, 1941, cartoon in the *Saturday Review of Literature* portrays a photographer in a pith helmet slung on a bamboo pole. As natives carry him away, he cries, "You can't do this to me—I'm from the *National Geographic*."

These cartoon "metapictures," as discussed in chapter 3, comment on the institutional management of *National Geographic* photographs, based as they are on an implicit belief in American exceptionalism and the inviolable heroism of the photographer. These images, however, subvert the institution's and the photographer's privileged status, taking evident delight in the photographer becoming the main course in a cannibal feast. Both the photographer's assumption of privilege ("You can't do this to me") and the magazine's legacy of manufacturing stereotyped images of cultural difference are lampooned. Similarly, in *Collier's* of March 19, 1954, another photographer in a pith helmet bound to a tree shouts at an angry chief in a grass skirt: "If you think for one minute, Mabongo, that you'll get another big spread in the *National Geographic*, you're crazy!" This cartoon, like the previous example, reverses the magazine's conventional dynamic between the passive ethnographic subject and the photographer as creative agent.

In every parody the photographer is vulnerable and powerless, literally suffering for his art at the hands of the cultures he documents. A 1971 *New Yorker* cartoon depicts two natives appealing to a monumental god: "We've run out of virgins, O Mighty One! Will you accept a photographer from the *National Geographic*?" All of these images disrupt the romance paradigm in which the camera's flash affirms the imperialist explorer's heroism. Instead, their humor derives from the obvious relish in making the photographer over into a buffoon. Each parody, moreover, takes pleasure in imagining the forms of punishment *National Geographic*'s ethnographic subjects might exact on its hunters with the lens. In sacrificing the photographer, these cartoons forestall the audience's identification with and vicarious participation in the photographer's exploits. By undoing the performative elements encoded within the magazine's representation of its photographers and explorers, camp artifacts remind readers of how carefully its masculine heroics were managed visually and textually.

The photographer's fall from exalted imperial icon into camp parody reflected the diminishing power of the natural sublime as an aesthetic category. Indeed, by the 1930s there was little on the globe left to explore. "To travel in modern space was to engage in a search for the already discovered," observe critics of the period's travel literature.[19] With so much of the unknown having been domesticated by *National Geographic* photographs, snapshots of the photographer confronting the catastrophic sublime no longer possessed the same visual excitement as they did in the 1912 photograph of Charles Martin. Camp, writes Sontag, is "a feat goaded on, in the last analysis, by the threat of boredom."[20] The loss of sublime aura, from sheer repetition and consequent boredom, makes the *National Geographic* photographer ripe for ironic repossession. Uniting their spectators in shared laughter at the photographer's predicament, cartoons affirm *National Geographic*'s iconic status in the popular imagination while signaling disfavor with its imperialist sympathies. Moreover, camp reprisals of the photographer-on-assignment genre also register a suspicion of photography's truth-telling potential and a rejection of its complicity in fostering an imperialist worldview. More provocatively, however, campified images of *National Geographic* photographers position them in the passive, feminine role typically occupied by their ethnographic subjects.

Camp adaptations of *National Geographic* reproduce the imperial stereotype in its fetishized form, that is, in its form as a sacred object of sexual desire.[21] In presenting to audiences the iconic image of the *National Geographic* photographer on assignment, now reconstituted as the object of visual desire or spectacle, camp cartoons expose two other conceptual antitheses. The vulnerability/invulnerability dyad is contained in the photographer's visual mastery of primitive subjects. Part of the pleasure in looking at such images, after all, is the possibility that the photographer might fail, which fuels a corresponding desire to see him triumph in the face of difficult odds. In other words, it is not just the vulnerability of an ethnographic present to modernity that salvage ethnography expresses, but the need to fix and render invulnerable both the present and the past of colonialism itself. Thus secured in the heroic rhetoric surrounding the photographer, and in the enduring images of dark bodies presented for display, another antithesis emerges: modern/primitive. Threatened by its own exposure of the forces of production, the modern is vulnerable, destabilized in part by the very primitive subjects it wishes to record. Primitive desires—a desire for the racialized Other and the "primitive," irrational element in the unconscious—pose a threat to the photographer's authority as an agent of civilization.

The catastrophic sublime and the theme of the lone explorer were perennial *National Geographic* motifs that supplied the drama that later camp productions exposed as shopworn. Camp adaptations of the magazine wittily undermine the magazine's visual management of imperial conquest by taking advantage of tensions between mastery and defeat, primitive and modern, already present within the magazine's institutional aesthetic. By reversing imperialism's narrative logic and sacrificing the photographer as its agent, cartoon parodies of *National Geographic* make the "primitive" reflect a modern, skeptical sensibility.

The Curious Career of Joseph Rock

Camp calls attention to how the explorer's heroism is already vulnerable in the original images and texts, as is the case in articles written by one of *National Geographic*'s most prolific prototypes of the lone adventurer, Joseph Rock (1884–1962), a botanist whose adventures in bandit-riddled China and Tibet inspired James Hilton's best-selling *Lost Horizon* (1933), whose hero, Hugh Conway, might be understood as a camp version of Rock. A self-styled "lone geographer," Rock published eleven articles in *National Geographic* between 1922 and 1935 in which he documented his botanical expeditions through Tibet's and China's border provinces.[22] In Rock, we see how contradictions within his role as cosmopolitan and *National Geographic* representative heroic "type" create fissures within the dramatic role in the "epic story" the magazine expected its explorers to fulfill.

Rock's background corresponded well to the American ideal of the untutored genius: the self-taught man whose inborn talents transcend humble birth and undistinguished schooling. From his boyhood he set his sights on world travel, particularly China. At eighteen, he defied his father's and his older sister's ambition to see him join the Catholic priesthood, and instead embarked on a tour of Europe and northern Africa. Eventually, he arrived in New York, and briefly worked as a dishwasher and traveled the American Southwest before settling in Hawaii, where his love of the outdoors and his penchant for taxonomy led him to pursue botany. He worked briefly for the Forest Service. Later, in a Gatsby-esque feat of con artistry, Rock convinced officials at the University of Hawaii of his credentials and became a professor of botany. Throughout his long career, he went on expeditions for the U.S. Department of Agriculture and *National Geographic,* and collected numerous plant specimens for Harvard's Arnold Arboretum. His true passion, however, was his study of the culture and language of the Naxi (pronounced Na-shi) tribe dwelling on the remote Tibetan border, whom he befriended on his many expeditions to China's border provinces. His letters and diaries supplied material for his articles in *Life* and *National Geographic,* among other popular publications.[23]

Despite his staid professorial appearance and demeanor, Rock—whose patronym itself so perfectly captured the stalwart individualism and pioneer spirit of the American frontier ethos—could have been none other than the swashbuckling explorer of romance fiction. He called himself the "lone geographer," yet he always traveled with a retinue of porters and servants. He crossed the most hostile regions of China and Tibet—dressed in a shirt and tie. He traveled with a phonograph for his opera and a cook for his Viennese dinners. Regardless of the location, Rock dined at a table with spotless linens.[24] Rock embodied both the genteel imperial adventurer and the American success story, but his refined aesthetic tastes and his dependency on an entourage of servants undercut his—and perhaps his adopted country's—image of rugged self-reliance.

At first glance, Rock's worldliness bespeaks cosmopolitan competence and mastery and recalls the anthropologist as a figure who historically revels in his own alienation.[25] Rock participated in a tradition of *National Geographic* lone adventurers that included the likes of Robert E. Peary, disputed discoverer of the North Pole; Hiram Bingham, the academician-archaeologist who rediscovered the Incan ruins of Machu Picchu in Peru; and Richard Evelyn Byrd, pilot and explorer of the Antarctic. As the cosmopolitan who is at home everywhere and nowhere, Rock is the figurative embodiment of the detached all-seeing self. Superficially, Rock stands as the prototype for *National Geographic*'s classy "gentleman-adventurer."[26] Such figures combined genteel sophistication with a stalwart frontier ethos, and the magazine's photographs and articles tended to magnify their "talent for embodying two contradictory models of manhood simultaneously—civilized manliness and primitive masculinity."[27]

Rock appears not to have personally embraced the Rooseveltian model of manliness and civilization, however. He presented the image of a wilderness dandy at a time when the term "cosmopolitan" was not always positively inflected. It was often invoked pejoratively "to label anyone who did not fit or conform, including intellectuals, Jews, homosexuals and aristocrats."[28] Instead, Rock's cosmopolitanism made him an enigmatic and ambiguous figure. Despite the heroic persona put forward in his articles, his friends thought him "queer," in both senses of the word. His sexuality was the subject of speculation. He never married nor, to anyone's knowledge, had any romantic attachments.[29] His refined aesthetic sensibilities, richly manifest in his baroque descriptions of the natural landscape, strangely diminished his masculine heroism. In turn, these tensions in Rock's persona between stalwart individualism and a genteel dependence on others' labor and on the trappings of culture open up more provocative readings.

Camp, we have seen, exploits paradoxes already present in the original image. In the case of Joseph Rock, his combination of fastidiousness and wily fortitude encapsulates paradoxes that made *National Geographic*'s lone adventurer types ripe for parody. In particular, his cosmopolitan glamour was shadowed by a striking effeminacy, while his sympathy with those he encountered actually highlighted an imperialist attitude rather than concealing or negating it. These ambiguities make Rock a precursor to campified images of *National Geographic*'s explorer-photographers. Viewed from a particular angle of vision, he is not just an agent of imperialism, but a more complex figure, where the performative aspects of masculinity and heroic adventure are sharply delineated.

Witness two versions of Rock's first *National Geographic* article, "Hunting the Chaulmoogra Tree" (March 1922), which recounts an expedition for seeds to cure leprosy that turned into a deadly encounter with a tiger. The published version, touched up by editors, reproduces *National Geographic*'s trademark theme of the catastrophic sublime, in the epic struggle between man and nature. The original, unpublished manuscript, however, shows how the editorial process tended to elide or alter details that would have dramatically undercut Rock's heroic stature as master of his environment.

In the published account, the expedition's altruistic aim of bringing back botanical specimens to cure leprosy marks the narrative starting point for profound local tragedy involving natural disaster and death. The wives and children of two men accompanying Rock on his expedition in his entourage were attacked by a tiger that clawed through their makeshift dwelling near the rice fields they were tending. The tiger maimed and killed all but a five-year-old boy who escaped and told his story to the village headman, who, in turn, relayed the tragic events to Rock just as he was preparing to return to America. Delaying his departure to help the men find the tiger, Rock described his attendance at "the scene of a tragedy" (276). He did not spare *National Geographic* readers the gory details of the devastation he witnessed. One woman was brutally killed, "her face literally bitten out and her neck severed," while the other had been dragged from the hut alive, "but with a ghastly face wound, her whole left cheek having been bitten out, exposing both jaws" (276). A little girl, likely killed, had disappeared altogether. Rock dressed the surviving woman's wounds, "But what was to be done about the tiger?" he wondered. "We had no arms save a Colt automatic, so we decided to build a trap. I shall never forget how the poor husbands of the slain women worked on that trap. One had lost all his family—his wife, sister, and little daughter" (276). While this traumatic incident and Rock's deep regret are palpable in the article, the drama surrounding the tiger's attack receives greater emphasis. Because it represents nature's catastrophic sublime, the tiger and its ultimate fate are essential to establishing Rock's heroism. In the published version, Rock assumes a heroic role by leading a hunt for the tiger.

But earlier page proofs show how *National Geographic* editors subtly massaged Rock's narrative to heighten his heroism—and the reader's vicarious participation in the spectacle. Rock's original description of the massacre's aftermath has him joining, rather than leading, the male villagers on their trek to the rice field where the family was slain. "All the male villagers gathered with spears and knives," he wrote, "and marching ahead of them we went to the scene of a tragedy which will remain indelibly impressed in my memory, [*sic*] a dreadful spectacle awaited our arrival."[30] The published version transforms Rock's portrait of community endeavor and its emphasis on "we," to the heroic "I," in which Rock does not march alongside the men, but leads their mission: "All the male villagers gathered with spears and knives and, marching ahead of them, *I* went to the scene of a tragedy. A dreadful spectacle awaited *me*" (273, my emphasis).

A still more fascinating alteration from the page proofs to the final copy had to do with the tiger, or rather, "tigress," as Rock put it in his first draft. When he and the villagers find the tiger, Rock remarked, "There he was or rather she, for it proved to be a female, prowling with anger and a terrible fierceness."[31] In the published version, all references to the tiger's sex vanish. In their place, the editors inserted the word "brute": "only a few minutes and the brute was no more, for 20 spears ended its savage existence" (276). It would not do, apparently, for a female to have wrought such destruction. Nor would it be at all chivalric had Rock and his men killed a female tiger. The alteration of "tigress" to "brute" subtly helps to express the catastrophic sublime through an attempt to masculinize the tiger and thus preserve Rock's heroic posture.

A precondition for camp is failed seriousness arising from cultural beliefs that can later be brought forth as ironic commentary on a cultural moment for which those beliefs have become outdated. Such is the case in Rock's "Land of the Yellow Lama" (April 1925), his treacherous journey through bandit-infested mountain passes along China's southwestern border to visit the king of a religious sect of high priests or "lamas." Appearing during the vogue of ethnographic "romantic primitivism," Rock's article masterfully combines modernity and the ancient customs revered by armchair anthropologists in ways that later became the source of campified popular entertainment.[32] Rock, following custom, dons his best attire for a visit to the lama king to pay his respects and present a gift of a gun and 250 rounds of ammunition. Tradition and modernity clash during this encounter as Rock and his entourage, amid the visual trappings of ancient custom, confront the unexpected intrusion of Western life. Rock and his cohort are "escorted to the palace square, which is surrounded by a temple, from which issued the discordant sounds of trumpets, conch shells, drums, and gongs, besides weird bass grumblings of officiating monks" (469). However, amid "all this Lamaistic splendor," Rock writes, "there was a Western touch" (475). As he and the king dine on yak butter tea served "in a porcelain cup set in exquisite silver filigree with a coral-studded silver cover" and moldy yak cheese "interspersed with hair" (474–75), Rock spies, "on the crimson-painted posts" of the king's palace, "clothes-hooks with white porcelain knobs, such as one would expect to find on trees in a cheap German beer garden" (475). The clash of local customs and Western items grows positively surreal when the king's servants rush away and return laden with boxes of photographic equipment. Gifts from a Chinese trader, these include state-of-the art

French and Kodak cameras equipped with portrait lenses, boxes of plates, printing paper, and enough photography supplies "to start a photographic shop" (476). Without ceremony, the lama king then orders Rock to teach his trembling servant photography. This strange brew of Western modernity and local cultural tradition would come to inform many subsequent popular cultural adaptations of *National Geographic's* visual aesthetic.

A crucial element of camp is that it exploits the artifice already present in the original, reminding readers that the "original" is itself a response to still other cultural performances. As the culmination of his heroic forebears of *National Geographic* lore, Rock anticipates future heroes of pulp fiction and the silver screen. Roosevelt could don leather breeches and forego his steel-rimmed spectacles to appear as a cowboy, but for Rock, who also wore spectacles, his ethnographic shape-shifting invites camp treatment. Shown in the regal attire of a Tibetan prince, Rock embodies the failed seriousness of naïve camp (fig. 24). With his deadpan expression and steely gaze, he enacts the codes of masculine strenuous effort embodied by Roosevelt and Rock's explorer forebears. At the same time, the sheer flamboyance and ridiculousness of his posture as a Tibetan prince heightens the disparity between the magazine's heroic aesthetic and the threat of camp to expose its theatrics—tacitly acknowledged by the fact that *National Geographic* ultimately did not publish this photograph of Rock. In Rock, we witness the inadvertent bifurcation of *National Geographic's* iconicity on the one hand toward self-importance, as figured by the catastrophic sublime—his encounters with man-eating tigers and treacherous mountain passes—and on the other hand toward self-parody—his pose as a Tibetan prince—that undermines it.

Ethnographic Parody: James Hilton's *Lost Horizon*

Camp has been famously proclaimed a "lie that tells the truth."[33] In James Hilton's best-selling novel *Lost Horizon,* Rock's popular exploits along Chinese and Tibetan border regions supply the fictive backdrop against which the novel subtly parodies *National Geographic's* romantic ethnography and high-cultural aspirations.[34] The novel's cast of characters—a British war hero and his admiring young protégée; an American businessman con artist; and a British woman missionary—are thrown unexpectedly together. The characters flee revolution in the British-occupied city of Baskul in an airplane en route to a safer colonial haven in Peshawar, Pakistan.[35] Decolonization forms the dramatic backdrop of a novel that turns the tables on imperial power relations.

Fig. 24 The botanist-explorer Joseph Rock dressed as a Tibetan prince. (Dr. Joseph F. Rock/National Geographic Image Collection)

The travelers' hijacked plane veers off course and crashes in an uncharted region of the Himalayas. They are rescued by a group of lamas who escort them to the sequestered realm of Shangri-La, or "snowy mountain pass," a haven for world-weary travelers seeking repose under the "gleaming pyramid of Karakal," which, "in the valley patois, means Blue Moon" (82).[36] In Shangri-La, the party's individual members are unwittingly made into the objects of a living ethnographic collection of human types. In displaying the consumers/producers of ethnographic culture—the swashbuckling adventurer, the missionary, and the wealthy businessman (the class of reader historically most drawn to *National Geographic*)—*Lost Horizon* renders visible the "poetics of detachment," the habit of wresting objects from their cultural contexts that has been a legacy of museum display and *National Geographic*'s romantic ethnography.[37]

Perhaps on the basis of its popularity and Hilton's reputation for writing for popular audiences (e.g., his *Goodbye, Mr. Chips*), Hilton's novel rarely receives scholarly interest. Since its 1933 publication, the novel has been discussed primarily as a publishing phenomenon that helped launch the "paperback revolution."[38] The novel's best-seller status, selling more than 1 million copies as a Book-of-the-Month Club selection and among the most successful of the Pocket Paperback editions, positions the magazine in the pulp genre of literary escapism, yet its historical context invites a reconsideration of the novel as cultural commentary. Published in 1933, in the midst of global economic depression and Hitler's rise to power in Nazi Germany, the novel anticipates the coming turmoil of the Second World War and the demise of the British empire as a consequence of decolonization. *Lost Horizon* seemingly salvages a fading Victorian ethos as it sorts culture's artifacts into the "highbrow"—the "best" that has been thought and said—and the "lowbrow" popular entertainments for the masses: the "dance bands, cinemas, electric signs" (74). The novel's modernist sensibility, however, parodies those nineteenth-century cultural institutions that also helped shape *National Geographic*'s worldview— scientific classification of humans by "types," museums of natural history, and an academic literary establishment—that serve as the connoisseurs of "Culture."

At first glance, *Lost Horizon* contains all of *National Geographic*'s visual and narrative motifs: the catastrophic sublime, the lone adventurer, the exotic woman of color, and cultural timelessness. Escape from Baskul in the midst of civil war, a hijacked plane that crashes in the icy splendor of an uncharted mountain range, the High Lama's apocalyptic vision of a second world war—supply the novel's catastrophic sublime elements. The novel's hero, modeled on Joseph Rock, is Hugh Conway, a British soldier who survived the First World War. He and his young subordinate, Charles Mallinson, are rivals for the affections of Lo-Tsen, a literally ageless Chinese beauty (Shangri-La's atmosphere arrests the aging process). Those who dwell in Shangri-La possess unmeasured leisure to pursue whatever they wish. Partaking of the apparent timelessness of old *National Geographic*s, Shangri-La is "miraculously preserved against time and death" (178). And like *National Geographic*, Shangri-La aspires toward an international cultural archive containing the best that has been thought and said throughout the world and throughout history.[39]

Lost Horizon's campy appeal lies in its exploitation of Rock's overly refined aesthetic sensibilities in the figure of Conway. Clever "but rather slack" (5), Conway is "bored by mere exploits" (43). In having "grown used to people liking him only because they misunderstood him" (84) and in not behaving as "one of those resolute, strong-jawed, hammer-and-tongs empire builders" (84), Conway occupies the marginal position of camp. Conway's resolute passivity, "a form of indolence, an unwillingness to interrupt his mere spectator's interest in what was happening" (57), marks an eschewal, and therefore exposure, of the showy theatrics that accompany male heroism. Mallinson, his hotheaded vice consul and protégé, frequently criticizes Conway for neglecting his heroic role and for a romantic attitude incompatible with manly heroics. When Shangri-La's mountainous horizon inspires Conway's lofty meditation on sublime grandeur, Mallinson scoffs, "Good God, Conway, d'you fancy you're pottering about the Alps?" (65).[40] Though the novel invokes Rock's longing for a spiritual homeland, where, as he once rhapsodized in a letter, "My soul still dwells in the great silences among the snow peaks," it does so in order to call into question the possibility for discovering a haven from civilization.[41]

Rather than swashbuckling heroics, what Conway finds expressed in Shangri-La is the possibility of ethnographic discovery. When he first beholds the rugged landscape, Conway shares the ethnographer's "glow of satisfaction that there were such places still left on earth, distant, inaccessible, as yet unhumanized" (42). He remarks to their local guide Chang, "A separate culture might flourish here without contamination from the outside world" (73). In keeping with the novel's critique of self-satisfied cosmopolitanism, Conway's romantic thralldom in the face of cultural difference is revealed as misguided and founded on ignorance. The novel mocks Conway's pride in having previously lived "for nearly a decade in China" and feeling "at home with the Chinese ways" (72). The "agreeable sensation of being at home" (73) Conway attributes to his cosmopolitanism is actually the result of Shangri-La's successful deterritorialization, a deadening sameness that accompanies culture's diffusion within a global marketplace.[42] The "atmosphere" he pompously regards as "Chinese rather than specifically Tibetan" (73) is later proven to be European. Conway wanders through a library housing "the world's best literature. . . . Volumes in English, French, German, and Russian abounded, and there were vast quantities of Chinese and other Eastern scripts. A section which interested him particularly was devoted to Tibetiana" (97–98). Shangri-La is no more than an "orchestrated fairyland" of Sung vases and lacquered paintings (97). Like the *National Geographic* its readers criticized in the

1930s, Shangri-La offers clichéd cosmopolitan tastes. Its hodgepodge eclecticism—where "Plato in Greek touched Omar in English; Nietzsche partnered Newton; Thomas More was there, and also Hannah More, Thomas Moore, George Moore, and even Old Moore" (114)—like camp's cousin, "kitsch," parodies "good" taste that embraces without discrimination everything considered "highbrow." Shangri-La is merely an exaggerated simulacrum of European cultural refinement. Consequently, there is no cultural difference to be embraced as Conway had hoped. Instead, Shangri-La is a moldering archive that pokes fun at nonpulp readers' pretensions to cultural sophistication. Conway feels at home for the same reasons *National Geographic*'s photographs of the estranging and exotic did not disturb armchair travelers enough to make them discontinue their memberships: he never really left home. In undercutting Conway's cosmopolitan authority, *Lost Horizon* also denies Conway's heroism.

This mania for the collection is more sharply parodied when it becomes clear that Shangri-La is little more than a human zoo. First, Chang reveals that Shangri-La's inhabitants are representatives of many nations. Then, in a private audience with Father Perrault—who reveals himself as the mysterious and aloof High Lama from whom the entourage has been held at bay—Conway discovers that he and his fellow travelers have been intentionally detained in order to fill out Shangri-La's human collection. Indeed, *Lost Horizon* burlesques conventional Victorian anthropology through characters who unwittingly parody its questionable ethnographic assumptions. Reflecting on the relative merits of Shangri-La's various interlopers, Father Perrault remarks that "our last visitor, a Japanese, arrived in 1912, and was not, to be candid, a very valuable acquisition" (157). Expressing his preference for European stock, Chang is delighted that at last Shangri-La has acquired an American, the swindling businessman Chalmers Bryant. And in a misguided effort to befriend Chang, Miss Brinklow, the Christian missionary within their group, patronizingly remarks that "'I'm broad-minded enough to admit that other people, foreigners, I mean, are quite often sincere in their views'" (75). By treating human beings—including "white" people—as collectible specimens, Shangri-La grotesquely replicates the magazine's inventory of human types and its commodification of exotic desire.

In these ways, *Lost Horizon* persistently ironizes the Victorian sensibilities of salvage ethnography and burlesques the Arnoldian high-cultural desire to preserve the best that has been thought and said. The "horizon" in the novel's title evokes the return for the longed-for frontier of Western mythology, suggesting unknown spaces available for exploration. It is also the elusive or receding horizon of the text, in which reading for pleasure occupies the space of leisure and contemplative pursuits embodied by Shangri-La. The atmosphere of Shangri-La, like the imaginative transport promised to readers of *National Geographic,* represents an escape from modernity, or from history itself. Like the salvage ethnographer, Father Perrault wants to preserve the perishable beauty of Shangri-La and its cultural artifacts against destruction: "He foresaw a time when men, exultant in the technique of homicide, would rage so hotly over the world that every precious thing would be in danger, every book and picture and harmony, every treasure garnered through two millenniums, the small, the delicate, the defenseless—all would be lost" (165). More than an asylum from modernity, Shangri-La, according to Perrault's dream, is one cultural repository that would protect the world's precious artifacts from historical violence. By salvaging cultural difference from modernity's ruins, Shangri-La's cultural archive highlights and intensifies an ideological problem in the magazine itself.

Yet the very gravity of that endeavor invites camp reprisal. Accordingly, *Lost Horizon* deploys the camp strategy of exaggeration and mocking self-seriousness as it upends conventional ethnographic accounts in which the anthropologist is the one in command. In an inversion that resembles the cartoon parodies of *National Geographic* photographers, *Lost Horizon* similarly makes Shangri-La's visitors the objects of cultural inquiry. Furthermore, in its strange juxtaposition of cultural artifacts spanning the globe and its amenities from other countries, Shangri-La epitomizes deterritorialized space, a space our own cultural moment knows so well as a landscape of strip malls, movie theaters, and fast-food chains. The irreducible paradox, however, is that despite its campy critique, the novel as a material artifact and publishing phenomenon actually contributed to the cultural erosion it decried. Like *National Geographic, Lost Horizon* was complicit in opening the region to tourism. In response to Hilton's novel, a number of villages in remote China renamed themselves "Shangri-La." Now a "brand-name" for restaurants, hotels, karaoke bars, and even an airport, "Shangri-La" has become a catch-phrase for Western tourists heading to China's once remote Himalayan villages.[43]

Camp renditions of *National Geographic* appeared at a moment when the magazine had achieved iconic stature as its readers' Shangri-La, a utopian space for achieving imaginative transport from the mundane. Small wonder, then, that the magazine survived the Depression years with little falloff in membership. Those who did give up the magazine found contentment in perusing their old issues. "I can always re-read the numbers I have," wrote a reader from Iowa. "They never grow old or out of date," adding, "On the receipt of the magazine I first read the pictures, then the text." As another observed, *National Geographic* was "a recreation that one can enjoy after a strenuous day in public. . . . so I will go back and review those I have, which will create the same pleasure and hand out that restful soothing feeling."[44] This reader's transport recalls the "deep anesthetizing tranquility" (69) and "soothing comfort of mind and body" (73) that *Lost Horizon*'s Conway experiences when he gazes upon the crystalline peaks of Karakal. This twofold stimulation and assurance supplies the unique narcotic formula of Shangri-La's magnetic attraction, whereby Conway derives "a combination of mental clarity and physical apathy that was not unpleasant" (42). These sensations recall Grosvenor's formulation of the *Geographic* as "mental relaxation without emotional stimulus."[45] Writers of the Frankfurt School would surely find Conway's and Grosvenor's comments an apt précis of the passive mental state encouraged by mass culture. By casting an ironic gaze on the popular by-products of the culture industry, however, camp revitalizes a critical intellect that resists passive identification with mass culture.

National Geographic Redux: Hemingway, the *New Yorker,* and Cosmopolitan Camp

National Geographic's global distribution of photographs of far-flung people and places helped consolidate an international membership based on shared commitment to a cosmopolitan ideal. By the 1930s, however, *National Geographic* had lost the cultural cachet it held in its first decades. The public grew increasingly aware that "membership" was a pretentious euphemism for "subscription."[46] No less a writer than Ernest Hemingway, spokesman for the "Lost Generation," found the occasion to satirize *National Geographic*'s most cherished markers of affiliation and belonging, its membership and cosmopolitanism in a scene in a Swiss train station from his "Homage to Switzerland" (1931). The story's camp treatment of the magazine addresses the futility of its attempts to forge an "imagined community" of cosmopolitans through the romantic spectacle of exploration and travel.[47]

"Homage to Switzerland" takes up the role of *National Geographic* photographs in hastening the process of deterritorialization, a theme reinforced by Switzerland's internationalism and political neutrality, and by the train station's function as a hub for cross-cultural contact. Within this deterritorialized space, a young American, Mr. Harris, who has just lost his father to suicide, is drawn into conversation by an elder Swiss professor, Mr. Wyer, who inquires whether Mr. Harris is a member of the National Geographic Society. Mr. Harris reveals he knows little about the NGS, its officers, or its headquarters in Washington, D.C. "You're not a member, then?" the Swiss gentleman concludes. "No," replies Harris, "But my father is. He's been a member for a great many years" (207). Harris decides to humor the gentleman by recollecting one of the magazine's most popular photographs.

> "Do you remember the panorama of the Sahara Desert?" Harris asked.
> "The Sahara desert? That was nearly fifteen years ago."
> "That's right. That was one of my father's favorites."
> "He doesn't prefer the newer numbers?"
> "He probably does. But he was very fond of the Sahara panorama."
> "It was excellent. But to me its artistic value far exceeded its scientific interest."
> "I don't know," said Harris. "The wind blowing all that sand and that Arab with his camel kneeling toward Mecca." (208)

In this exchange, Hemingway invokes perhaps one of *National Geographic*'s most campy visual images. Originally part of a 1911 *National Geographic* photographic panorama, "The Hour of Prayer," featuring a Bedouin sheik and his camel in the Sahara desert, appeared in advertising circulars and newspaper articles celebrating *National Geographic*'s artistic photographs.[48] Hemingway invokes this clichéd image in order to recall another figure of camp, T. E. Lawrence, for his outlandish cross-dressing as an Arabian sheik and his not quite closeted homosexuality, in addition to his popular accounts of Arabia.[49] Rather than function as yet another example of imperialist stereotyping, "The Hour of Prayer," as it appears in Hemingway's short story, then, signals both the magazine's iconic status and camp's expression of public disenchantment with the magazine's old-fashioned sensibilities.

This, of course, is what the encounter in Hemingway's short story parodies in calling attention to the failed seriousness of the magazine's membership enterprise. Wyer's desire to secure another member and continue the great work of the NGS stands for the Victorian sensibilities with which Hemingway's generation had grown disillusioned. The Swiss gentleman's deep pride in his NGS membership and his unself-conscious zeal—"I have nominated a scientist from Vevey and a colleague of mine from Lausanne and they were both elected. I believe they would be very pleased if I nominated Colonel Lawrence" (208)—reveals the generational divide between them. Hemingway lightly satirizes the magazine's romantic, "rose-colored" philosophy through Wyer's naïve belief in the sanctity of cultural institutions and their power to create social cohesion. Yet Harris, a figure of the Lost Generation and its repudiation of old systems and values, lacks the energy to confront Wyer's generation or divest it of its comforting belief in heroism, honor, and, most of all, a sense of cultural stability and belonging. Loathe to destroy his elder's illusions, Harris replies, "It's a splendid idea" (208). Just when Dr. Wyer expresses his interest in meeting Harris's father and making a pilgrimage to NGS headquarters, Harris reveals that his father has committed suicide. The story's denouement, concluding in an image of Wyer's NGS membership card, comments ironically on the fading value of NGS membership in shaping identity—let alone promoting international sympathy and cultural cohesion.

A critique of the global mediascape that promotes sensational representations of cultural difference is built into Hemingway's portrait of failed cosmopolitanism, as it is in *Lost Horizon*. Nor was it lost on *National Geographic* readers who recognized the darker potential beneath the magazine's glossy surface. George C. Stokes of Illinois declared the NGS's membership campaign a "hoax" that lured readers with a "false pretense of superiority." Accusing the NGS of being no better than "the rest of the money-grubbing publishing concerns," Stokes presciently anticipates later critiques of the culture industry. "Good bye," he said, "to the integrity, the superiority of the National Geographic Society." Membership had become another ploy "useful to befuddle the minds of the people and make them subservient to all sorts of nefarious promotional schemes for the benefit of the few and at the expense of the many."[50] Meanwhile, readers from England, Mexico, and the Netherlands complained of dated photographs and misleading articles. One reader said he would never put the magazine "in the hands of my son," lest it lead him wrongly to conclude that Americans are "the cleverest people" instead of being "still in the middle ages . . . Prohibition, Comstock Laws, prosecutions for teaching evolution!"[51] Readers' criticism acknowledged the fractures already present in the original magazine, which made it vulnerable to appropriation as camp.

More than a critique of ersatz cosmopolitanism and the imperialist imagination, however, camp registers the danger progressive educator John Dewey perceived in education that insists on making the "main material of education" the past. To do so, Dewey argued, would "make the past a rival of the present and the present a more or less futile imitation of the past." "Under such circumstances," wrote Dewey, "culture becomes an ornament and solace; a refuge and an asylum."[52] Camp persistently exhumes the magazine's dated sensibilities so that they cannot be taken as scientific gospel. As Flannery O'Connor once noted, the pages of *National Geographic* gave off an "unforgettable transcendent apotheotic"—and, she punned, "very grave odor."[53]

By keeping readers alive to the contradictions present in the institutions and customs it lampoons, camp fulfills an important ethnographic function. It reminds readers that historical artifacts are representations of a particular order and tied to a particular cultural moment. By inviting laughter at the pretensions of the arbiters of culture, camp promotes a more self-conscious consumption of popular culture. Camp productions remind the public that the values and customs portrayed in popular culture, rather than triggering automatic responses, can instead be continually revisited and revised by their audiences in imaginative and critical ways.

National Geographic as Camp Icon

Published spoofs of the magazine's conventions give public recognition to criticisms already voiced by its readership. The various mass-cultural adaptations of *National Geographic* reveal the process by which an institution invested in the production of visual emblems of ethnographic difference became grist for the machine it helped to create. Illustrations parodying the magazine's visual pantheon of "savages" and photographer-explorers indicate the magazine's transformation from novelty to camp. "Give me the *National Geographic* and a copy of 'Indian Love Lyrics' and I'll write you any romantic novel," quipped a cartoon in the *Saturday Review of Literature* for October 13, 1934, in recognition of the artifice behind *National Geographic*'s romance with the exotic.

Cartoon parodies of *National Geographic* fall into roughly four categories: (1) those that critique the magazine's habit of depicting the Third

World as primitive and unchanging; (2) those that mock or reflect anxiety regarding anthro-pornographic images of bare breasts, or reproduce such icons of African tribal ornamentation as neck rings and lip plugs; (3) those that take revenge on the photographer as an agent of the magazine's imperialism; and (4) those that poke fun at the magazine's readership and the cultural phenomenon of collecting *National Geographic*.[54] For the moment, I will focus on parodies appearing in the *New Yorker*, which delighted in lampooning *National Geographic*'s conventions and middlebrow readership.

National Geographic's local color and exoticism were often parodied in the *New Yorker*, which published thirteen joke references to the magazine between 1930 and 1999. The motto of the magazine that *New Yorker* founder Harold Ross introduced in the 1930s, "Not for the old lady in Dubuque," was *National Geographic*'s antithesis in both content and implied or intended readership. While both publications could be said to appeal to the nation's "Upper Masses," as discussed in chapter 5, nuclear families comprised much of the *Geographic*'s membership base, while the *New Yorker* subscribership consisted mainly of singles or childless couples, "mobile urbanites" who identified with cosmopolitan consumer tastes.[55] With its mascot, the dandy Eustace Tilley, as "an ironic symbol of contemporary sophistication" on its inaugural 1925 cover, the *New Yorker* mascot parodied the nineteenth-century dandy, which Sontag defines as the paragon of a camp outlook and aesthetics.[56]

Showing various "jungle types" "participating in the common rituals of western European cosmopolitan culture" was a staple of *New Yorker* humor, as cautious editors not only perceived "natives" as acceptable substitutes for caricatures of African Americans, but also heightened the inherent "foolishness" of imperial exploits themselves.[57] A Carl Rose cartoon from 1934, for example, depicts an African chief and gentleman in a pith helmet looking at a *National Geographic*, with a stack of old issues at their feet. Calling to mind the 1926 photograph "Seeing Himself as Others See Him," the cartoon highlights the absurdity of the magazine's adherence to an aesthetic of ethnographic timelessness, now shown as obsolete in an increasingly sophisticated global mediascape. "That was in '26," remarks the native. "Now here I am again in the spring of '29" (fig. 25).[58] A year later, Charles Addams portrayed a tribesman in hot pursuit of his mate. "Geographic readers don't *want* that sort of thing, I tell you!" argues a disgruntled White Hunter standing behind a *National Geographic* photographer squinting into his viewfinder.[59] If, for *National*

"That was in '26. Now here I am again in the spring of '29."

Geographic, romanticizing the Other helped to preserve the tenuous psychological borders that deterritorialization and cross-cultural contact had begun to erode, by calling attention to the institutional stage management of those borders, *New Yorker* parodies deflate *National Geographic's* savage romance.

Consider an April 1944 *New Yorker* cartoon by Richard Taylor that depicts a roomful of models awaiting a fashion cattle call. The lone black woman among them is entirely nude except for gold rings spiraling around her neck. She explains confidingly to the woman seated next to her, "Practically all my calls come from the *National Geographic*" (fig. 26). This cartoon deploys the *New Yorker's* "humor of anachronism," the result of the "tension between content and context."[60] In this case, the cartoon relocates the primitive African woman from the grass hut to a modern urban high-rise, where she appears as poised and sophisticated as her white counterparts. The cartoon's anachronistic humor acknowledges the magazine's strategies for eroticizing racial difference by mimicking fashion photography as well as the role its exotic women have filled as pin-ups.[61] But the cartoon does not reinforce *National Geographic*'s ethnographic timelessness. In salvaging the magazine's racial eroticism, it enacts a modernist subversion of middle-class sexual double standards. The bourgeoisie could politely titter at the magazine's publication of nude photographs under the lofty auspices of science, but the *New Yorker* showed how that laughter itself was based on repressing the possibility that the primitive was no longer "primitive," but had become modern. The tittering, elbowing, and winking of "polite" society signaled just how far behind the times *National Geographic*'s readers were.

In the same spirit as the *New Yorker*, a 1950 cartoon in *Esquire* mocks *National Geographic*'s representations of the erotic and exotic outside history. Like a typical *National Geographic* ethnographic photo-documentary, the cartoon takes its viewer-voyeurs inside the domestic space of an African hut. Closest to the entrance sits a full-figured woman in a grass skirt and bikini top. She squats on the floor with downcast eyes, preoccupied with the task of pounding something in a bowl. Another woman, fully clothed in modern Western attire, appears to be preening before a mirror. A third woman, also in a grass skirt, stands between the two and glances back at the one wearing Western clothes. As if to avert disaster, she says, "Quick, slip that dress off! Here come a couple of photographers from the *National Geographic*." These images function as "metapictures" that both comment on the constructed nature of *National Geographic*'s photographs and critique its construction of the ethnographic Other as the antithesis of Western modernity. By portraying the exotic woman of color in modern settings and Western attire, the images ironize *National Geographic*'s fixation with primitive "culture" as a counterforce to Western "civilization."

Cartoons in which the stock words and images of cultural imperialism are registered, and then forcibly rejected as artifice, record the ambivalence that postcolonial scholars locate in colonialist representations of racial difference. By laying bare the aesthetic and ideological processes by which imperialism constructs its ethnographic objects of desire, cartoon parodies in the *New Yorker* and elsewhere make visible "that 'otherness' which is at once the object of desire and derision, an articulation of difference contained within the fantasy of origin and identity."[62] This way of reading enables resistance on the part of the colonized. It also, however,

"Practically all my calls come from the 'National Geographic.'"

Fig. 26 Richard Taylor cartoon from the *New Yorker,* April 1944. (© The New Yorker Collection 1944 Richard Taylor from cartoonbank.com, All Rights Reserved)

mobilizes resistance from within dominant cultures to colonialist visual rhetoric. Cartoon parodies demonstrate how perceptive readers not only register the ambivalence encoded within images of imperial desire, but also resist the colonizing ideology of the culture industry that promotes such images.

Cartoon images featuring familiar *National Geographic* subjects express a collective sense that the magazine had grown passé and that its reputation as scientific authority and cultural standard-bearer could not be taken seriously. As the unknown parts of the globe increasingly diminished, in large measure because of *National Geographic* itself, narratives of exploration and adventure gradually lost their novelty. Moreover, with greater public awareness that *National Geographic* was not just an educational enterprise but a commercial one, membership in the NGS no longer simply symbolized the cosmopolitan ideal. By exploiting an ironic gap between the familiar *National Geographic* representations and their deeper narrative structures, cartoon images perform an important civic role in underscoring imperialism's mythological basis in images of power and technological supremacy. Moreover, these cartoons, like letters from

NGS members, register criticisms of the many kinds of "culture" *National Geographic* reproduced and exhibited in its pages.

A trademark quality of the iconic image is its appeal to spectators' emotions. What makes iconic images so compelling is their power as emotional catalysts.[63] The emotional appeal that makes the iconic image reach across various national and political constituencies, however, also renders it vulnerable to other appropriations and public revisions that recast its narratives in a more critical light. Camp adaptations take advantage of this vulnerability and divest the original image of its emotional content. In stripping the iconic photograph of its original emotional appeal, camp adaptations foster a more critical sensibility.

These cartoons hint at the magazine readers' increasing dissatisfaction with *National Geographic*'s photographic and ethnographic redundancies. As early as 1925, readers began signaling their boredom with natural history and local color. Dr. Perry G. Vago of Rochester, New York, revoked his membership dues and suggested the magazine be renamed "the 'Botanist Monthly' or the 'Monthly Bird Guide.'" In a letter dated January 22, 1935, a colonel in the U.S. Marine Corps, who had been a member for many years, articulated perhaps the most common reason that readers gave for not renewing their Society memberships. "I . . . find so little in the magazine now that is new and interesting that would justify my continuing my subscription," he wrote. "I have even come to the point where I readily recognize photographs published in preceding years."[64] By the 1930s, *National Geographic*'s themes had become so redundant as to approach self-parody, yet the producers of camp are not always aware that they are producing it.

The skepticism and parodic impulse extended to the concept of NGS membership, and once again the *New Yorker* took the lead. "Brothers in N.G.S.," a spoof in the June 24, 1933, issue, parodies the magazine's pretension to exclusivity by portraying membership as if it were a fraternity rush. The new pledge Marc Connelly writes his senior brother Frank Sullivan for "the lowdown on the inside political situation there, so that I shan't embarrass you or any of the other fellows who stood by me during the pledge period" (13). Sullivan responds with hearty congratulations: "Why, you old potato, I'm tickled pink" (13). After describing how chance encounters with NGS brethren helped him through several narrow escapes ("When I was with the Fuller Brush Company" in the Gobi Desert and "When I was with the Hoover Vacuum people" in the Galapagos Islands), Sullivan issues a series of warnings. He tells "Old Con" always to keep a copy of the magazine with him, "even when you bathe," a jocular reference to the magazine's reputation as ethnographic porn. Mocking the near sacredness of the magazine to its members, he tells Old Con that "A fellow is supposed to give his copy only to the girl he's engaged to" (13). And, if he wants to remain in good standing, he will be called upon to "go out for something." For instance, "Either dig up some old ruins, or take a trip across the Atlantic in a twenty-foot yawl, or race Alan Villiers around the Horn in a ketch" (14). "Brothers in N.G.S." deploys camp's strategies of exaggeration and irony to deflate members' potential identification with imperialism's heroic "types."

Though more subtle than "Brothers in N.G.S.," Geoffrey T. Hellman's three-part series "Geography Unshackled," which appeared in the *New Yorker* in September and October of 1943, profiled Gilbert Grosvenor's long reign as *National Geographic* editor and Society president and exemplified the pleasure the *New Yorker* took in lampooning the magazine's middlebrow readership and its Victorian sensibilities. Hellman's series was both a tribute to and a send-up of the musty stamp Grosvenor's editorship had placed on the magazine. The first installment in Hellman's series invokes much of the celebratory rhetoric in Grosvenor's institutional history. The end of the article, however, gives a foretaste of the chiding to come, as Hellman points to Grosvenor's "Achilles heel," a penchant for birds rendered especially vivid in the most self-parodying of titles: "Nature's Children," "Our Policemen of the Air," "Birds of Town and Country" and "Birds May Bring You More Happiness than the Wealth of the Indies."[65] "Brothers in N.G.S." should have tipped Grosvenor off, perhaps, to the ironic tone his own profile would take, but then irony was never Grosvenor's, or his magazine's, strong suit.

"Geography Unshackled" makes it clear that *National Geographic*'s unintended campiness originated with Grosvenor's editorial dictatorship and the predictability of his preferred content and style. Grosvenor "does not believe," Hellman writes, "that his magazine's text and captions are poor or that his authors, of whom he is one, are not all they should be." Such self-seriousness, of course, demands a camp response. So Grosvenor's editorial imperative to publish only topics of a "kindly nature" is shown in all its self-parodying splendor in titles that resound with the failed gravity of naïve camp: "Guernsey, the Friendly Island," "Friendly Crows in Festive Panoply," "Friendly Journeys in Japan," "Friends of Our Forests," "Our Friend the Frog," "Our Friends, the Bees," "Our Friends, the French," "The Crow, Bird Citizen of Every Land: A Feathered Rogue

Who Has Many Fascinating Traits and Many Admirable Qualities Despite His Marauding Propensities."[66] But Grosvenor was not one to tinker with a successful formula, regardless of how hackneyed it had become to his readers.

Increasingly caricatured line drawings of Grosvenor over the course of the series symbolically capture the magazine's degeneration into camp. The first is a sketch that presents a realistic and serious, even flattering, drawing of Grosvenor, then approaching his sixty-eighth birthday. The next two, however, are caricatured in ways that dramatize the magazine's transformation from a respectable magazine with lofty aspirations to a quaint and endearing relic. The second profile in the series is a simple line drawing in which its key features—a balding head, elongated face, receding chin, and serious gaze framed by spectacles—present Grosvenor as a throwback to the Victorian era. The simplest, most abstract of the three, the final image makes Grosvenor less formidable, with scrunched-up eyes and a slight smile lurking beneath his moustache. He appears in more whimsical fashion, as if in his dotage. Birds and clouds take flight around the hat perched on his head. As Grosvenor's portrait devolves from realism to caricature over the course of Hellman's series, it perfectly dramatizes *National Geographic*'s decades-long transformation into a camp artifact.

New Yorker parodies of *National Geographic* should be understood not just as a backhanded compliment paid by the cultural elite to a middle-brow cultural icon, but as an expression of broader dissent, even hostility, toward the magazine's rose-tinted window on the world. Readers were well aware that beneath the magazine's editorial kindliness, there lurked a simplistic humanism. Although its concept of membership aspired toward exclusivity, it pandered to unsophisticated tastes. In its celebration of quaint, traditional customs, *National Geographic* promoted a naïve, superficial belief that reading a magazine could make one a cosmopolitan, part of an in-crowd of world travelers. By promoting photographs as a "universal language" to transcend cultural difference, the magazine actually transcribed difference into type. In response, camp reveals how membership, rather than stimulating a genuine cosmopolitan willingness to embrace cultural difference, can encourage identification with a corporation specifically, or with the mass generally, of which camp itself is suspicious. In turning *National Geographic* back on itself and thus reversing the roles of observer and observed, camp imagines an alternative dynamic, one in which photography's ethnographic subjects are in control and set the terms of representation, one in which the consumers of the culture industry are not consumed by it.

Nevertheless, there were some international readers who found relief from provincialism in the iteration of *National Geographic*'s visual narratives. Readers from South Africa, France, and New Zealand, for example, praised the magazine and promptly renewed their membership dues.[67] Vicarious participation through *National Geographic* afforded readers the "conceptual mobility" of Hemingway's privileged fictional protagonists.[68] Even as it offered an ersatz cosmopolitanism derived from often stereotypical representations of racial and cultural difference, rather than from lived experience, the magazine afforded an opportunity for its readers to *feel* cosmopolitan; it opened up positive ways of making audiences more aware of and more attuned to cultural difference. At the same time, it also gave people a false sense of mastery, exemplified by photographs promoting the technological expertise of the photographer.

This failure among its other shortcomings, from clichéd articles and titles that approached self-parody to its praise of fascist nations, however, as we have seen, was not lost on its critical readership. A 1939 letter from the composer David Raskin written from Fox Film Studios in Hollywood wittily captures the spirit of the many camp parodies of *National Geographic* and its failure to keep pace with the times:

> How, in a world of constantly shifting borders and political alignments (which bear so much more strongly upon you than upon ordinary men) the magazine can contrive to maintain a position somewhere between a travelogue, a cracker-barrel philosopher, a gaga tourist, and a Leibnizian armchair geographer, I do not know, but somehow it manages to do so.

> If the energy you now waste in sycophantic cleaving to a dying tradition, lampooned even in film cartoons (and as the sun sinks into the Silly Sea, we bid a fond *adieu* to the Island of Blaha!), if this energy were expended to further the progress of the great science you now fall far short of representing, clichés in your columns and wolves at your door would no longer be present . . . This is 1939 A.D., and the world does move, and in neglecting to consider its movements, you are falling into the category of useless appendages of society. . . . There is need for such a magazine today—not for an audience of permanent adolescents, but for the builders of tomorrow, who must know the world of today.[69]

What readers critiqued was the magazine's persistent disavowal of global interconnectedness and complexity, the "constantly shifting borders and political alignments" to which Raskin's letter on the eve of the Second World War calls attention. The magazine's overall tone changed little in the next twenty years of *National Geographic*'s editorial leadership. This emphasis on the noncontroversial persisted under John Oliver La Gorce, who briefly succeeded Gilbert H. Grosvenor, and under Grosvenor's son Melville Bell Grosvenor, who assumed the helm from 1957 to 1967. The magazine reinforced national media portrayals of the United States as "good eggs" in its coverage of the Korean War, while it eschewed coverage of the Soviet Union and other communist nations and anticolonial independence movements. Dissent at home was equally abhorrent. Accordingly, the magazine ignored the geographic consequences of the civil rights movement in the drawing of racial lines around urban and suburban districts. Well into the 1970s the popular press continued to reflect audience critique of *National Geographic*'s trivialized portraits of national and global events. *Wordsmith* comic strip in 1976 joked about *National Geographic* articles on "The Happy Ghetto: Training Ground for the NBA" and "Backpacking on the Ho Chi Minh Trail."[70] That the magazine avoided controversy to the point of inanity had become an acknowledged element of *National Geographic*'s iconicity.

Camp, therefore, is also about criticizing the middlebrow presumption to cosmopolitan mastery, as witnessed in *New Yorker* cartoons that satirize the tastes of *National Geographic* readers, the magazine's status as waiting-room literature, its routine fare of savages and heroes, and the staid conventionality of its signature themes. This is not to argue that readers themselves were always naïve, but to suggest instead that parodies recognize and voice criticisms and concerns already expressed by an alert readership. The content that gets commented on most negatively by readers are those things that nearly parody themselves, content that is so local as to be banal, like chickens, or that was once novel but has grown clichéd, like the Arab and camel in the desert. Camp calls attention to the "banality of difference" that potentially undermines otherwise positive efforts to institutionalize multiculturalism.[71]

By parodying both the local scene and the global panorama, camp seeks to restore the world's strangeness, its dramatic otherness, particularly that which lies within the culture to which one is closest. It reverses the "museum effect" by training an ethnographic lens on the production of cultural representations. In so doing, "One becomes increasingly exotic to oneself, as one imagines how others might view that which we consider normal."[72] It shows how characters in *National Geographic* perform their identities, how they are part of its institutional machinery, and yet it also shows the instability of these performances. The fact that its visual motifs have to be repeated over and over again in issue after issue hints at an instability in the ideas or themes that demands their continual reassertion visually and textually. Hence camp's seriality: its habitual orientation toward the redundant, the clichéd, the predictable.

The Bridges of Madison County: Camp Seriality and the *National Geographic* Photographer

For a time, the magazine's new leadership took heed of *National Geographic*'s flagging self-image. An edgier editorial policy emerged in the 1970s and 1980s that did not shy from controversy. While *National Geographic* still showed a world brightly colored, it became more invested in the underlying complexities of global politics, publishing, for example, the first photographs of American military activities in Vietnam.[73] Editor Gilbert M. Grosvenor, the grandson of the president who initiated the magazine's editorial policies of kindliness and nonpartisanship in 1915, pursued a more rigorous application of the editorial tenets of timeliness and objectivity. But when conservative trustees censored him for publishing articles on Cuba under Fidel Castro, South African apartheid, and Harlem, he capitulated by publishing an editorial statement repudiating "advocacy journalism."[74] When Grosvenor's successor, Wilbur Garrett, assumed the editorship in 1980, he continued to publish articles of both topical and controversial interest until his firing in 1990. It was then that the board chose to base the magazine's content on market research indicating reader preference for brief articles on American themes over troubling international and social issues. By the 1990s, then, write Lutz and Collins, "Politeness seemed to be more marketable than politics."[75]

It is in this context of the magazine's shift from its more political editorial agenda of the 1970s to the palatable in the 1990s that I turn to that Robert Waller's best-selling *The Bridges of Madison County* (1992), whose romantic hero is a *National Geographic* photographer, as an illustration of the banal seriality that camp exploits. The popular 1995 film adaptation directed by Clint Eastwood, who plays opposite Meryl Streep, concerns Francesca Johnson, an Italian immigrant now trapped in Iowa as a farmwife, and Robert Kincaid, the *National Geographic* photographer with whom she has a romantic tryst. In both the novel and the film, each functions as a *National Geographic* "type." She plays the exotic female Other to his nomadic explorer in ways that undermine the magazine's aesthetic and ideological ethos.

Like their cartoon predecessors, however, both novel and film rework and subtly critique a host of "romance" themes addressed in this book: the cowboy photographer (intensified in the film by Clint Eastwood's spaghetti western legacy) and the exotic woman, pictorial photography, and the institution's self-documentary photographs. Both the novel's and the film's high seriousness classify *The Bridges of Madison County* as naïve camp, whose "failed seriousness" has something to do with the way in which its nostalgic reprisal of the romance of *National Geographic* reveals the scripted nature of gender performance. Both Kincaid and Francesca self-consciously appropriate the "exotic" to perform their respective gender roles.

Kincaid's journey to America's heartland becomes a quest for what we might term the "internal exotic," wherein Francesca Johnson, an Italian who immigrated to America after the Second World War, embodies a forgotten past that Kincaid must, through his lens, "rediscover."[76] As Francesca, Meryl Streep's sinuous gait and thick accent present an unselfconsciously camped-up version of exoticism. For his part, Eastwood fulfills the seriality of camp by being doubly iconic as the hero of spaghetti westerns who now attempts to infuse with seriousness a book unabashedly catering to the unfulfilled dreams of middle-aged women.

The novel and film both embrace the image of the *National Geographic* photographer as a latter-day frontiersman, the "last cowboy" (101) of the Old West, revealing how the magazine's themes of romance adventure continued to resonate powerfully in American culture, despite their campiness. Kincaid's masculinity, for Francesca, similarly has to do with his exoticism. Appearing "something of a gypsy" (4) and a "magician of sorts" (27), like the first American advertisers, traffickers in the exotic, the mysterious, and the forbidden, Kincaid represents the *National Geographic* photographer as magazine ad-man, a "peddler" of its exotic wares.[77] Through Francesca's eyes, Kincaid fulfills the frontier archetypes of cowboy and native American, with a little Walt Whitman thrown in for good measure.[78] Francesca observes that his nose "was like that she had seen on Indian men during a vacation" (32). A refined yet rugged cosmopolite, equally at home in civilization or nature, Kincaid "fished and swam and walked and lay in long grass listening to distant voices he fancied only he could hear" (10). Francesca repeatedly links his masculinity to the primitive and animalistic. Francesca notes that he moves "with a peculiar, animal-like grace" (30) and has the "smell of a civilized man who seemed, in some part of himself, aboriginal" (99). The embodiment of a nineteenth-century manliness that incorporates attributes of the primitive frontier, Kincaid himself is both savage and civilized.

Kincaid's real fascination, for Francesca, is that he possesses the power to make her imagine herself in the role of the exotic female. Kincaid's performance as *National Geographic*'s masculine archetype has its counterpart in Francesca's self-conscious efforts to resemble the magazine's exotic women. In an evocation of *National Geographic*'s notorious focus on breasts, Francesca recalls that when Kincaid photographed her she deliberately chose not to wear a bra so that her breasts might show through her white t-shirt. His photography becomes, to her imagination, a form of extended foreplay: "He had smiled at her, saying how fine and warm she looked in early light, asked her to lean against the post, and then moved around her in a wide arc, shooting from knee level, then standing, then lying on his back with the camera pointed up at her" (25). In this latter-day ethnographic fantasy of discovery and conquest, Francesca appropriates the nineteenth-century ethnography that links unbound breasts (and up-thrust camera/phallus) to primitive female sexuality as a means of liberating herself from the Western management of female bodies. The fantasy is complete, moreover, with Camel cigarettes and "the gold hoop earrings Richard said made her look like a hussy and a gold bracelet" (45). In the novel, she silently wonders, "How many sets of long fingernails had he watched delicately pointing toward him from the stems of brandy glasses, how many pairs of blue-round and brown-oval eyes had looked at him through foreign evenings, while anchored sailboats rocked offshore and water slapped against the quays of ancient ports?" (63). Here, Francesca's meditations invoke the "romance" behind *National Geographic,* in which the photographic collection of women of color involves the endless reproduction of the same exotic "type" to satisfy market demands. These images are part of the recognized visual grammar of Middle East exoticism, as reflected, for example, in a February 1970 *Playboy* spread ("How Other Magazines Would Photograph a Playmate") that emulates *National Geographic* style with its topless blond wearing a veil, draped with gold jewelry, and posed in front of a camel.[79]

In exposing putatively "original" pictures as self-conscious reproductions of preexisting images, concepts, and themes, camp serves a vital ethnographic function. "The transgressiveness of camp," it has been remarked, "relies on its privilege of the secondary and derivative . . . of serial reproduction over the original, showing that the secondary is always already a copy of a copy."[80] Accordingly, *National Geographic's* eroticized images of women of color have supplied Francesca with models for heightening her sexual appeal. Her dangling earrings and bared breasts allow her to assume the same exoticism she imagines that Kincaid admires: she plays the foreign gypsy in Iowa, the nation's backyard. Francesca's confrontation of Kincaid thus underlines the ways in which he already inhabits a role—one that Roosevelt, Rock, and numerous other *National Geographic* explorers defined before him.

Francesca's search for his photograph in the magazine transforms Kincaid into another of the ethnographic subjects captured in the pages of *National Geographic.* She even encounters *National Geographic's* genre of "self-documentary" photograph in which Kincaid appears "by a river in East Africa, facing the camera and up close to it, squatting down, getting ready to take a photograph of something" (130). What Kincaid photographs is less important, of course, than the fact that he himself is photographed—that his heroic aura is reconstituted each time she searches out "the back page of the magazine," in its "On Assignment" column, which debuted in December 1981: "He was there sometimes. . . . In the Kalahari, at the walls of Jaipur in India, in a canoe in Guatemala, in Northern Canada. The road and the cowboy" (129). Reversing the expected order of photographic subject and object, the camera's lens focuses on Kincaid's performance in front of the camera; the machinery behind the institution continues its relentless objectification of the subject. It is a process that forbids intimacy and real knowledge—that is, knowledge of the "details" that compose the ordinary life and that forestall its absorption into romance. At the same time, the constant effort to recuperate the photographer's heroism heightens our sense of its tenuousness, of its frailty in the face of an artifice from which it cannot escape.

Even naïve camp renditions of the magazine's favored themes reflect a savvy awareness of its artifice, while also hinting at a desire to rehabilitate some of the magazine's original appeal. Kincaid's plea to Francesca at the film's end to "Come away with me," distills *National Geographic's* psychological force into once sentence. The magazine invites readers to "come away" with the photographer, to escape routine and embrace the exotic and erotic possibilities of travel. Kincaid's photographs of the covered bridges of Madison County may salvage the picturesque characteristics of local color, but the exotic is not far away. It materializes in Francesca, the Italian immigrant made over as the "local exotic." Waller's book seems to have succeeded as a refuge for the magazine's faded glory, for *National Geographic* was soon besieged with requests for a nonexistent issue on covered bridges.[81] *National Geographic* had never produced an article on covered bridges, but it could have, the subject so suited its quaint local-color themes. More importantly, the book's nostalgia for the romance of *National Geographic* expresses a longing for the emotional particularities of place, rather than the foreign and exotic associated with an increasingly globalized culture.

The pattern of subverting the photographer's conquest, or of undermining the magazine's ethnographic realism by exposing its artifice, suggests that camp adaptations of *National Geographic* form a complex reaction to globalization. One consequence of the twentieth-century "pictorial turn" is that the world came to seem a smaller and more familiar place precisely through the efforts of media outlets like the *National Geographic*.[82] *National Geographic*'s photographs contributed to expanding its readers' awareness of unknown parts of the world and diminishing the scope of the unexplored. Its images hastened globalization and contributed to a psychological feeling of deterritorialization, a growing sense that the particularities of cultural place and space were constantly shifting, or being lost, that local customs and rituals were giving way to forms of "complex connectivity" joining all parts of the globe. In response, camp, by joining audiences in laughter, reaffirms the frail borders between self and other and affirms cultural membership through humor. By recovering the detritus of cast-off cultural forms, its camp artifacts mark an attempt to reinvest the abstractions of deterritorialized space with the specificities of shared cultural rituals and beliefs.

In its effort to reclaim and redeem popular culture's refuse, camp obliquely aligns itself with salvage ethnography, which aims to rescue doomed culture from modernity. The primitive and the exotic, the faded glory of the *National Geographic,* its hackneyed primitivism and celebration of the commonplace—all these can be salvaged through camp as "symbols of a spent historical mode of production."[83] The possibility of redeeming outmoded (i.e., primitive) images and ideals brings camp and salvage ethnography into alignment. By showing the magazine and its motifs reconstituted as camp, parodies of *National Geographic* put the institution in the same position as the African chieftain beholding a sketch of himself. In that original image, the photographer stands offstage as a figure of worldly wisdom, experience, and knowledge, while the chieftain

Fig. 27 "The 'Better Halves' of a Mangebetou Chief, Lined up in Order of Preference." (National Geographic Society)

seems to be coming into an awareness of his own representation, the figure emerging out of innocence, so to speak. In parallel terms, the campy parodies of *National Geographic* can be said to represent the clear-eyed wisdom of the magazine's skeptical readership, while the object of representation, the magazine, is forced to confront itself in a similarly disconcerting encounter.

The corrupted innocence that characterizes camp nonetheless posits a relationship to its original that is innocent in its initial sincerity. Many of *National Geographic*'s visual motifs are campy only in retrospect. Camp's objects are often "old fashioned, out-of-date," notes Sontag, not from nostalgia, but because "the process of aging or deterioration provides the necessary detachment" that "arouses a necessary sympathy" (285). For instance, a June 1926 photograph titled "The 'Better Halves' of a Mangebetou Chief, Lined up in Order of Preference" (716) (fig. 27) vividly comments on *National Geographic*'s photographic mass production, the seriality or redundancy that opened the magazine to camp appropriation. In his epic poem of Paterson, New Jersey, the American poet William Carlos Williams creatively reconstructed this same *National Geographic* photograph, which he translated into a more sexually evocative image: The wives appear in a "descending scale of freshness," "semi-naked / astraddle" an "official log."[84] In the original, each woman is perched one behind the other on a small stool. With their profiles averted from the camera, the women appear identical, as if on an assembly line.

Yet time and distance from *National Geographic*'s earliest cultural moments lend audiences a more knowing perspective on its visual repertoire. "Thus, things are campy," writes Sontag, "not when they become old—but when we become less involved in them, and can enjoy, instead of be frustrated by, the failure of the attempt." The difference between "intentional and unintentional camp," maintains another critic, is a difference in subject position. Unintentional camp privileges the ironic gaze of the reader's "deliberate misunderstanding," while intentional camp affirms the "self-recognition of *understanding*" when insiders communicate their insider status to other insiders through camp.[85] In other words, camp consolidates its audience members on the basis of a shared pleasure in dissent. Camp affirms the power of the marginalized. By denigrating and corrupting those modes of power it adopts, camp's agents claim power through an appropriation that is simultaneously a rejection through humor. In each of their manifestations, parodies of *National Geographic* serve a reflexive role by making visible the aesthetic processes that mobilize its institutional narratives. Taking pleasure in the *New Yorker*'s and other magazines' spoofs of *National Geographic*'s high seriousness, then, does not signal passivity in the face of its imperialist legacy. Rather, it recognizes the failure of those politics to take hold of the popular imagination.

Notes

Abbreviations

AGB   Alexander Graham Bell
GFP   Grosvenor Family Papers
GHG   Gilbert H. Grosvenor
LC   Library of Congress
NGM   *National Geographic Magazine*
NGS   National Geographic Society
NGSA   National Geographic Society Archives

Prologue

1. See Hariman and Lucaites's reading of "Migrant Mother" in chapter 3 of *No Caption Needed.*

2. Ibid., 31–37.

3. Spurr, *Rhetoric of Empire,* 52; Newman, "Special Report," 10.

4. Hesford and Kozol, *Just Advocacy?* 6; Spurr, *Rhetoric of Empire,* 53; see also Whitlock, *Soft Weapons,* 71.

5. Newman, "Special Report," 13.

6. Schulten, *Geographical Imagination,* 239.

7. Joe Narush, Vancouver, British Columbia, October 14, 1985, Microfilm Division, Microfiche File No: 510-2.6034, NGSA.

8. Hilario Vite, Mexico City, June 26, 1985; Trevor W. Kidby, England, August 16, 1985; Mrs. Bharati Banerjee, West Germany, July 15, 1985; J. O. Helmerson, Fan Anda, British Columbia, June 28, 1985; Microfiche File No: 510-2.6034, Records Division, NGSA.

9. Under the photograph appears the heading, "Paris in Afghanistan," followed by a quote from the celebrity, 'I'm here to party my fucking ass off'" (*Harvard Lampoon,* March 30, 2007, 94).

10. Ibid.

11. Hariman and Lucaites, *No Caption Needed,* 241.

12. Held and McGrew, *Globalization/Anti-Globalization,* 103–4.

13. The fund established in 2002 has been put to use in an Education and Training Center (ASCHIANA) and works with the Afghan Ministry of Education and the nongovernmental Asia Foundation to provide computer training and books in English,

Dari, and Pashto (2006 Afghan Girls Fund Stewardship Report, microfilm, Records Division, NGSA).

14. Gula's husband is a baker who supports the family of five on a "dollar a day." Newman, "Special Report," 12; Held and McGrew, *Globalization/Anti-Globalization,* 79.

15. http://scorchedtruth.blogspot.com/2007/04/new-tattoo.html.

16. Lutz and Collins, Reading *"National Geographic,"* xii.

17. Bauman, "Performance," 262–63. Hariman and Lucaites also draw on this definition of performance.

18. See Butler, *Precarious Life,* 143.

19. Alexander Graham Bell to Gilbert H. Grosvenor, April 4, 1904, "NGS Correspondence," Box 267, GFP, Manuscript Division, LC; Held and McGrew, *Globalization/Anti-Globalization,* 36.

1. National Geographic

1. *Harvard Lampoon,* March 30, 2008, 6.

2. Appadurai, "Disjuncture and Difference," 299; Tomlinson, *Globalization and Culture,* 2–3.

3. Appadurai, "Disjuncture and Difference," 299.

4. Hereafter, I abbreviate National Geographic Society as NGS. See Bryan, *National Geographic Society;* and Poole, *Explorer's House.*

5. Rothenberg, *Presenting America's World,* 16.

6. C. Wilson, "The Rhetoric of Consumption," 43.

7. Rothenberg, *Presenting America's World,* 169. See also Haraway, *Primate Visions;* Gero and Root, "Public Presentations and Private Concerns"; and Hadziselimovic, "Snowy Domes and Gay Turbans."

8. Alfred Koch, Bowden, Alberta, Canada, March 19, 1926, Commendations and Criticisms, 1921–26, microfilm, Records Division, NGSA.

9. The ad appears in Lutz and Collins, Reading *"National Geographic,"* as an example of *National Geographic*'s strategic placement as a "symbol of good taste and wealth" (*Reading "National Geographic,"* 8).

10. Brink, "Secular Icons," 139–43.

11. Hariman and Lucaites, *No Caption Needed,* 29–30.

12. Ibid., 33.

13. Watson R. Sperry, Hartford, Conn., December 1924, Commendations and Criticisms, 1921–31; E. M. DeShar, Albany, N.Y., September 30, 1921; Myra Hedges, Philadelphia, Pa., August 24, 1914, Commendations and Criticisms, 1912–22, microfilm, Records Division, NGSA.

14. Hannerz, "Cosmopolitans and Locals," 239. See Bramen, *Uses of Variety.*

15. Horace R. Sturgis, Riverside, Me., April 3, 1920; W. H. Burhans, Arapahoe, Wyo., October 14, 1920; Alice B. Dewson, Brooklyn, N.Y., March 10, 1920; J. R. Levy, Florence, S.C., undated, Commendations and Criticisms, 1912–21, microfilm, Records Division, NGSA.

16. Rothenberg, *Presenting America's World,* 21.

17. Wayland Ramsey, Los Angeles, Calif., April 28, 1926, Commendations and Criticisms, 1912–22, microfilm, Records Division, NGSA.

18. Anderson, *Imagined Communities*, 6, 33.

19. Bhabha, "DissemiNation," 297.

20. Ibid., 292.

21. Skrbis, Kendall, and Woodward, "Locating Cosmopolitanism," 124.

22. See Adorno and Horkheimer, "Culture Industry," 99.

23. Tomlinson, *Globalization and Culture*, 18–19;

24. Delanty, "Theorising Citizenship," 24.

25. See May, *Homeward Bound*.

26. Tomlinson, *Globalization and Culture*, 29, 118.

27. Elizabeth Bishop, "In the Waiting Room," in *Geography III*, by Bishop (New York: Farrar, Straus, and Giroux, 1976), 4–6.

28. Ibid., 7.

29. Tomlinson, *Globalization and Culture*, 118.

30. Edensor, *National Identity*, 89.

31. Mrs. Elisabeth Howe Terflinger, Logansport, Ind., December 1, 1940, Commendations and Criticisms, 1912–21, microfilm, Records Division, NGSA.

32. Urry, *Tourist Gaze*, 12–14; Tomlinson, *Globalization and Culture*, 43.

33. Strain, *Public Places, Private Journeys*, 39.

34. See Said, *Orientalism* and *Culture and Imperialism*.

35. Raymond Williams, *Keywords* (New York: Oxford University Press, 1983), 275–76.

36. Most notably, Trinh, *Woman, Native, Other*; Said, *Culture and Imperialism*; and Chakrabarty, *Provincializing Europe*.

37. Thompson, *Ideology and Modern Culture*, 105. See, for example, Morley, *The Nationwide Audience*; Radway, *Reading the Romance*; Ang, *Watching Dallas*; Fiske, *Television Culture*; and Hermes, *Reading Women's Magazines*.

38. Cigarette and alcohol advertisements were eliminated from *National Geographic* advertising pages, not because of Grosvenor's disapproval (see Abramson, *National Geographic*, 147–49), but in response to its readers. An April 1920 issue that featured ads for two different cigarette brands drew forth a number of reader complaints (see Mrs. B. Lethe Scovell, Minneapolis, Minn., June 2, 1920, Commendations and Criticisms, 1912–21, microfilm, Records Division, NGSA).

39. Judith Yaross Lee, "From the Field: The Future of *American Periodicals* and American Periodicals Research," *American Periodicals* 15.2 (2005): 199.

40. "Report of the Director and Editor of the NGS for 1919," GFP, Box 160, Manuscript Division, LC.

41. Douglas Kellner, *Media Culture* (London and New York: Routledge, 1995).

2. Training the "I" to See

1. Becker, "Witwatersrand and the Revolt of the Uitlanders, 355.

2. Rothenberg, *Presenting America's World*, 6.

3. Lewis Hosea, Cincinnati, Ohio, November 30, 1914, Commendations and Criticisms, 1912–21, microfilm, Records Division, NGSA.

4. Margaret H. Wilson, undated letter, India, Burma, Ceylon, Commendations and

Criticisms, 1921–26, microfilm, Records Division, NGSA. Also in Schulten, *Geographical Imagination,* 8.

5. Griffiths, *Wondrous Difference,* 13.

6. Conn, *Museums and American Intellectual Life,* 4–5; Griffiths, *Wondrous Difference,* 11–13.

7. Grosvenor, *NGS and Its Magazine* (1936), 40.

8. Hyde, "Introductory," 2.

9. *NGM* 10.9 (September 1899).

10. McSweeney, "The Character of Our Immigration, Past and Present," *NGM* 16.1 (January 1905): 11; Higham, *Strangers in the Land,* 110; Popkewitz, *Cosmopolitanism and the Age of School Reform;* McGee, "American Geographic Education," 305.

11. Cremin, *Transformation of the School,* 129–30; Hubbard, "Introductory Address," 10.

12. Hyde, "Introductory," 2.

13. For *National Geographic's* role during the Spanish-American War, see Tuason, "Ideology of Empire"; Schulten, *Geographical Imagination;* and Rothenberg, *Presenting America's World.*

14. Marien, *Photography and Its Critics,* 134.

15. AGB to GHG, April 4, 1904, GFP, Box 99, Manuscripts Division, LC. Also in Pauly, "World and All That Is in It"; Schulten, *Geographical Imagination;* and Rothenberg, *Presenting America's World.*

16. Darwin, *Origin of Species* (New York: Modern Library, 1936), 100. See Gillian Beer, *Darwin's Plots* (London: Routledge and Kegan Paul, 1983).

17. See Bramen, *Uses of Variety.*

18. Strain, *Public Places, Private Journeys,* 32, 79.

19. William Morris Davis, "The Improvement of Geographical Teaching," *NGM* 4 (July 1893): 70–71.

20. W. J. McGee, "Work of the National Geographic Society," *NGM* 7.8 (August 1896): 354.

21. For Powell, geographic reading would help young readers better appreciate the nation's literary achievements: "A large part of our literature can be understood and appreciated only by him who has been properly prepared to study geography aright" ("Geographic Instruction," 153).

22. Harris, *Cultural Excursions,* 342.

23. The magazine thus reflects Panofsky's interdisciplinary tenets for art history in *Meaning in the Visual Arts* (24–25).

24. See Mitchell, *Iconology,* on the icon as representative of the division between material image and spiritual likeness (31–35, 39).

25. Estelle M. Hurll, "Picture Study in Education," *Outlook* 61.3 (January 21, 1899), 176; Brink, "Secular Icons," 139, 143.

26. AGB to GHG, April 4, 1904, NGS Correspondence, Box 267; Home Notes, October–December 1907; Oct. 23, 1907, NGS Correspondence, Box 267, GFP, Manuscript Division, LC.

27. "Does Editorial Appeal Win?" Advertising Collection, NGSA.

28. See Barthes, *Camera Lucida.*

29. See Tagg, *Burden of Representation;* and Sekula, "The Body and the Archive."

30. Rothenberg, *Presenting America's World,* 75–78.

31. Schulten, *Geographical Imagination,* 111–14.

32. AGB to GHG, September 18, 1899, NGS Correspondence, Box 267, GFP, Manuscript Division, LC.

33. See Austin, "Colonial Systems of the World."

34. Austin, "Queer Methods of Travel," 689. See, for example, Adams, "East Indians in the New World," which draws erroneous comparisons between Native Americans and East Indians.

35. Pauly, "World and All That Is in It," 528.

36. Boon, *Anthropological Romance of Bali,* 3–4.

37. Tebbel and Zuckerman, *Magazine in America,* 57.

38. Mott, *A History of American Magazines,* vol. 4, *1885–1905,* 2.

39. Ibid., 3–5.

40. AGB to GHG, March 5, 1900, GFP, Box 6, Folder 19, Manuscript Division, LC.

41. "Members of the NGS," *NGM* 14.1 (January 1903): 45–75.

42. AGB to GHG, July 13, 1899, GFP, Box 99, Manuscript Division, LC.

43. Ibid.

44. Glazener, *Reading for Realism,* 266; Ohmann, *Selling Culture,* 118–19.

45. A clipping from *E. W. Howe's Monthly,* sent by a reader from Atcherson, Kans., March 1912, Commendations and Criticisms, 1912–22, microfilm, Records Division, NGSA.

46. Burrall, "Sight-Seeing," 500.

47. Reverend J. W. Schoech, Menfro, Mo., October 16, 1914, Commendations and Criticisms, 1912–21, microfilm, Records Division, NGSA.

48. Edgerton, "Recent Experiment," 278; Simons, "American Literature and the Modern Magazine," 360–61.

49. Engleman, "Outside Reading," 20.

50. Ibid., 21–22.

51. Grosvenor, "Report of the Director and Editor," 319.

52. AGB to GHG, February 3, 1909, Bell Papers, Box 78, Manuscript Division, LC; Grosvenor, "Report of the Director and Editor," 319.

53. Mott, *History of American Magazines,* 4:8.

54. In 1915, the *Manufacturer's Record* praised the magazine's recruitment of members amid declining circulations as "a notable record of achievement in journalism." From 1907 to 1910, it noted that membership had increased by 335.9 percent, the "result of what may be termed intensive cultivation in magazine work" (April 15, 1915, Commendations and Criticisms, 1912–22, microfilm, Records Division, NGSA; "Report of the Director and Editor of the NGS for 1919," GFP, Box 160, Folder 1, Manuscript Division, LC).

55. *Library Journal,* June 15, 1926, Commendations and Criticisms, 1912–22, microfilm, Records Division, NGSA; Tebbel and Zuckerman, *Magazine in America,* 57; "The *NGM* 1953 Distribution Analysis," Advertising Collection, NGSA; Kozol, *"Life"'s America,* 35.

56. James K. Stinson, Hammond, Ind., September 21, 1926; Margaret C. Calvert,

Kit Carson, Colo., April 6, 1926, Commendations and Criticisms, 1921–26, microfilm, Records Division, NGSA.

57. Grosvenor, *NGS and Its Magazine* (1936), 1; GFP, Box 159, Manuscript Division, LC; "Facts for Advertising Analysts" (1928–36), Advertising Collection, NGSA.

58. "Are You an Advertising Wise Man or a Whittler of Sticks?" (1919); "Facts for Advertising Analysts" (1924); "The Geographic's Upper Masses" (1930); "Graphic Evidence" (1955), Advertising Collection, NGSA.

59. Europe (131,971); Canada (74,595); Australia and New Zealand (41,482); Mexico, Central, and South America (29,755); Asia (14,157); and Africa (13,786) ("*NGM* 1953 Distribution Analysis," Advertising Division, NGSA).

60. GHG to Norman A. Brittin of Seattle, Wash., April 6, 1946. Grosvenor responded to Brittin's February 16, 1946, complaint that the magazine had changed little in the thirty years he had been a member.

61. Schulten, *Geographical Imagination*, 170.

62. Readers praised, for example, Ralph Stock's "The Dream Ship: The Story of a Voyage of Adventure More Than Half around the World in a 47-Foot Lifeboat," *NGM* 39.1 (January 1921); and Robert F. Griggs's "Our Greatest National Monument: An Account of the NGS's Completion of its Explorations in the Valley of Ten Thousand Smokes," *NGM* 39.9 (September 1921).

63. Stocking, "Ethnographic Sensibility," 209.

64. Paul Boyd, Schenectady, N.Y., December 1, 1920, Commendations and Criticisms, 1912–21; Mrs. S. G. Roadcap, February 4, 1926, Commendations and Criticisms, 1921–26; George Fullerton Evans, June 23, 1920, Commendations and Criticisms, 1912–1921, microfilm, Records Division, NGSA.

65. D. A. Saw, Amsterdam, Calif., February 8, 1915, Commendations and Criticisms, 1912–21; George M. Jenkins, Yetholm, Roxburghshire, Scotland, October 3, 1933, Commendations and Criticisms, 1932–35, microfilm, Records Division, NGSA.

66. A graph showed that from 1904 to 1908, membership had increased almost eightfold, growing from a meager 3,256 in 1904 to 38,698 in 1908 ("From 1,000 in 1899 to More Than 750,000 Subscribers in 1920," advertising circulars from 1925 and 1935, Advertising Collection, NGSA).

67. L. E. Wettling, Lincoln, Nebr., July 23, 1914; Charles Gerhardt, Circleville, Ohio, August 28, 1914, Commendations and Criticisms, 1912–22; Alexander Ralph, Mt. Albert, Auckland, New Zealand, August 1, 1926; Charles S. Muir, Philadelphia, Pa., undated, Commendations and Criticisms, 1921–26, microfilm, Records Division, NGSA.

68. James D. Kent, Garden City, N.Y., December 8, 1913, Commendations and Criticisms, 1912–21, microfilm, Records Division, NGSA.

69. Rev. R. Cahill, Le Sueur, Minn., June 7, 1919, Commendations and Criticisms, 1912–21; A. E. McKee, Columbus, Ohio, March 23, 1928, Commendations and Criticisms 1921–26, microfilm, Records Division, NGSA.

70. Benjamin R. Landis, no address, May 20, 1917, Commendations and Criticisms, 1912–21. Mrs. George F. Merryman echoed Landis's comment, writing, "Two books always seen on our library table are the Bible and the *Geographic Magazine*" (Indianapolis, Ind., May 11, 1926). Louis W. Spradling, a doctor from Athens, Tenn., similarly wrote: "I find 'The *Geographic*' about as much of an essential around my household, as

is the Bible" (September 8, 1926), Commendations and Criticisms, 1921–26, microfilm, Records Division, NGSA.

71. Siegel, "Talking through the 'Fotygraft Album,'" 243, 249.

72. O. R. Goldman, Gadsden, Ala., July 8, 1918, Commendations and Criticisms, 1912–22; D. B. Evans, Gold Coast, Africa, November 6, 1926, Commendations and Criticisms, 1921–26, microfilm, Records Division, NGSA.

73. Buxbaum, *Collecting National Geographic Magazines,* (1935), 63, 48. In 1956, and again in 1962, Buxbaum turned out an enormously expanded second edition of the *Collector's Guide* (*Collector's Guide* [1962], 11).

74. Mrs. L. B. Greenfield, Springdale, Ark., October 29, 1921, Commendations and Criticisms, 1912–21; Rev. A. Peterson, Joliette, Quebec, March 22, 1926; V. de Lacy Evans, Longwarry, Victoria, Australia, January 25, 1926, Commendations and Criticisms, 1921–26, microfilm, Records Division, NGSA.

75. R. A. Warden, Mill Valley, Calif., November 2, 1930; Miss R. Tallantyre, New Orleans, La., November 22, 1930, Commendations and Criticisms, 1930–32, microfilm, Records Division, NGSA; Hannerz, "Cosmopolitans and Locals in World Culture," 239.

76. W. C. Allen, Santa Rosa, Calif., April 23, 1926, Commendations and Criticisms, 1921–26, microfilm, Records Division, NGSA; Friday, *Aesthetics and Photography,* 34.

77. A. S. Juncken, Kingswood, South Australia, May 15, 1918, Commendations and Criticisms, 1912–22, microfilm, Records Division, NGSA. The same photograph taken by Underwood, and Underwood appears without the plane in *American Review of Reviews* 57.1 (January 1918): 49.

78. C. P. Sherman, Philadelphia, Pa., March 6, 1914; H. G. Buehler, Lakeville, Conn., November 5, 1919, Commendations and Criticisms, 1912–22, microfilm, Records Division, NGSA.

79. Elizabeth Sutton Brown, Denver, Colo., April 25, 1917. Several readers noted the same error: Frank Shell, Newman, Ill., April 20, 1917; O. J. Salo, Red Lodge, Mont., April 15, 1917, Commendations and Criticisms, 1912–22, microfilm, Records Division, NGSA.

80. Kono Hikotaro, New York, N.Y., October 6, 1924; E. H. Twamley, Davenport, Iowa, August 28, 1925, Commendations and Criticisms, 1921–26, microfilm, Records Division, NGSA.

81. Schulten, *Geographical Imagination,* 153.

82. See I. Ross, "Geography, Inc."

83. Harris, *Cultural Excursions,* 311.

84. Banks and Morphy, *Rethinking Visual Anthropology,* 21.

85. I borrow this term from the separate, but not entirely unrelated, context of autobiographical realism in Paul John Eakin's *Touching the World: Reference in Autobiography* (Princeton: Princeton University Press, 1992), 52.

3. Savage Visions

1. Leander C. Claflin, Commendations and Criticisms, 1912–1921, microfilm, Records Division, NGSA.

2. On dating the culture concept, see Evans, *Before Cultures,* 3.

3. See Evans's discussion of "circulating culture" in *Before Cultures,* 20.

4. *Selected Writings of Gertrude Stein* (New York: Vintage, 1990), 258.

5. Torgovnick, *Gone Primitive,* 8

6. Elliott, *Culture Concept,* 74.

7. Glazener, *Reading for Realism,* 160.

8. Elliott, *Culture Concept,* 61.

9. Rev. R. Pawlikowski, Passaic, N.J., January 14, 1921, Commendations and Criticisms, 1912–21; Frank J. Mayr, Erie, Pa., May 31, 1926, Commendations and Criticisms, 1921–26, microfilm, Records Division, NGSA.

10. Young, *Colonial Desire,* 41.

11. See also "The Texas Delta of an American Nile," *NGM* 75.1 (January 1939).

12. Torgovnick, *Gone Primitive,* 8.

13. Clifford, "On Ethnographic Allegory," 112.

14. Lears, *No Place of Grace,* 5.

15. Advertising pages, *NGM* 24.12 (December 1913); "A Latter Day Fable of the Three Wise Men" (1919), Advertising Collection, NGSA.

16. Chapin, "Glimpses of Korea," 895, 902. The term "local color" as a designation for the quaint and picturesque appears throughout *National Geographic* history (see "In Quaint, Curious Croatia" *NGM* 19.12 [December 1908]; "The Transformation of Turkey" *NGM* 75.1 [January 1939]; and "Down Mark Twain's River on a Raft" *NGM* 93.4 [April 1948]).

17. "Adventures with a Camera," 90, my emphasis; Steet, *Veils and Daggers,* 54. Many such images are indebted to the circulation of imperial postcards (see Alloula, *Colonial Harem*).

18. M. Williams, "Adventures with a Camera," 111.

19. Frederick Simpich, "Along the Nile, through Egypt and the Sudan," *NGM* 42.4 (October 1922): 400.

20. Sekula, "The Body and the Archive," 351.

21. See Kate Chopin, *The Awakening,* chap. 12. Michelle A. Brinbaum, "'Alien Hands': Kate Chopin and the Colonization of Race." *American Literature* 66.2 (June 1994): 301–23; Evans, *Before Cultures,* 144.

22. Carleton R. S. Malcolm, Argyll, Scotland, May 22, 1926, Commendations and Criticisms, 1921–26, microfilm, Records Division, NGSA; Murphy, "Romance of Science in Polynesia," 370.

23. For a history of the aesthetic arts movement in relation to local-color fiction, see Evans, *Before Culture,* 147–51.

24. "The Society in 1903: A General Overview," *National Geographic Timeline,* http://inside.ngs.org/intranet/history.nsf, November 11, 2004, Records Division, NGSA.

25. Evans, *Before Cultures,* 134. Maxfield Parrish's August 1897 poster for the *Century Illustrated Monthly* depicts a nude white woman in a forested glade. Her hands are clasped around her knees as she gazes reflectively up at the sky.

26. White, "Nude in Photography," 80.

27. Florence A. Bright, no address, November 7, 1919, Commendations and Criticisms, 1912–21, microfilm, Records Division, NGSA.

28. According to the *Oxford English Dictionary,* the word "queer" had already acquired homoerotic connotations by 1914.

29. See West, *Back to Africa;* Liebenow, *Liberia: The Quest for Democracy;* and Moran, *Liberia: The Violence of Democracy.*

30. Johnston and Lyon, "Black Republic," 339.

31. Folkner, "Conditions in Liberia," 735.

32. Gellner, *Nations and Nationalism,* 7.

33. West, *Back to Africa,* 257. See also Henry S. Villard's 1948 article "Rubber-Cushioned Liberia," which provides visual testimony of just how closely Firestone's plantation approximated the slave quarters of the South.

34. Lutz and Collins, *Reading "National Geographic,"* 29.

35. Cartier-Bresson, *Mind's Eye,* 23. In the 1980s, *National Geographic* photographers saw themselves as heirs to Cartier-Bresson (see Lutz and Collins, *Reading "National Geographic,"* 59).

36. Ammons and Rohy, *American Local Color Writing,* 7–30; Bunnell, *Photographic Vision,* 1–7.

37. Hine's photographs appear in Graves, "Human Emotion Recorded by Photography." "North American Indians" (July 1907), features fourteen of Curtis's photographs. Warner's "Country Where Going to America Is an Industry" (December 1909) features twenty-six of von Gloeden's portraits.

38. Tagg's *Burden of Representation* articulates a Marxist-Foucaldian argument that has predominated in studies of nineteenth-century photography.

39. Marien, *Photography and Its Critics,* 83–85.

40. Strain, *Public Places, Private Journeys,* 75.

41. Robinson, *Pictorial Effect in Photography,* 18, 13–14.

42. Bunnell, introduction to *A Photographic Vision,* 1–7.

43. "The Washington Salon and Art Photographic Exhibit of 1896," National Museum of American History, Smithsonian Institute, http://americanhistory.si.edu/1896/index.htm.

44. Livingston, Fralin, and Haun, *Odyssey,* 20.

45. White, "Nude in Photography," 81.

46. Warner, "A Country," 1069.

47. Ibid., 1093, 1083. For more on von Gloeden's homoerotic photographs, see Jason Goldman, "'The Golden Age of Gay Porn': Nostalgia and the Photography of Wilhelm von Gloeden," *GLQ* 12.2 (2006): 237–58.

48. E. Edwards, "Image as Anthropological Document," 243.

49. Conner, "Forgotten Ruins of Indo-China," 216.

50. Alpers, "Museum as a Way of Seeing," 27.

51. Kirshenblatt-Gimblett, "Objects of Ethnography," 410.

52. Haardt, "Through the Deserts and Jungles," 703.

53. Griffiths, *Wondrous Difference,* 17–22.

54. Lutz and Collins, *Reading "National Geographic,"* 207–8.

55. Mitchell, *Picture Theory,* 57.

56. Clifford, "On Ethnographic Allegory," 100–101.

57. James Bryce, "The Scenery of North America," *NGM* 41.4 (April 1922): 385. See Foley, *Spectres of 1919.*

58. Shay, "From Cairo to Cape Town Overland," 245.

59. Jones, *Strange Talk,* 137.

60. Burgin, "Looking at Photographs," 56.

61. Bramen, *Uses of Variety,* 207.

62. Bell, "A Few Thoughts Concerning Eugenics," 12.

63. Ward belonged to the Immigration Restriction League and was a secretary of the American Breeders' Association, a eugenicist society (Higham, *Strangers in the Land,* 152; Haller, *Eugenics*).

64. Marlatt, "Pests and Parasites," 208, 213.

65. Gannett, "Movement of Our Population," 37; Ward, "Our Immigration Laws," 12.

66. Fairchild, "Book of Monsters," 98.

67. Benjamin, "Work of Art," 246.

68. Fairchild, "Book of Monsters," 91.

69. Godlewska and Smith, "Critical Histories of Geography," 2.

70. Pratt, *Imperial Eyes;* Rothenberg, *Presenting America's World,* 100–103.

71. Sontag, *On Photography,* 14; Cleaves, "Hunting with the Lens," 1.

72. M. Williams, "Adventures with a Camera," 87; Kopper, "*National Geographic* Photographers," 15.

73. Bederman, *Manliness and Civilization,* 191–93.

74. Haraway, *Primate Visions,* 29, 28–29.

75. Clifford, "On Ethnographic Allegory," 112.

76. For a related argument, see Dunaway, *Natural Visions;* he does not address the camera's presence in wildlife photography.

77. Novak, *Nature and Culture,* 200.

78. Lutz and Collins found that between 1967 and 1986, canoes in *National Geographic* symbolized "a route out of a traditional life-style," while serving equally "as an icon for it" (*Reading "National Geographic,"* 137).

79. Novak, *Nature and Culture,* 171.

80. Harris, *Cultural Excursions,* 313.

81. Ibid.

82. Worcester, "Taal Volcano," 346; Kolb and Kolb, "Experiences in the Grand Canyon," 128.

83. Kaplan, *Anarchy of Empire,* 117.

84. Livingston, Fralin, and Haun, *Odyssey,* 33.

85. Finley, "Hunting Birds," 160.

86. *NGS and Its Magazine* (1957), 324.

87. Stevens, "Exploring the Valley of the Amazon," 359.

88. Metz, "The Imaginary Signifier," 735; Strain, *Public Places, Private Journeys,* 19.

89. Metz, "The Imaginary Signifier," 735.

4. Fracturing the Global Family Romance

1. Perry, *Young America,* 3–6; Sanchez-Eppler, *Dependent States,* 189.

2. Lansing, "Prussianism," 456, 552.

3. Higham, *Strangers in the Land,* 215.

4. Koon, *Believe, Obey, Fight,* xv.

5. See Blake, *Beloved Community.*

6. Higham, *Strangers in the Land,* 214.

7. Myra Hedges, Philadelphia, Pa., August 24, 1914; Lewis Hosea, Cincinnati, Ohio, November 30, 1914, Commendations and Criticisms, 1912–21, microfilm, Records Division, NGSA.

8. Perry, *Young America,* 2.

9. Sànchez-Eppler, *Dependent States,* xv.

10. Gellner, *Nations and Nationalism,* 1.

11. Dewey, *Democracy and Education,* 163; Bourne, "Trans-National America," 120.

12. Bramen, *Uses of Variety,* 13.

13. Schulten, *Geographical Imagination,* 166–67.

14. Higham, *Strangers in the Land,* 196.

15. Adams, "In French Lorraine," 504; Taft, "Health and Morale," 235; "Races of Europe," 597.

16. Reinhold Jentzsch, no address, February 14, 1919; E. G. Huttmann, Ashley, N.D., September 18, 1919, Commendations and Criticisms, 1912–22, microfilm, Records Division, NGSA.

17. Showalter, "America's New Soldier Cities," 474.

18. Sanchez-Eppler, *Dependent States,* 225. Between 1916 and 1919, 90 percent of Rockwell's illustrations for *Saturday Evening Post* were of children (Thomas S. Buechner, *Norman Rockwell: A Sixty Year Retrospective* [New York: Abrams, 1972], 52).

19. Susman, *Culture as History,* 273.

20. Hazel Lane, Davenport, Iowa, May 13, 1917; Eugene Wehmeyr, New York, N.Y., May 15, 1917; Rev. Thomas Petersen, Marion, Tex., November 25, 1917; A. E. Breen, Mt. Morris, N.Y., May 7, 1917; Reverend C. Meyer, Therasa, Wisc., June 1919, Commendations and Criticisms, 1912–22, microfilm, Records Division, NGSA.

21. Higham, *Strangers in the Land,* 211.

22. See Tuason, "Ideology of Empire"; Schulten, *Geographical Imagination;* and Rothenberg, *Presenting America's World.*

23. Johnson, "Self-Determining Haiti II," 265.

24. Henry G. Wincor, no address, December 1920; Hugo Mueller, Rosholt, Wisc., December 1920, Commendations and Criticisms, 1912–22, microfilm, Records Division, NGSA. For more on the *Nation's* public repudiation of *National Geographic,* see Rothenberg, *Presenting America's World,* 64.

25. J. Williams, "Ties That Bind," 281–82.

26. Walter Collins, Voltaire, Calif., May 21, 1917; Lucy C. Donoghue, July 7, 1917, Seattle, Wash., Commendations and Criticisms, 1912–22, microfilm, Records Division, NGSA.

27. Mrs. C. R. Daniels, June 18, 1917, Islington, Mass.; A. E. Breen, Mt. Morris, N.Y., May 7, 1917; E. A. Brenholtz, Turnersville, Tex., July 20, 1917, Commendations and Criticisms, 1912–22, microfilm, Records Division, NGSA.

28. Washburn, "Russian Situation," 377, 382.

29. Held and McGrew, *Globalization/Anti-Globalization,* 131.

30. Taft, "A Poisoned World," 460; Baker, "America's Duty," 453.

31. Tindall and Shi, *America: A Narrative History,* 935.

32. See, for example, Alfred M. Hitchcock, "The Relation of the Picture Play to Literature," *English Journal* 4.5 (May 1915): 292–98; and J. O. Engleman, "Outside Reading," *English Journal* 6.1 (January 1917): 20–27.

33. Schulten, *Geographical Imagination,* 8.

34. Ibid., 166–67.

35. Ibid., 85.

36. Krysto, "Bringing the World," 82–83.

37. GHG to JLB, June 15, 1915, GHG Collection, 1914–15, microfilm, Records Division, NGSA.

38. "Climbing the Greased Pole"; "Rides a Sorrel Horse"; "Transplanting Rice," Pictorial Geography, Records Division, NGSA.

39. JLB to GHG, October 7, 1914, GHG Collection, 1914–15, microfilm, Records Division, NGSA.

40. "Birth of the 'School Bulletin,'" Records Division, NGSA.

41. GNB, October 13, 1919, reprinted from the *Brooklyn Eagle,* September 27, 1919; GNB, November 3, 1919; GNB, October 4, 1920; GNB, January 24, 1921, Records Division, NGSA.

42. J. W. Gamel, Roswell, N.M., November 20, 1920; McCluer H. Parker, no address, 1921, Commendations and Criticisms, 1912–22, microfilm, Records Division, NGSA.

43. Higham, *Strangers in the Land,* 223–25.

44. GHG to AGB, May 14, 1917; GHG to AGB, May 13, 1921, GFP Box 100, Manuscript Collection, LC.

45. Paxton, *Anatomy of Fascism,* 23.

46. See Arendt's *Eichmann in Jerusalem: A Report on the Banality of Evil* (1963); see also Paxton, *Anatomy of Fascism;* Carsten, *Rise of Fascism;* and Payne, *History of Fascism.*

47. See Higham, *Strangers in the Land,* 142; and Paxton, *Anatomy of Fascism,* 34.

48. Freud, "Family Romances," 240–41.

49. Zalampas, *Hitler and the Third Reich,* 2–3, 8.

50. Quoted in Poole, *Explorer's House,* 118; Higham, *Strangers in the Land,* 279.

51. See Gellner, *Nations and Nationalism,* 143–46.

52. Zalampas, *Hitler and the Third Reich,* 17; Payne, *History of Fascism,* 230, 231–32, 218.

53. In his recognition of Germany's consolidation of the economic and social systems of production, i.e., "rationalization," Eyre invokes Max Weber, who uses the term in his *Protestant Ethic and the Spirit of Capitalism* (1930).

54. See Bergmeier and Lotz, *Hitler's Airwaves;* and J. Edwards, *Berlin Calling.*

55. Payne, *History of Fascism,* 9.

56. Quoted in Poole, *Explorer's House,* 175.

57. Frederick H. Vosburgh, unpublished memoirs, November 30, 1998, Records Division, NGSA.

58. Bartoletti, *Hitler Youth,* 40–43, 46.

59. For more on Mussolini's modernization of Italy, see, for example, Gelasio Caetani's "Redemption of the Pontine Marshes," *NGM* 66.2 (August 1934).

60. Patric, "Imperial Rome," 280.

61. Hariman and Lucaites, *No Caption Needed,* 35–36.

62. Koon, *Believe, Obey, Fight,* xvii.

63. Arthur Koegel, Chicago, Ill., March 23, 1937; Mrs. Fay Wilson, Fort Worth, Tex., February 15, 1937, Commendations and Criticisms, 1937–38, microfilm, Records Division, NGSA.

64. A. L. Dell, August 23, 1938; M. G. Dubois, Newark, N.J., February 16, 1938, Commendations and Criticisms, 1937–38, microfilm, Records Division, NGSA.

65. Bartoletti, *Hitler Youth,* 110–11; Koon, *Believe, Obey, Fight,* xx–xxi.

66. Mason Hawkins, "A Plea for World Culture," *Journal of Negro History* 19.1 (January 1934): 44.

67. Mary Elizabeth Smith, "Periodicals in the Classroom," *English Journal* 28.5 (May 1939): 372; Arno Jewett, "Detecting and Analyzing Propaganda," *English Journal* 29.2 (February 1940): 105–6.

68. Minnie C. Squire, "We Read behind the Lines," *English Journal* 29.7 (September 1940): 556, 558. See, for example, Dora V. Smith, "Today's Challenge to Teachers of English," *English Journal* 30.2 (February 1941): 101–13; Harold A. Anderson et al., "Basic Aims for English Instruction in American Schools," *English Journal* 31.1. (January 1942): 40–55; Vivian E. Bergland, "A Study of Prejudice for High-School English Classes," *English Journal* 34.8 (October 1945): 444–47; Nathaniel Tillman, "Literacy in a Democracy," *Phylon* 7.3 (3rd quarter 1946): 284–88.

69. Bourne, "Trans-National America," 120. The term "melting pot" derived from Israel Zangwill's popular 1908 play by that name (see Bramen, *Uses of Variety,* 11, 17).

5. Jungle Housekeeping

1. The term "White Hunter" was a common name for the white male guides who accompanied travelers on safari (Shay, "From Cairo to Cape Town," 195–96).

2. Harnden, "Keeping House in Majorca," 425; Stocking, "Ethnographic Sensibility," 216.

3. Calvin, "Nakwasina Goes North," 1; Tambs, "Modern Saga of the Seas," 649.

4. Albee and Albee, "Family Afoot in Yukon Wilds," 589.

5. Mrs. W. R. Poulterer, Audubon, N.J., February 9, 1934, Commendations and Criticisms, 1932–35, microfilm, Records Division, NGSA.

6. Butler, *Gender Trouble,* 176.

7. Bauman, "Performance," 262–63.

8. Companionate marriage was popularized by Ben B. Lindsay and Wainright Evans in their 1925 *Revolt of Modern Youth.* See Mintz and Kellogg, *Domestic Revolutions,* 115.

9. See Bauman and Briggs, "Poetics and Performance," 61.

10. Bauman, "Performance," 266.

11. Marcus and Fischer, *Anthropology as Cultural Critique,* 32–33.

12. Tomlinson, *Globalization and Culture,* 161.

13. See Mintz and Kellogg, *Domestic Revolutions;* Matthews, *Just a Housewife;* Tobey, *Technology as Freedom;* and Kyvig, *Daily Life in the United States, 1920–1940.* See also Lears, *Fables of Abundance.*

14. *NGM* 51.1 (January 1927); Mrs. Evelyn M. Mance, Chelmsford, England, December 29, 1930, Commendations and Criticisms, 1930–32, microfilm, Records Division, NGSA.

15. Hamilton, "Keeping House in Borneo," 316. Travel as if by "time machine" to human origins is a familiar ethnographic motif (see Rony, *The Third Eye*, 10).

16. Bates, "Keeping House for a Biologist in Columbia," 260, 252–53. For similar language, see Hamilton, "Keeping House in Borneo"; and Tambs, "A Modern Saga of the Seas."

17. Fabian, *Time and the Other*, 30.

18. McClintock, *Imperial Leather*, 30, 40; Strain, *Public Places, Private Journeys*, 27; Fabian, *Time and the Other*, 31.

19. See Pratt, "Fieldwork in Common Places," 36.

20. Daniel Defoe's novel *Robinson Crusoe* inspired Johan David Wyss's *Der Schweizerische Robinson* (1819), later produced in English translation by William H. G. Kingston at the height of British imperialism in 1879.

21. Mills, *Discourses of Difference*, 27.

22. Hoover, "Keeping House," 505.

23. Gill, "Mrs. Robinson Crusoe," 143.

24. Mintz and Kellogg, *Domestic Revolutions*, 133.

25. "The Geographic's Upper Masses," 1930, Advertising Collection, NGSA.

26. Advertising circulars from 1925 and 1935, respectively, Advertising Collection, NGSA.

27. Mintz and Kellogg, *Domestic Revolutions*, 134.

28. W. F. Schrader, Fort Wayne, Ind., November 23, 1932; Mrs. O. D. Nelson, Greensboro, N.C., November 23, 1932; Edith DuBois Meyer, Toms River, N.J., November 26, 1932, Commendations and Criticisms, 1930–32, microfilm, Records Division, NGSA.

29. Cooper, "Two Fighting Tribes," 473.

30. G. R. Carlin, April 11, 1930, Halifax, England, Commendations and Criticisms, 1930–32, microfilm, Records Division, NGSA.

31. Imperato and Imperato, *They Married Adventure*, 168. See, for example, "Three Fulah-kunda Women Present the African 'Permanent Wave,'" in De Chételat, "My Domestic Life," 703.

32. See Rothenberg, "*National Geographic*'s World," 124.

33. Rose Scorgie, February 6, 1925, Richmond, Va.; C. L. McDavitt, February 17, 1925, Fort Wayne, Ind.; M. W. Cadwallader, February 1925, Waterloo, Ind., NGS Archives, Commendations and Criticisms, 1921–26, microfilm, Records Division, NGSA.

34. G. Savels, February 10, 1925, Alameda, Calif., Commendations and Criticisms, 1921–26, microfilm, Records Division, NGSA.

35. See Rony, *Third Eye*, 4.

36. Pratt, *Imperial Eyes*, 213.

37. Mills, *Discourses of Difference*, 23; *Imperial Eyes*, 215; Wexler, *Tender Violence*, 8–9.

38. Schmitt, "Voyage to the Island Home," 353, 355.

39. Shor and Shor, "We Took the Highroad," 675.

40. Lockley, "We Live Alone," 265.

41. Imperato and Imperato, *They Married Adventure*, 101, 74.

42. Matthews, *Just a Housewife*, 200–201.

43. Kaplan, *Anarchy of Empire*, 111.

44. Shor and Shor, "We Took the Highroad," 680; see also Shor and Shor, "We Dwelt in Kashgai Tents," 810.

45. Siemel, "Jungle Was My Home," 701.

46. See Mills, *Discourses of Difference.*

47. Wexler, *Tender Violence,* 10.

48. Stoler, "Intimidations of Empire," 2.

49. Ibid., 11.

50. Anne Morrow Lindbergh served as her husband's copilot throughout their 1933 circumnavigation of the Atlantic (see Lindbergh, "Flying around the North Atlantic").

51. See Stocking, "Ethnographic Sensibility"; Geertz, *Works and Lives;* and Marcus and Fischer, *Anthropology as Cultural Critique.*

52. Wexler, *Tender Violence,* 11.

53. Geertz, *Works and Lives,* 106.

54. Marion Stirling, "Jungle Housekeeping," 319; Hamilton, "Keeping House in Borneo," 309, 316.

55. See, for example, Langley, "I Kept House in a Jungle," 100.

56. Edensor, *National Identity,* 63.

57. Hamilton, "Keeping House in Borneo," 301.

58. Langley, "I Kept House in a Jungle," 115.

59. Bauman, "Performance," 266.

60. Barthes, *Camera Lucida,* 26–27, 32.

61. Lutz and Collins, *Reading "National Geographic,"* 64.

62. M. Williams, "Adventures with a Camera," 92–93.

63. Latour, "Give Me a Laboratory," 259.

64. Ruby, *Picturing Culture,* 170.

65. Grimshaw, "Eye in the Door," 46.

66. Grosvenor, *NGS and Its Magazine,* 96.

67. Benjamin, "Work of Art," 236–37.

68. Wilson, "Rhetoric of Consumption," 43.

69. See Said, *Orientalism.*

70. May, *Homeward Bound,* 105.

71. See, for example, Frank Craighead and John Craighead, "We Survive on a Pacific Atoll."

72. Lutz and Collins, *Reading "National Geographic,"* 36.

73. Steet, *Veils and Daggers,* 79.

74. Cresson, "We Lived in Turbulent Tehran," 707.

75. Cresson and Cresson, "American Family in Afghanistan," 417. See, for example, Mary Mills Patrick's, "The Emancipation of Mohammedan Women" (January 1909), where she describes women's active role in Turkey's modernization (42–43); and Ella C. Sykes's "A Talk about Persia and Its Women" (October 1910), in which she describes how the architecture of Persian women's homes reflects their political and social containment.

76. Steet, *Veils and Daggers,* 79, 107.

77. See Patric, "Imperial Rome."

78. Glissant, *Poetics of Relation,* 8.

79. Matthew Stirling, "Exploring the Past," 374.

80. "The *National Geographic Magazine* 1953 Distribution Analysis," Advertising Collection, NGSA. For *Life*'s subscription statistics, see Kozol, *"Life"'s America,* 35.

81. Mrs. Claire Ashkin, November 6, 1951, Pittsburgh, Pa., Commendations and Criticisms, 1946–54, microfilm, Records Division, NGSA.

6. *National Geographic*'s **Romance in Ruins**

1. C. A. Ferriss, Brinnon, Wash., April 20, 1927; unattributed author, Lansing, Mich., April 27, 1927; Judge Robert L. Henry, Bulkeley, Egypt, November 19, 1927, 1927 Criticism, microfilm, Records Division, NGSA.

2. Signed "Member," no address, November 26, 1927, microfilm, Records Division, NGSA.

3. Mrs. Reone Nabours, Los Angeles, Calif., October 31, 1949, Commendations and Criticism, 1949–52, microfilm, Records Division, NGSA.

4. Hariman and Lucaites, *No Caption Needed,* 39.

5. Ibid., 120, 116–17.

6. Sontag, "Notes on 'Camp,'" 280.

7. While not explicitly referencing the term, "camp," Judith Butler's *Gender Trouble* comments on drag as a form of "gender parody" (175) that reflects ironically on the various cultural scripts informing gendered behaviors.

8. Clifford, "Ethnographic Allegory," 112.

9. Ross, "Uses of Camp," 320.

10. Core, *Camp,* 205; Sontag, "Notes on 'Camp,'" 277.

11. Sontag, "Notes on 'Camp,'" 282.

12. Lutz and Collins call *National Geographic* "high middlebrow" in its cultural sensibilities (*Reading "National Geographic,"* 7).

13. Sontag, "Notes on 'Camp,'" 283.

14. Abrams, *Natural Supernaturalism,* 97–113. See also Nicolson, *Mountain Gloom,* 15–16.

15. Volcanoes and earthquakes are prime examples of *National Geographic*'s "catastrophic sublime." In the cumulative index for 1899 to 1940, there are forty-eight entries for "volcano" and eighteen for "earthquake."

16. Worcester, "Taal Volcano," 345, 334.

17. Kaplan, *Anarchy of Empire,* 114.

18. See Mulvey, "Visual Pleasure," 750.

19. Burdett and Duncan, *Cultural Encounters,* 6.

20. Sontag, "Notes on 'Camp,'" 289.

21. See Bhabha, "Other Question," 107.

22. Rock, "Experiences of a Lone Geographer."

23. Sutton, *China's Border Provinces,* 29–34.

24. Ibid., 15.

25. Hannerz, "Cosmopolitans and Locals," 241; Sontag, "Anthropologist as Hero," 74.

26. Lutz and Collins, *Reading "National Geographic,"* 69.

27. Bederman, *Manliness and Civilization,* 44.

28. Skrbis, Kendall, and Woodward, "Locating Cosmopolitanism," 122.

29. Sutton, *China's Border Provinces*, 106–7.

30. My emphasis. Rock, "Hunting the Chaulmoogra Tree," File No: 20.1352, microfilm, Records Division, NGSA.

31. Ibid.

32. Stocking, "Ethnographic Sensibility," 245.

33. Core, *Camp*.

34. See "Shangri-La Paradise Lost, Found, Relocated," *China Online*, March 16, 2001; and "Chinese Government Puts Shangri-la on the Map," *Reuters English News Service*, January 7, 2002 (Courtesy NGSA). See Allen, *Search for Shangri-La*, 40–41, which confirms Hilton's familiarity with Rock's travels published in *Life* and *National Geographic*.

35. Although Baskul is a city in present-day Iran, in Hilton's novel Baskul is the name of a fictive city somewhere near the Afghanistan and Pakistan border with China.

36. "Shangri-La" was Hilton's coinage (see Allen, *Search for Shangri-La*, 40–41).

37. Kirshenblatt-Gimblett, "Objects of Ethnography," 434.

38. See Charles S. Braden, "The Novelist Discovers the Orient," *Far Eastern Quarterly* 7.2 (February 1948): 169; and Warren French, "The First Year of the Paperback Revolution," *College English* 25.4 (January 1964): 256.

39. See Thomas Richards, "Archive and Utopia," *Representations* 37 (Winter 1992): 104–35.

40. For such lofty descriptions, see Rock, "Through the Great River Trenches," 185.

41. Sutton, *China's Border Provinces*, 77.

42. Tomlinson, *Global Culture*, 107–11.

43. "Shangri-La Paradise, Lost, Found, Relocated," *China Online*, March 16, 2001 (Courtesy Mark Jenkins, NGSA).

44. H. M. Pratt. Fort Dodge, Iowa, September 28, 1933, Commendations and Criticisms, 1932–35; Glyda J. Fish, Kendallville, Ind., February 8, 1932, Commendations and Criticisms, 1930–32, microfilm, Records Division, NGSA.

45. "NGS Correspondence," GFP, Box 267, Manuscript Division, LC.

46. I. Ross, "Geography, Inc.," 614.

47. See Anderson, *Imagined Communities*.

48. Some of these clippings appear in "NGS Correspondence," GFP, Box 267, Manuscripts Division, LC.

49. Core, *Camp*, 119. The image recalls Lawrence's fanciful descriptions of the Middle East in his *Seven Pillars of Wisdom* (1926) (see Spurr, *Rhetoric of Empire*, 130).

50. George C. Stokes, Streator, Ill., January 4, 1930, Commendations and Criticisms, 1929–30, microfilm, Records Division, NGSA.

51. Pedro Espinosa, Mazatlan, Mexico, June 27, 1930; Mrs. Margaret Warendorf-Konijn, Netherlands, June 2, 1930; S. Edwardes, Katha, Upper Burma, June 21, 1930, Commendations and Criticisms, 1930–32, microfilm, Records Division, NGSA.

52. Dewey, *Democracy and Education*, 58.

53. Letter to unknown recipient, dated June 28, 1956, in *The Habit of Being: Letters of Flannery O'Connor*, ed. Sally Fitzgerald (New York: Farrar, Straus, and Giroux, 1979), 164.

54. See a Garret Price cartoon in the *New Yorker*, December 5, 1931, showing a wife standing above a morose husband. A *National Geographic* dangles from his hand as he

stares vacantly at the floor. She admonishes him, "If you don't quit your mooning, not another 'National Geographic' comes into this house." See also *Esquire* 33.1 (January 1950), in which a caveman dragging a woman by the feet remarks, "Smile, honey. He says it's for the *National Geographic.*" See also the *Christian Science Monitor,* May 28, 1952, in which a husband asks his scowling wife, "What's my collection of *National Geographics* doing down here?" A gaping hole in the ceiling answers the question.

55. Lee, *"New Yorker" Humor,* 40; Corey, *World through a Monocle,* 5–6.

56. Lee, *"New Yorker" Humor,* 288; Sontag, "Notes on 'Camp,'" 288.

57. Corey, *World through a Monocle,* 83.

58. *New Yorker,* July 21, 1934, 49.

59. Ibid., June 29, 1935, 34.

60. Lee, *"New Yorker" Humor,* 168.

61. Lutz and Collins, *Reading "National Geographic,"* 146.

62. Bhabha, "Other Question," 96.

63. Brink, "Secular Icons," 138; Hariman and Lucaites, "Performing Civic Identity," 372.

64. Commendations and Criticisms, 1921–26, H. C. Reisinger, Commendations and Criticisms, 1935, microfilm, Records Division, NGSA.

65. "Geography Unshackled—I," *New Yorker,* September 25, 1943, 32. See June 1932, June 1913, May 1914, and June 1913 issues, respectively.

66. Hellman, "Geography Unshackled—III," *New Yorker,* October 2, 1943, 27–28.

67. A. J. de Waal, Uiterwyk, Vlottenberg, South Africa, June 13, 1933; Mrs. Alice Thomassey, Haute-Saone, France, November 30, 1933; Wallace Shrimpton, Hawkis Bay, New Zealand, November 10, 1933, Commendations and Criticisms, 1932–35, microfilm, Records Division, NGSA.

68. Moddelmog, *Reading Desire,* 100.

69. July 4, 1939, Commendations and Criticisms, 1939, microfilm, Records Division, NGSA.

70. Lutz and Collins, *Reading "National Geographic,"* 37–40, 44.

71. Kirshenblatt-Gimblett, "Objects of Ethnography," 433.

72. Ibid., 410.

73. Lutz and Collins, *Reading "National Geographic,"* 41–42.

74. See Fred Ward's "Inside Cuba Today" (January 1977); Frank Hercules's "To Live in Harlem" (February 1977); "One Canada—or Two?" (April 1977); and "South Africa's Lonely Ordeal" (June 1977), commented on in Lutz and Collins, *Reading "National Geographic,"* 42–43.

75. Lutz and Collins, *Reading "National Geographic,"* 45–46.

76. Francesca's passion and vulnerability to Kincaid's romantic conquest recalls "The Italian Race" (January 1918) and "Italy, Land of History and Romance" (April 1924), in which Italians figure as hot-blooded types whose natures make them vulnerable to Greek conquest.

77. See Lears, *Fables,* 66.

78. See Jim Sanderson and Cecil Johnson. "Clint Eastwood's Last Cowboy: *The Bridges of Madison County,*" *Post Script* 15.3 (Winter 1995): 41–57. Jim Welsh, "Fixing *The Bridges of Madison County,*" *Literature/Film Quarterly* 23.3 (Winter 1995): 154, 228.

79. "NGS Scrapbook: References to the Geographic Serious and Otherwise," Records Division, NGSA.

80. Cleto, "Introduction: Queering the Camp," 20.

81. NGS archivist Renee Braden recalled that the archives department helped produce a mock cover of the covered bridges issue for the film. The seeming authenticity of the cover provoked numerous requests for the "original" *National Geographic* issue (Braden, interview by the author, August 2007).

82. Mitchell, *Picture Theory*, 13.

83. A. Ross, "Uses of Camp," 320.

84. William Carlos Williams, *Paterson* (New York: New Directions, 1963), 13.

85. Sontag, "Notes on 'Camp,'" 285; Cleto, "Introduction: Queering the Camp," 32.

Bibliography

Manuscript Sources

LIBRARY OF CONGRESS, WASHINGTON, D.C.
  Bell Papers
  Grosvenor Family Papers
NATIONAL GEOGRAPHIC SOCIETY ARCHIVES
  Advertising Collection
  Commendations and Criticisms, 1912–22, 1921–26, 1927, 1929–30, 1930–32, 1932–35, 1935, 1936–37, 1937–38, 1939, 1946–54
  GHG Collection, 1914–15
  Microfiche File No. 510-2.6034

Other Sources

Abrams, M. H. *Natural Supernaturalism: Tradition and Revolution in Romantic Literature.* New York: Norton, 1973.

Abramson, Howard S. *"National Geographic": Behind America's Lens on the World.* New York: Crown, 1987.

Adams, Harriet Chalmers. "East Indians in the New World." *NGM* 18.7 (July 1907): 484–92.

———. "In French Lorraine." *NGM* 32.5–6 (November–December 1917): 499–518.

Adorno, Theodor W., and Max Horkheimer. "The Culture Industry: Enlightenment as Mass Deception." In *Dialectic of Enlightenment: Philosophical Fragments,* edited by Gunzelin Schmid Noerr, translated by Edmund Jephcott, 94–136. Stanford, Calif.: Stanford University Press, 2002.

Albee, Ruth, and William Albee. "Family Afoot in Yukon Wilds." *NGM* 81.5 (May 1942): 589–616.

Allen, Charles. *The Search for Shangri-La: A Journey into Tibetan History.* London: Little, Brown, 1999.

Alloula, Malek. *The Colonial Harem: Images of Subconscious Eroticism.* Minneapolis: University of Minnesota Press, 1986.

Alpers, Svetlana. "The Museum as a Way of Seeing." In *Exhibiting Cultures: The Poetics and Politics of Museum Display,* edited by Ivan Karp and Steven D. Lavine, 25–32. Washington, D.C., and London: Smithsonian Institution Press, 1991.

Ammons, Elizabeth, and Valerie Rohy. Introduction to *American Local Color Writing, 1880–1920*, edited by Ammons and Rohy. New York: Penguin, 1998.

Anderson, Benedict. *Imagined Communities: Reflections on the Origin and Spread of Nationalism.* Rev. ed. London and New York: Verso, 1999.

Ang, Ien. *Watching Dallas: Soap Opera and the Melodramatic Imagination.* Translated by Della Couling. New York and London: Routledge, 1985.

Appadurai, Arjun. "Disjuncture and Difference in the Global Cultural Economy." In *Global Culture: Nationalism, Globalization and Modernity*, edited by Mike Featherstone, 295–310. London: Sage, 1990.

Asquith, Herbert Henry. "A Tribute to America." NGM 31.4 (April 1917): 295–96.

Austin, O. P. "An Around-the-World American Exposition." *NGM* 12.2 (February 1901): 49–53.

———. "Colonial Systems of the World." *NGM* 10.1 (January 1899): 21–26.

———. "Queer Methods of Travel in Curious Corners of the World." NGM 18.11 (November 1907): 687–715.

Baker, Newton D. "America's Duty." *NGM* 31.5 (May 1917): 453–57.

Banks, Marcus, and Howard Morphy. Introduction to *Rethinking Visual Anthropology*, edited by Banks and Morphy. New Haven and London: Yale University Press, 1997.

Barthes, Roland. *Camera Lucida: Reflections on Photography.* Translated by Richard Howard. New York: Hill and Wang, 1981.

Bartoletti, Susan Campbell. *Hitler Youth: Growing Up in Hitler's Shadow.* New York: Scholastic, 2005.

Bates, Nancy Bell Fairchild. "Keeping House for a Biologist in Columbia." *NGM* 94.8 (August 1948): 251–74.

Bauman, Richard. "Performance." In *International Encyclopedia of Communications*, vol. 3. New York and Oxford: Oxford University Press, 1989.

Bauman, Richard, and Charles L. Briggs. "Poetics and Performance as Critical Perspectives on Language and Social Life." *Annual Review of Anthropology* 19 (1990): 59–88.

Becker, George F. "The Witwatersrand and the Revolt of the Uitlanders." *NGM* 7.11 (November 1896): 349–67.

Bederman, Gail. *Manliness and Civilization: A Cultural History of Gender and Race in the United States, 1880–1917.* Chicago and London: University of Chicago Press, 1995.

Bell, Alexander Graham. "A Few Thoughts Concerning Eugenics." *NGM* 19.1 (January 1908): 119–23.

Benjamin, Walter. "The Work of Art in the Age of Mechanical Reproduction." In *Illuminations*, by Benjamin, edited by Hannah Arendt, translated by Harry Zohn, 217–51. New York: Schocken, 1969.

Bergmeier, Horst J. P., and Rainer E. Lotz. *Hitler's Airwaves: The Inside Story of Nazi Radio Broadcasting and Propaganda Swing.* New Haven and London: Yale University Press, 1997.

Bhabha, Homi K. "DisseminNation: Time, Narrative, and the Margins of the Modern Nation." In *Nation and Narration*, edited by Bhabha, 291–322. New York and London: Routledge, 2007.

——— . "The Other Question: Stereotype, Discrimination and the Discourse of

Colonialism." In *The Location of Culture*, edited by Bhabha, 94–120. London and New York: Routledge, 2007.

Bishop, Peter. *The Myth of Shangri-La: Tibet, Travel Writing, and the Western Creation of Sacred Landscape*. Berkeley and Los Angeles: University of California Press, 1989.

Blake, Casey Nelson. *Beloved Community: The Cultural Criticism of Randolph Bourne, Van Wyck Brooks, Waldo Frank, and Lewis Mumford*. Chapel Hill: University of North Carolina Press, 1990.

Blanchard, C. J. "The Call of the West." *NGM* 20.5 (May 1909): 403–37.

Bloom, Lisa. "Constructing Whiteness: Popular Science and *National Geographic* in the Age of Multiculturalism." *Configurations* 2.1 (1994): 15–32.

———. *Gender on Ice: American Ideologies of Polar Expeditions*. Minneapolis: University of Minnesota Press, 1993.

Bohlman, H. T. "Hunting Birds with a Camera." *NGM* 44.2 (August 1923): 161–201.

Boon, James A. *The Anthropological Romance of Bali, 1597–1972: Dynamic Perspectives in Marriage and Caste, Politics and Religion*. London: Cambridge University Press, 1977.

Booth, Mark. "*Campe-Toi!* On the Origins and Definitions of Camp." In *Camp: Queer Aesthetics and the Performing Subject: A Reader*, edited by Fabio Cleto, 66–79. Ann Arbor: University of Michigan Press, 1999.

Bourdieu, Pierre. *Photography: A Middle-brow Art*. Stanford: Stanford University Press, 1990.

Bourne, Randolph S. "Trans-National America." In *War and the Intellectuals: Collected Essays, 1915–1919*, edited by Carl Resek, 105–23. New York: Harper and Row, 1964.

Bramen, Carrie Tirado. *The Uses of Variety: Modern Americanism and the Quest for National Distinctiveness*. Cambridge: Harvard University Press, 2000.

Brink, Cordelia. "Secular Icons: Looking at Photographs from Nazi Concentration Camps." *History and Memory* 12.1 (Spring/Summer 2000): 135–50.

Bryan, C. D. B. *The National Geographic Society: 100 Years of Adventure and Discovery*. New York: Abrams, 1987.

Bunnell, Peter C. Introduction to *A Photographic Vision: Pictorial Photography, 1889–1923*, edited by Bunnell. Salt Lake City: Peregrine Smith, 1980.

Burdett, Charles, and Derek Duncan. *Cultural Encounters: European Travel Writing in the 1930s*. New York and Oxford: Berghahn, 2002.

Burgin, Victor. "Looking at Photographs." In *Thinking Photography*, edited by Burgin, 142–53. New York: Macmillan, 1984.

Burrall, Jessie L. "Sight-Seeing in School: Taking Twenty Million Children on a Picture Tour of the World." *NGM* 35.6 (June 1919): 489–500.

Butler, Judith. *Gender Trouble: Feminism and the Subversion of Identity*. New York and London: Routledge, 1999.

———. *Precarious Life: The Powers of Mourning and Violence*. New York and London: Verso, 2006.

Buxbaum, Edwin C. *Collecting "National Geographic" Magazines*. Milwaukee: Box Tree Press, 1935.

———. *Collector's Guide to the "National Geographic" Magazine*. Wilmington, Del., 1962.

Calvin, Jack. "Nakwasina Goes North." *NGM* 64.1 (July 1933): 1–42.

Carsten, F. L. *The Rise of Fascism.* 2nd ed. Berkeley and Los Angeles: University of California Press, 1982.

Cartier-Bresson, Henri. *The Mind's Eye: Writings on Photography and Photographers.* Millerton, N.Y.: Aperture, 1999.

Chakrabarty, Dipesh. *Provincializing Europe: Postcolonial Thought and Historical Difference.* Princeton and Oxford: Princeton University Press, 2000.

Chapin, William W. "Glimpses of Holland." *NGM* 27.1 (January 1915): 1–29.

———. "Glimpses of Korea and China." *NGM* 21.11 (November 1910): 895–934.

Chester, M. "Haiti: A Degenerating Island." *NGM* 19 (March 1908): 200–217.

Cleaves, Howard H. "Hunting with the Lens." *NGM* 26.1 (July 1914): 1–35.

Cleto, Fabio. "Queering the Camp." Introduction to *Camp: Queer Aesthetics and the Performing Subject: A Reader,* edited by Cleto, 1–42. Ann Arbor: University of Michigan Press, 1999.

Clifford, James. "On Ethnographic Allegory." In *Writing Culture: The Poetics and Politics of Ethnography,* edited by Clifford and George E. Marcus, 98–121. Berkeley and Los Angeles: University of California Press, 1986.

———. *The Predicament of Culture: Twentieth-Century Ethnography, Literature, and Art.* Cambridge: Harvard University Press, 1988.

Conn, Steven. *Museums and American Intellectual Life, 1876–1926.* Chicago and London: University of Chicago Press, 1998.

Conner, Jacob E. "The Forgotten Ruins of Indo-China." *NGM* 23.3 (March 1912): 209–72.

Cooper, Merian C. "Two Fighting Tribes of the Sudan." *NGM* 56.4 (October 1929): 465–86.

Core, Philip. *Camp: The Lie That Tells the Truth.* New York: Delilah, 1984.

Corey, Mary F. *The World through a Monocle: "The New Yorker" at Midcentury.* Cambridge and London: Harvard University Press, 1999.

Craighead, Frank, Jr., and John Craighead. "We Survive on a Pacific Atoll." *NGM* 93.1 (January 1948): 73–94.

Cremin, Lawrence. *The Transformation of the School: Progressivism in American Education, 1876–1957.* New York: Knopf, 1961.

Cresson, Osborn C., and Rebecca Shannon Cresson. "American Family in Afghanistan." *NGM* 103.3 (September 1953): 417–32.

Cresson, Rebecca Shannon. "We Lived in Turbulent Tehran." (November 1953): 707–20.

Day, Gladys. "Flying the World." *NGM* 61.6 (June 1932): 655–90.

De Chételat, Eleanor. "My Domestic Life in French Guinea." *NGM* 67.6 (June 1935): 695–730.

Dewey, John. *Democracy and Education: An Introduction to the Philosophy of Education.* 1916. Champaign, Ill.: Project Gutenberg, 1997.

Delanty, Gerard. "Theorising Citizenship in a Global Age." In *Globalization and Citizenship: The Transnational Challenge,* edited by Wayne Hudson and Steven Slaughter, 15–29. London and New York: Routledge, 2007.

Denker, Debra. "Along Afghanistan's War-Torn Frontier." *NGM* 167.6 (June 1985): 772–97.

Dunway, Finis. *Natural Visions: The Power of Images in American Environmental Reform.* Chicago: University of Chicago Press, 2005.

Edensor, Tim. *National Identity, Popular Culture and Everyday Life.* Oxford and New York: Berg, 2002.

Edgerton, William Frederick. "A Recent Experiment with Magazine Literature." *English Journal* 1.5 (May 1912): 278–83.

Edwards, Elizabeth. "The Image as Anthropological Document, Photographic 'Types': The Pursuit of Method." *Visual Anthropology* 3 (1990): 235–58.

Edwards, John Carver. *Berlin Calling: American Broadcasters in Service to the Third Reich.* New York: Praeger, 1991.

Elliott, Michael A. *The Culture Concept: Writing and Difference in the Age of Realism.* Minneapolis: University of Minnesota Press, 2002.

Engleman, J. O. "Outside Reading." *English Journal* 6.1 (January 1917): 20–27.

Evans, Brad. *Before Cultures: The Ethnographic Imagination in American Literature, 1865–1920.* Chicago and London: University of Chicago Press, 2005.

Fabian, Johannes. *Time and the Other: How Anthropology Makes Its Object.* New York: Columbia University Press, 2002.

Fairchild, David. "Book of Monsters." *NGM* 26 (July 1914): 89–98.

———. "Monsters of Our Backyards." *NGM* 24 (May 1913): 575–626.

———. "New Plant Immigrants." *NGM* 22.10 (October 1911): 879–907.

———. "Our Plant Immigrants." *NGM* 17.4 (April 1906): 179–201.

Finley, William L. "Hunting Birds with a Camera." *NGM* 44.2 (August 1923): 161–202.

Fiske, John. *Television Culture.* New York and London: Routledge, 1988.

Foley, Barbara. *Spectres of 1919: Class and Nation in the Making of the New Negro.* Urbana and Chicago: University of Illinois Press, 2003.

Folkner, Roland P. "Conditions in Liberia." With George Salee and Emmet J. Scott. *NGM* 21.9 (September 1910): 729–74.

Forbes, Edgar Allen. "Notes on the Only American Colony in the World." *NGM* 21.9 (September 1910): 719–29.

Fortescue, Granville. "The Burden France Has Borne." *NGM* 31.4 (April 1917): 323–44.

French, Warren. "The First Year of the Paperback Revolution." *College English* 25.4 (January 1964): 255–60.

Freud, Sigmund. "Family Romances." In *The Standard Edition of the Complete Psychological Works of Sigmund Freud,* translated by James Strachey, 9:240–41. London: Hogarth Press, 1959.

Friday, Jonathan. *Aesthetics and Photography.* London: Ashgate, 2002.

Gannett, Henry. "The Annexation Fever." *NGM* 8.12 (December 1897): 354–58.

———. "Movement of Our Population." *NGM* 5 (March 1893): 21–44.

Geertz, Clifford. *Works and Lives: The Anthropologist as Author.* Stanford: Stanford University Press, 1988.

Gellner, Ernest. *Nations and Nationalism.* Ithaca and London: Cornell University Press, 1983.

Gero, Joan, and Delores Root. "Public Presentations and Private Concerns: Archaeology in the Pages of *National Geographic.*" In *The Politics of the Past,* edited by Peter Gathercole and David Lowenthal, 19–37. London: Unwin Hyman, 1990.

Gill, Mrs. Richard C. "Mrs. Robinson Crusoe in Ecuador." *NGM* 65.2 (February 1934): 133–72.

Gilliard, E. Thomas. "New Guinea's Rare Birds and Stone Age Men." *NGM* 103.4 (April 1953): 421–88.

Glazener, Nancy. *Reading for Realism: The History of a U.S. Literary Institution, 1850–1910.* Durham and London: Duke University Press, 1997.

Glissant, Édouard. *Poetics of Relation.* Translated by Betsy Wing. Ann Arbor: University of Michigan Press, 1997.

Godlewska, Anne, and Neil Smith. "Critical Histories of Geography." Introduction to *Geography and Empire,* edited by Godlewska and Smith. Oxford and Cambridge: Blackwell, 1994.

Graves, Ralph A. "Fearful Famines of the Past." *NGM* (July 1917): 69–90.

——— . "Human Emotion Recorded by Photography." *NGM* 38.4 (October 1920): 281–300.

Greeley, A. W. "The Great Populous Centers of the World." *NGM* 4 (July 1893): 89–92.

Griffiths, Alison. *Wondrous Difference: Cinema, Anthropology, and Turn-of-the-Century Visual Culture.* New York: Columbia University Press, 2002.

Grimshaw, Anna. "The Eye in the Door: Anthropology, Film and the Exploration of Interior Space." In *Rethinking Visual Anthropology,* edited by Marcus Banks and Howard Morphy, 36–52. New Haven and London: Yale University Press, 1997.

Grosvenor, Edwin. "The Races of Europe." *NGM* 34.6 (December 1918): 441–534.

Grosvenor, Gilbert. *The National Geographic Society and Its Magazine.* Washington, D.C.: National Geographic Society, 1936.

——— . *The National Geographic Society and Its Magazine.* Washington, D.C.: National Geographic Society, 1957.

——— . "The National Geographic Society and Its New Building." *NGM* 25.4 (April 1914): 454–70.

——— . "Our Flag Issue." *NGM* 32.4 (October 1917): 281–85.

——— . "Practical Patriotism." *NGM* 32.3 (September 1917): 279–80.

——— . "Report of the Director and Editor of the National Geographic Society for the Year 1914." *NGM* 27.3 (March 1915): 318–20.

——— . "The Spirit of the *Geographic.*" *NGM* 34.5 (November 1918): 434–40.

Haardt, Georges-Marie. "Through the Deserts and Jungles of Africa by Motor." *NGM* 49.6 (June 1926): 650–720.

Hadziselimovic, Omer. "Snowy Domes and Gay Turbans: American Travelers on Bosnia, 1897–1941." *East European Quarterly* 36.1 (March 2002): 27–38.

"Haiti and Its Regeneration by the United States." *NGM* 38 (December 1920): 497–511.

Haller, Mark H. *Eugenics: Hereditarian Attitudes in American Thought.* New Brunswick, N.J., and London: Rutgers University Press, 1963.

Hamilton, Virginia. "Keeping House in Borneo." *NGM* 88.9 (September 1945): 293–324.

Hannerz, Ulf. "Cosmopolitans and Locals in World Culture." In *Global Culture: Nationalism, Globalization and Modernity,* edited by Mike Featherstone, 237–51. London: Sage, 1990.

Haraway, Donna. *Primate Visions: Gender, Race, and Nature in the World of Modern Science.* New York and London: Routledge, 1989.

Hariman, Robert, and John Louis Lucaites. *No Caption Needed: Iconic Photographs,*

Public Culture, and Liberal Democracy. Chicago and London: University of Chicago Press, 2007.

———. "Performing Civic Identity: The Iconic Photograph of the Flag Raising on Iwo Jima." *Quarterly Journal of Speech* 88.4 (2002): 363–92.

Harnden, Phoebe Binney. "Keeping House in Majorca." *NGM* 45.4 (April 1924): 425–40.

Harris, Neil. *Cultural Excursions: Marketing Appetites and Cultural Tastes in Modern America.* Chicago: University of Chicago Press, 1990.

Held, David, and Anthony McGrew. *Globalization/Anti-Globalization.* Cambridge: Polity Press, 2002.

Hemingway, Ernest. "Homage to Switzerland." *Scribner's Magazine.* 93.4 (April 1933): 204–8.

Hermes, Joke. *Reading Women's Magazines: An Analysis of Everyday Media Use.* Cambridge: Polity Press, 1995.

Hesford, Wendy S., and Wendy Kozol. *Just Advocacy?: Women's Human Rights, Transnational Feminisms, and the Politics of Representation.* New Brunswick, N.J., and London: Rutgers University Press, 2005.

Higham, John. *Strangers in the Land: Patterns of American Nativism, 1860–1925.* New York: Atheneum, 1967.

Hilton, James. *Lost Horizon.* New York: Perennial, 2004.

Hirsch, Marianne. *Family Frames: Photography, Narrative and Postmemory.* Cambridge: Harvard University Press, 1997.

Holly, Michael Ann. *Panofsky and the Foundations of Art History.* Ithaca and London: Cornell University Press, 1984.

Hoover, Mrs. William H. "Keeping House for the Shepherds of the Sun." *NGM* 57.4 (April 1930): 483–506.

"How the World Is Shod." *NGM* 19.9 (September 1908): 649–60.

Hubbard, Gardiner Greene. "Introductory Address by the President, Mr. Gardiner G. Hubbard." *NGM* 1.1 (October 1888): 3–10.

Hyde, John. "Introductory: The Editor." *NGM* 7.1 (January 1896): 1–2.

Imperato, Pascal James, and Eleanor M. Imperato. *They Married Adventure: The Wandering Lives of Martin and Osa Johnson.* New Brunswick, N.J., and London: Rutgers University Press, 1992.

Johnson, James Weldon. "Self-Determining Haiti I: The American Occupation." *Nation* 111 (August 28, 1920): 236–38.

———. "Self-Determining Haiti II: What the United States Has Accomplished." *Nation* 111 (September 4, 1920): 265–67.

———. "Self-Determining Haiti III: Government of, by, and for the National City Bank." *Nation* 111 (September 11, 1920): 295–97.

Johnston, Sir Harry, and U.S. Minister Lyon of Monrovia. "The Black Republic, Liberia." *NGM* 18 (May 1907): 334–43.

Jones, Gavin. *Strange Talk: The Politics of Dialect Literature in Gilded Age America.* Berkeley and Los Angeles: University of California Press, 1999.

Kaplan, Amy. *The Anarchy of Empire in the Making of U.S. Culture.* Cambridge: Harvard University Press, 2002.

Kirshenblatt-Gimblett, Barbara. "Objects of Ethnography." In *Exhibiting Cultures: The Poetics and Politics of Museum Display,* edited by Ivan Karp and Steven D. Lavine, 386–443. Washington, D.C., and London: Smithsonian Institution Press, 1991.

Kolb, Ellsworth, and Emery Kolb. "Experiences in the Grand Canyon." *NGM* 26.2 (August 1914): 99–184.

Koon, Tracy H. *Believe, Obey, Fight: Political Socialization of Youth in Fascist Italy, 1922–1943.* Chapel Hill and London: University of North Carolina Press, 1985.

Kopper, Philip. "The *National Geographic* Photographers: The Gang That Better Shoot Straight." *Washington Post,* July 7, 1974.

Kozol, Wendy. *"Life"'s America: Family and Nation in Postwar Photojournalism.* Philadelphia: Temple University Press, 1994.

Krysto, Christina. "Bringing the World to Our Foreign-Language Soldiers: How a Military Training Camp Is Solving a Seemingly Unsurmountable Problem by Using the *Geographic.*" *NGM* 34.2 (August 1918): 81–90.

Kyvig, David E. *Daily Life in the United States, 1920–1940.* Chicago: Ivan R. Dee, 2000.

Lane, Franklin K. "What Is It to Be an American?" *NGM* 33.4 (April 1918): 348–54.

Langley, Anne Rainey. "I Kept House in a Jungle." *NGM* 75.1 (January 1939): 97–132.

Lansing, Robert. "Prussianism." *NGM* 33.6 (June 1918): 546–58.

Latour, Bruno. "Give Me a Laboratory and I Will Raise the World." In *The Science Studies Reader,* edited by Mario Biagioli, 258–75. New York: Routledge, 1999.

Lears, T. J. Jackson. *Fables of Abundance: A Cultural History of Advertising in America.* New York: Basic Books, 1994.

———. *No Place of Grace: Antimodernism and the Transformation of American Culture, 1880–1920.* New York: Pantheon, 1981.

Lee, Judith Yaross. *Defining "New Yorker" Humor.* Jackson: University of Mississippi Press, 2000.

Lehan, Richard. *Realism and Naturalism: The Novel in Age of Transition.* Madison: University of Wisconsin Press, 2005.

Liebenow, J. Gus. *Liberia: The Quest for Democracy.* Bloomington: Indiana University Press, 1987.

Lindbergh, Anne Morrow. "Flying around the North Atlantic." *NGM* 66.3 (September 1934): 259–337.

"Little Citizens of the World." NGM 31.2 (February 1917): 115–28.

Livingston, Jane, Frances Fralin, and Declan Haun. *Odyssey: The Art of Photography at "National Geographic."* Charlottesville, Va.: Thomasson-Grant, 1988.

Lockley, R. M. "We Live Alone, and Like It—On an Island." *NGM* 74.2 (August 1938): 252–78.

Lutz, Catherine A., and Jane L. Collins. *Reading "National Geographic."* Chicago: University of Chicago Press, 1993.

"Madonnas of Many Lands." *NGM* 31.6 (June 1917): 549–64.

Marcus, George E., and Michael M. Fischer. *Anthropology as Cultural Critique.* Chicago and London: University of Chicago Press, 1999.

Marien, Mary Warner. *Photography and Its Critics: A Cultural History, 1839–1900.* Cambridge: Cambridge University Press, 1997.

Marlatt, Charles Lester. "Pests and Parasites: Why We Need a National Law to

Prevent the Importation of Insect-Infested and Diseased Plants." *NGM* 22 (April 1911): 321–46.

———. "Protecting the United States from Plant Pests." *NGM* 40.2 (August 1921): 205–18.

Matthews, Glenna. *"Just a Housewife": The Rise and Fall of Domesticity in America.* New York: Oxford University Press, 1987.

May, Elaine Tyler. *Homeward Bound: American Families in the Cold War Era.* New York: Basic Books, 1988.

McBride, Harry. "The Land of the Free in Africa." *NGM* 42 (October 1922): 411–30.

McBride, Ruth Q. "Keeping House on the Congo." *NGM* 72.11 (November 1937): 643–70.

McClintock, Anne. *Imperial Leather: Race, Gender and Sexuality in the Colonial Conquest.* New York and London: Routledge, 1995.

McGee, W. J. "American Geographic Education." *NGM* 9.7 (July 1898): 305–7.

———. "National Growth and National Character." *NGM* 10.6 (June 1899): 185–206.

McSweeny, Z. F. "The Character of Our Immigration, Past and Present." *NGM* 16.1 (January 1905): 1–15.

Metz, Christian. "The Imaginary Signifier." In *Film Theory and Criticism: Introductory Readings,* edited by Gerald Mast, Marshall Cohen, and Leo Braudy, 4th ed., 730–45. New York and Oxford: Oxford University Press, 1992.

Mills, Sara. *Discourses of Difference: An Analysis of Women's Travel Writing and Colonialism.* London and New York: Routledge, 1991.

Mintz, Steven, and Susan Kellogg. *Domestic Revolutions: A Social History of American Family Life.* New York: Free Press, 1988.

Mitchell, W. J. T. *Iconology: Image, Text, Ideology.* Chicago and London: University of Chicago Press, 1986.

———. *Picture Theory.* Chicago and London: University of Chicago Press, 1994.

Moddelmog, Debra. *Reading Desire: In Pursuit of Ernest Hemingway.* Ithaca: Cornell University Press, 1999.

Moran, Mary H. *Liberia: The Violence of Democracy.* Philadelphia: University of Pennsylvania Press, 2006.

Morley, David. *The Nationwide Audience: Structure and Decoding.* London: British Film Institute, 1980.

Mott, Frank Luther. *A History of American Magazines.* Vol. 3, *1865–1885.* Cambridge: Harvard University Press, 1938.

———. *A History of American Magazines.* Vol. 4, *1885–1905.* Cambridge: Belknap Press of Harvard University Press, 1957.

Mulvey, Laura. "Visual Pleasure and Narrative Cinema." In *Film Theory and Criticism,* edited by Gerald Mast and Marshall Cohen, 803–16. New York: Oxford University Press, 1985.

Murphy, Robert Cushman. "The Romance of Science in Polynesia: An Account of Five Years of Cruising among the South Sea Islands." *NGM* 48.4 (October 1925): 355–402.

Newman, Cathy. "Special Report." *NGM* 201.4 (April 2002): 9–13.

———. *Women Photographers at National Geographic.* Washington, D.C.: National Geographic, 2000.

Nicolson, Marjorie Hope. *Mountain Gloom and Mountain Glory: The Development of the Aesthetics of the Infinite*. Seattle and London: University of Washington Press, 1997.

"North American Indians." *NGM* 18.7 (July 1907): 469–84.

Novak, Barbara. *Nature and Culture: American Landscape Painting, 1825–1875*. New York and Oxford: Oxford University Press, 1980.

Ohmann, Richard. *Selling Culture: Magazines, Markets, and Class at the Turn of the Century*. New York and London: Verso, 1996.

"Our Foreign-Born Citizens." *NGM* 31.2 (February 1917): 95–130.

"Our Imperialist Propaganda: The *National Geographic*'s Anti-Haitian Campaign." *Nation* 112 (April 6, 1921): 508.

"Our Narrowing World." *NGM* 100.6 (December 1951): 751–54.

Panofsky, Erwin. *Meaning in the Visual Arts*. London and Chicago: University of Chicago Press, 1982.

Patric, John. "Imperial Rome Reborn." *NGM* 61.3 (March 1937): 269-325.

Pauly, Philip J. "The World and All That Is in It: The National Geographic Society, 1888–1918." *American Quarterly* 31.4 (Autumn 1979): 517–32.

Paxton, Robert O. *The Anatomy of Fascism*. New York: Knopf, 2004.

Payne, Stanley G. *A History of Fascism, 1914–1945*. Madison: University of Wisconsin Press, 1995.

Perry, Claire. *Young America: Childhood in 19th-Century Art and Culture*. New Haven and London: Yale University Press, 2005.

Poole, Robert M. *Explorer's House: "National Geographic" and the World It Made*. New York: Penguin, 2004.

Popkewitz, Thomas S. *Cosmopolitanism and the Age of School Reform: Science, Education, and Making Society by Making the Child*. New York and London: Routledge, 2008.

Powell, W. B. "Geographic Instruction in the Public Schools." *NGM* 5.1 (January 1894): 137–53.

Pratt, Mary Louise. "Fieldwork in Common Places." In *Writing Culture: The Poetics and Politics of Ethnography*, edited by James Clifford and George E. Marcus. Berkeley and Los Angeles: University of California Press, 1986.

———. *Imperial Eyes: Travel Writing and Transculturation*. New York: Routledge, 1992.

Radway, Janice A. *Reading the Romance: Women, Patriarchy, and Popular Literature*. Chapel Hill and London: University of North Carolina Press, 1984.

Renan, Ernest. "What Is a Nation?" In *Nation and Narration*, edited by Homi Bhabha, 8–22. New York and London: Routledge, 2007.

Richards, Thomas. "Archive and Utopia." *Representations* 37 (Winter 1992): 104–35.

Robinson, Henry Peach. *Pictorial Effect in Photography, Being Hints on Composition and Chiaroscuro for Photographers*. London: Piper and Carter; Pawlet, Vt.: Helios, 1971.

Rock, Joseph. "Experiences of a Lone Geographer." *NGM* 48.3 (September 1925): 334–47.

———. "Hunting the Chaulmoogra Tree." *NGM* 41.3 (March 1922): 243–76.

———. "The Land of the Yellow Lama." *NGM* 47.4 (April 1925): 447–91.

———. "Seeking the Mountains of Mystery." *NGM* 57.2 (February 1930): 131–85.

————. "Through the Great River Trenches of Asia." *NGM* 50.2 (August 1926): 133–86.

Rony, Fatimah Tobing. *The Third Eye: Race, Cinema, and Ethnographic Spectacle.* Durham and London: Duke University Press, 1996.

Roosevelt, Theodore. "Wild Man and Wild Beast in Africa." *NGM* 22.1 (January 1911): 1–33.

Ross, Andrew. "Uses of Camp." In *Camp: Queer Aesthetics and the Performing Subject: A Reader,* edited by Fabio Cleto, 308–29. Ann Arbor: University of Michigan Press, 1999.

Ross, Ishbel "Geography, Inc." *Scribner's Magazine* 103.6 (June 1938): 23–27, 57.

Rothenberg, Tamar. "*National Geographic*'s World: The Politics of Popular Geography, 1888–1945." Ph.D. diss., Rutgers University, 1999.

————. *Presenting America's World: Strategies of Innocence in "National Geographic Magazine."* Hampshire, England, and Burlington, Vt.: Ashgate, 2007.

Ruby, Jay. *Picturing Culture: Explorations of Film and Anthropology.* Chicago and London: Chicago University Press, 2000.

Said, Edward W. *Culture and Imperialism.* New York: Knopf, 1993.

————. *Orientalism.* New York: Vintage, 1979.

Sànchez-Eppler, Karen. *Dependent States: The Child's Part in Nineteenth-Century American Culture.* Chicago and London: University of Chicago Press, 2005.

"Scene in Liberia." *NGM* 20.3 (March 1909): 299.

Schmitt, Waldo L. "A Voyage to the Island Home of Robinson Crusoe." *NGM* 104.3 (September 1928): 353–70.

Schulten, Susan. *The Geographical Imagination in America, 1880–1950.* Chicago: University of Chicago Press, 2001.

Sekula, Allan. "The Body and the Archive." In *The Contest of Meaning: Critical Histories of Photography,* edited by Richard Boltin, 344–89. London and Cambridge: MIT Press, 1990.

————. "On the Invention of Photographic Meaning." In *Thinking Photography,* edited by Victor Burgin, 84–109. New York: Macmillan, 1984.

Shay, Felix. "Cairo to Cape Town Overland." *NGM* 47.2 (February 1925): 123–260.

Shiras, George, III. "Photographing Wild Game with Flashlight and Camera." *NGM* 17.7 (July 1906): 367–423.

Shor, Franc, and Jean Shor. "We Took the Highroad in Afghanistan." *NGM* 98.5 (November 1950): 673–706.

————. "We Dwelt in Kashgai Tents." *NGM* 101.6 (June 1952): 805–32.

Shuttleworth, Sally. "Victorian Childhood." *Journal of Victorian Culture* 9.1 (Spring 2004): 107–13.

Siemel, Sasha. "The Jungle Was My Home." *NGM* 101.11 (November 1952): 695–712.

Simons, Sarah E. "American Literature and the Modern Magazine in the High-School Course." *English Journal* 2.6 (June 1913): 357–61.

Showalter, William Joseph. "America's New Soldier Cities." *NGM* 32.5–6 (November–December 1917): 439–76.

Siegel, Elizabeth. "Talking through the 'Fotygraft Album.'" In *Phototextualities: Intersections of Photography and Narrative,* edited by Alex Hughes and Andrea Noble, 239–70. Albuquerque: University of New Mexico Press, 2003.

Skrbis, Zlatko, Gavin Kendall, and Ian Woodward. "Locating Cosmopolitanism: Between Humanist Ideal and Grounded Social Category." *Theory, Culture and Society* 21.6 (2004): 115–36.

Sollors, Werner. *Neither Black nor White yet Both: Thematic Explorations of Interracial Literature.* New York: Oxford University Press, 1997.

Sontag, Susan. "The Anthropologist as Hero." In *Against Interpretation and Other Essays,* by Sontag, 69–81. New York: Farrar, Straus, and Giroux, 1966.

———. "Notes on 'Camp.'" In *Against Interpretation and Other Essays,* by Sontag, 275–92. New York: Farrar, Straus, and Giroux, 1966.

———. *On Photography.* New York: Farrar, Straus, and Giroux, 1977.

Spurr, David. *The Rhetoric of Empire: Colonial Discourse in Journalism, Travel Writing, and Imperial Administration.* Durham and London: Duke University Press, 1993.

Staples, Amy J. "Safari Adventure: Forgotten Cinematic Journeys in Africa." *Film History* 18 (2006): 392–411.

Steet, Linda. *Veils and Daggers: A Century of "National Geographic"'s Representation of the Arab World.* Philadelphia: Temple University Press, 2000.

Stevens, Albert W. "Exploring the Valley of the Amazon in a Hydroplane." *NGM* 49.4 (April 1926): 353–420.

Stirling, Marion. "Jungle Housekeeping for a Geographic Expedition." *NGM* 80.9 (September 1941): 303–27.

Stirling, Matthew W. "Exploring the Past in Panama." *NGM* 95.3 (March 1949): 373–99.

Stocking, George W., Jr. *The Ethnographer's Magic and Other Essays in the History of Anthropology.* Madison: University of Wisconsin Press, 1992.

———. "The Ethnographic Sensibility of the 1920s and the Dualism of the Anthropological Tradition." In *Romantic Motives: Essays on Anthropological Sensibility,* edited by George Stocking, 208–75. History of Anthropology vol. 6. Madison: University of Wisconsin Press, 1989.

———. *Race, Culture, and Evolution: Essays in the History of Anthropology.* New York: Free Press, 1968.

———. *Victorian Anthropology.* New York: Free Press, 1987.

Stoler, Ann Laura. "Intimidations of Empire: Predicaments of the Tactile and Unseen." In *Haunted by Empire: Geographies of Intimacy in North American History,* edited by Stoler, 1–22. Durham and London: Duke University Press, 2006.

Storey, John. *Cultural Consumption and Everyday Life.* London: Arnold, 1999.

———. *Inventing Popular Culture: From Folklore to Globalization.* Malden, Mass., and Oxford: Blackwell, 2003.

Stott, William. *Documentary Expression and Thirties America.* New York: Oxford University Press, 1973.

Strain, Ellen. *Public Places, Private Journeys: Ethnography, Entertainment, and the Tourist Gaze.* New Brunswick, N.J.: Rutgers University Press, 2003.

Susman, Warren I. *Culture as History: The Transformation of American Society in the Twentieth Century.* New York: Pantheon, 1984.

Sutton, S. B. *In China's Border Provinces: The Turbulent Career of Joseph Rock, Botanist-Explorer.* New York: Hastings House, 1974.

Taft, William Howard. "The Health and Morale of America's Citizen Army." NGM 33.3 (March 1918): 219–45.

———. "The League of Nations, What It Means and Why It Must Be." NGM 35.1 (January 1919): 43–66.

———. "A Poisoned World." NGM 31.5 (May 1917): 459–67.

Tagg, John. The Burden of Representation: Essays on Photographies and Histories. Amherst: University of Massachusetts Press, 1988.

Tambs, Erling. "A Modern Saga of the Seas." NGM 60.6 (December 1931): 645–88.

Tebbel, John, and Mary Ellen Zuckerman. The Magazine in America: 1741–1990. New York: Oxford University Press, 1991.

Thompson, John B. Ideology and Modern Culture: Critical Social Theory in the Era of Mass Communication. Stanford: Stanford University Press, 1990.

Tindall, George Brown, and David Emory Shi. America: A Narrative History. 7th ed. Vol. 2. New York: Norton, 2007.

Tobey, Ronald C. Technology as Freedom: The New Deal and the Electrical Modernization of the American Home. Berkeley and Los Angeles: University of California Press, 1996.

Tomlinson, John. Globalization and Culture. Chicago and London: University of Chicago Press, 1999.

Torgovnick, Marianna. Gone Primitive: Savage Intellects, Primitive Lives. Chicago and London: University of Chicago Press, 1990.

Trachtenberg, Alan. "From Image to Story: Reading the File." In Documenting America, 1935–1943, edited by Carl Fleischhauer and Beverly W. Brannan, 43–75. Berkeley and Los Angeles: University of California Press, 1988.

———. Reading American Photographs: Images as History, Mathew Brady to Walker Evans. New York: Hill and Wang, 1989.

Trinh, T. Minh-ha. Woman, Native, Other: Writing Postcoloniality and Feminism. Bloomington and Indianapolis: Indiana University Press, 1989.

Tuason, Julie A. "The Ideology of Empire in National Geographic Magazine's Coverage of the Philippines, 1898–1908." Geographical Review 89.1 (January 1999): 34–53.

Turner, Frederick Jackson. "The Significance of the American Frontier in American History." 1893. Reprint, North Stratford, N.H.: Irvington Reprint Series, 1991.

"Typical Men and Women of Cambodia." NGM 23.3 (March 1912): 216.

Urry, John. Sociology beyond Societies: Mobilities for the Twenty-first Century. New York and London: Routledge, 2000.

———. The Tourist Gaze. London: Sage, 2002.

"Useful Facts about the Countries of the World." NGM 18.6 (June 1907): 424–25.

Villard, Henry S. "Rubber-Cushioned Liberia." NGM 93 (February 1948): 201–28.

Waller, Robert James. The Bridges of Madison County. New York: Warner, 1992.

Ward, Robert De C. "Our Immigration Laws from the View Point of National Eugenics." NGM 23.1 (January 1912): 38–41.

"Wards of the United States." NGM 30 (August 1916): 143–77.

Warner, Arthur H. "A Country Where Going to America Is an Industry." NGM 20.12 (December 1909): 1063–102.

Washburn, Stanley. "The Russian Situation and Its Significance to America." *NGM* 31.4 (April 917): 371–82.

West, Richard. *Back to Africa: A History of Sierra Leone and Liberia.* New York: Holt, Rinehart and Winston, 1970.

Wexler, Laura. *Tender Violence: Domestic Visions in an Age of U.S. Imperialism.* Chapel Hill: University of North Carolina Press, 2000.

White, Gleeson. "The Nude in Photography." 1897. In *A Photographic Vision: Pictorial Photography, 1889–1923,* edited by Peter C. Bunnell, 78–84. Salt Lake City: Peregrine Smith 1980.

Whitlock, Gillian. *Soft Weapons: Autobiography in Transit.* Chicago and London: University of Chicago Press, 2007.

Williams, John Sharp. "The Ties That Bind." *NGM* 31.3 (March 1917): 281–86.

Williams, Maynard Owen. "Adventures with a Camera in Many Lands." *NGM* 40.1 (July 1921): 87–112.

Wilson, Christopher P. "The Rhetoric of Consumption: Mass-Market Magazines and the Demise of the Gentle Reader, 1880–1920." In *The Culture of Consumption: Critical Essays in American History, 1880–1980,* edited by Richard Wightman Fox and T. J. Jackson Lears, 41–64. New York: Pantheon, 1983.

Wilson, Woodrow. "Do Your Bit for America." *NGM* 31.4 (April 1917): 289–93.

Worcester, Dean C. "Taal Volcano and Its Recent Destructive Eruption." *NGM* 23.4 (April 1912): 313–67.

Young, Robert J. C. *Colonial Desire: Hybridity in Theory, Culture and Race.* New York: Routledge, 1995.

Zalampas, Michael. *Adolf Hitler and the Third Reich in American Magazines, 1923–1939.* Bowling Green: Bowling Green State University Popular Press, 1989.

Index

Italicized page numbers refer to illustrations.

Family of Man (Steichen), 13, 28
family romance, 123, 129
fascism: and anti-communism, 124;
  defined, 122–23; and "family romance,"
  123; and representation in *National
  Geographic*, 121–31. *See also* local
  color; romance
flag (U.S.), 6, 14, 109–10, *111*
foreign-born. *See* immigrants
Fossey, Dian, 8
Frankfurt School, 190
Freud, Sigmund, 123

Garrett, Wilbur, 203
Gauguin, Paul, 72
Gellner, Ernest, 75
gender: and instability of traditional
  roles, 136, 151–53, 158, 170; and
  masculine frontier heroics, 144–45;
  and photographer's heroism, 95–96;
  "primitivist performance," 136–38
geography: and body as landscape, 39;
  and citizenship, 34–35; and comparative method, 35–38; as current
  events, 39; eighteenth-century colonial
  origins of, 91; as "epic story," 32–33;
  and interpretation of symbols, 37–38,
  58; and "racial geography," 34, 87–88;
  as world history, 37. *See also* visual
  literacy
Gill, Mr. and Mrs. Richard C., 144–46, *147*
globalization: and citizenship, 18–19;
  as "complex connectivity," 9,
  19–20, 55, 57, 105, 108, 207; and
  deterritorialization of space, 19–20,
  187, 189, 191, 195, 207; dystopian and
  utopian possibilities of, 18, 20; and
  global civic culture, 5, 7, 18–19
Goodall, Jane, 8
Grosvenor, Edwin, 108–9
Grosvenor, Gilbert H., 22–23, 33, 50, 190,
  199–200, 202; anti-Semitism of, 104,
  124; editorial principles of, 47–48; *New
  Yorker* caricature of, 200
Grosvenor, Gilbert M., 203

Grosvenor, Melville Bell, 202
Gula, Sharbat: and "Afghan Women's
  Fund," 5; appropriation in popular
  culture, 4; NGS rediscovery of, 1–7;
  parodies of, 4–5, 6; photograph of, 2

Haggard, H. Rider, 137
Haiti, U.S. occupation of, 112–14
Haraway, Donna, 93
Hariman, Robert, and John Louis
  Lucaites, 2, 4, 21, 134, 172, 210n1,
  210n11
Harper's Monthly (magazine), 44, 48
Harris, Joel Chandler, 65, 75
Harris, Neil, 60
Harvard Lampoon (magazine), 4–5, 8
Hearn, Lafcadio, 72
Heart of Darkness, The (Conrad), 86
Hemingway, Ernest, 152, 190
Hilton, James, 179, 184–86. See also *Lost
  Horizon* (Hilton)
Hilton, Paris, 4, 8, 210n9
Hine, Lewis, 76, 120, 219n37
Hirsch, Marianne, 28
Hitler, Adolph, 104, 127, 186; in Ameri-
  can magazines, 123–24; and Hitler
  Youth, 104, 126, 131. *See also* fascism
"Homage to Switzerland" (Hemingway),
  190–92
Hoover, Herbert, 146; and Hoovervilles,
  146
Hoover, Mr. and Mrs. William H., 143–
  44; William, *145*
Howells, William Dean, 44
Hubbard, Gardiner Greene, 35–36, 43, 78
Hyde, John, 33, 34–35, 72

iconic photographs, 198; circulation
  of, 1; as civic performance, 2, 21; as
  emotional catalysts of public sentiment,
  1–2; and global civic ethic, 5, 7; Iwo
  Jima flag-raising, 13, 173; popular appropriation of, 13. *See also* Gula, Sharbat;
  Hariman, Robert, and John Louis
  Lucaites; "Migrant Mother" (Lange)

demographics of, 50–51; economics of, 52–53; and exclusivity, 44, 51–52; and global kinship, 31; and the Great Depression, 146–47, 189–90; and inclusivity, 43–45; internationalism of, 216n59; and *National Geographic* reader identification, 11; and *National Geographic* subscription rates, 48, 216n66; and nationalism, 51–51; by nomination, 44; privileges of, 25, 31. *See also* family

metapicture, 84, 177, 196

Metz, Christian, 99

Mickey Mouse, 128, 169

Middle East, 166–69, 205

"Migrant Mother" (Lange), 1, 175

Mitchell, W. J. T., 84. *See also* metapicture

Mott, Frank Luther, 42

museum: in *Lost Horizon*, 187–89; and "museum effect," 82–84, *83*, 202; *National Geographic* distinguished from, 32–34; and "poetics of detachment," 185

Museum of Natural History, 64

Mussolini, Benito, 104, 123–24, 128

Nation (magazine), 113, 123, 132

National Geographic Magazine; advertising, 14, 45, 50, 52–53, 139, 146, 191; as anthro-pornography, 8, 194; as art, 53–54; in classrooms, 45–47, *46*, 54–55; as collectible, 53–56; compared to Bible, 55; cosmopolitanism of form, 33; cover, *6*, 13, 45; disordering of globe, 15, 33; faked photographs, 58; as guidebook, 54–55; iconicity of, 13, 39, 55, 202; institutional aesthetic, 13, 45, 47–48; institutional gaze, 159–65; magazine competitors, 48–49; and mental relaxation, 190; modernism of, 14, 63, 68–69, 83–84, 100; parodies of, 8, 177–78, 184, *195*, *197*; photographers on assignment, 63, 91–101, 159–65, 206; popular articles, 51; public display of, 55;

reader criticisms of, 15, 25–26, 51–52, 58, 73, 110, 113–15, 130–32, 148–49, 172–73, 198, 200–203, 213n38; and recycled photographs, 58–59, 148, *195*, 198; reliance on commercial or "stock" photographs, 29; tensions between science and art in, 11, 23, 42, 76–79, 85, 91; as textbook, 40, 54–55; as vicarious travel, 14–17, 22, 56–57; visual discord of, 63. *See also* icons; membership (NGS); photography; readership (*National Geographic*); visual literacy

National Geographic Society (NGS): archive of unpublished readers' letters, 12, 26; flag, *170*; founding of, 34–35; Geographic News Bulletins, 121; and internationalism, 12; and nationalism, 7, 12, 16–17; "Pictorial Geography," 54, 116–21; policy of editorial nonpartisanship, 47–48, 58, 108, 150

nativism: and immigration, 105; and nationalism; 104–11, 114; during World War I, 105–11

natural disaster, 24, 175–76. *See also* sublime, the: "catastrophic sublime"

New Republic (magazine), 132

Newsweek (magazine), 132

New Yorker (magazine): as antithesis of *National Geographic*, 194; cartoons, 194, *195*, *197*, 202, 227–28n54; "Geography Unshackled," 199–200; "humor of anachronism," 195–96; spoof on NGS membership campaign, 198–99

New York Times Magazine, 12

nostalgia: and anti-modernism, 137; and childhood, 94, 107; critical function of, 6; and photography 25; for preindustrial past, 137, 141. *See also* anthropology; children; primitivism

O'Connor, Flannery, 193

Orientalism, 167

Outlook (magazine), 48

painting: Hudson River school, 94–95; landscape, 97; and *National Geographic* photographs, 94–95

Panofsky, Erwin, 214n23

parody, 8, 149, 173–209; unintentional, 41, 199, 202. *See also* "camp" aesthetic

Parrish, Maxfield, 72, 218n25

pastoral, 94, 79, 81. *See also* local color; romance

Patterns of Culture (Benedict), 154

Pan American Exposition (Buffalo, New York), 64

Pauly, Philip J., 9–10, 41

Peary, Robert E., 180

performance: and aesthetic of "camp," 174–75; civic, 2, 21, 129; and cultural framing, 6–7, 137–38; and improvisation, 160

photography: as "collaboration" between subject and photographer, 162; contradictions between caption and image in, 61; documentary, 2, 159, 162; ethnographic, 79–82; and fantasy, 77; fashion, 2, 4, 196; history of, 23–24, 27, 95–96; as "living-picture," 7, 24, 56; of nudes, 15, 28, 72–74, 176, 196; of photographers, 97, 99, 100, 162, 165; pictorial, 24, 72–74, 76–80, 164, 204; and production of iconic racial "types," 13, 23, 39–40, 63, 69, 76, 80–81, 82, 86, 92, 159, 204, 205; and science, 40, 64, 77–78; as secular icon, 13, 38–39; and self-documentary in *National Geographic*, 63, 159–65, 174, 204, 206; and self-reflexivity, 84, 99–100, 163, 165, 176; as story, 14, 39, 58, 60, 69–70, 76–77; and travel, 15, 21; and vicarious participation, 36, 56–57, 98, 178, 182; wildlife, 92–93, 98

photojournalism, 95–96

Playboy (magazine), 205

Powell, W. B., 37–38

primitivism: as cultural commodity, 23, 151; ethnographic imagination, 62; and historical violence, 141, 150, 168;

and modernity, 139–42, 168–69, 179, 183, 196; as performance, 136–38, 143–45; stereotypes of, 13, 29, 70–71, 135–37, 148, 174–75, 194–96, 205; as time travel, 139–40. *See also* anthropology; "camp" aesthetic; children; nostalgia

progressive education: and assimilation, 34, 119; and critical media consumption, 34, 45–47, 131–34. *See also* children; visual literacy

Prussianism, 103–4

Reader's Digest (magazine), 123

readership (*National Geographic*): alertness to inconsistencies, 59; and consent, 10–11, 25; cosmopolitanism of, 12, 15, 59; critical reading practices of, 57–61; and culture of dissent, 11–13, 53, 105; democratic values of, 51; and demographics of, 49–51; identification with NGS, 4, 12, 16, 18; and "mediascape," 9; *National Geographic's* "first million," 53; rituals of *National Geographic* consumption, 17, 53–77. *See also* African Americans; immigrants; spectatorship

realism: aesthetic of, 2; fusion with realism, 95; literary, 61; and photography, 40, 60, 76–79; and science, 64, 77, 171; and "type" 69. *See also* local color

reflexivity, 21, 209. *See also* photography

Review of Reviews (magazine), 48, 58, 123

Riis, Jacob, 120

Robinson, Henry Peach (H. P.), 78, 95

Robinson Crusoe (Defoe), 142, 144–45, 150–51

Rock, Joseph, 179–84, 185, 206

Rockwell, Norman, 109, 221n18

romance: and anti-romance, 152; defined, 24; and fascism, 123; and imperialism, 24; in literature, 65, 205; *National Geographic's* romance of adventure, 6, 62; of the real, 61. *See also* anthropology

romanticism: and concept of "folk," 125; distinguished from romance, 24; and eugenics, 90. *See also* sublime, the

Roosevelt, Theodore, 12, 51, 93, 184, 206

Rose, Carl, 194; cartoon by, *195*

Rosenthal, Joe, 175

Ross, Betsy, 6–7, 109; parody of, *6*

Rothenberg, Tamar, 15

Russia, 114, 115–16

Said, Edward, 23

Saturday Evening Post (magazine), 48, 109, 132

Saturday Review of Literature (magazine), 177, 193

Schoedsack, Ernest B., 150. *See also* Cooper, Merian C.

Schulten, Susan, 10

Scribner's Monthly (magazine), 43, 52

Sedition Act (1918), 110

September 11, 2001, 3, 4, 7, 18

Shields, Brooke, 2. *See also* photography: fashion

Shiras, George, 95; photograph by, *96*

"Short Happy Life of Francis Macomber, The" (Hemingway), 152

Smithsonian Institution, 64

"Snows of Kilimanjaro, The" (Hemingway), 152

Sontag, Susan, 174–75, 178, 194, 208–9

Spanish-American War, 14, 19, 35, 78

spectatorship: and "distanced immersion," 36; and "familial look," 28; and "political spectatorship," 10; and "punctum," 162–65; and "tourist gaze," 22

Steet, Linda, 10

Steichen, Edward, 28. *See also* Family of Man (Steichen)

stereograph, 77

Stieglitz, Alfred, 78

Stocking, George, 51, 94

Strain, Ellen, 36, 99

Streep, Meryl, 203

sublime, the: "catastrophic sublime," 175–79, 181–83, 184, 186–87, 226n15; and romanticism, 24, 98

suburbia, 166–67

Swiss Family Robinson, 142, 151

Taft, William Howard, 116

Tarzan of the Apes (Burroughs), 137

Taylor, Richard, 195; cartoon by, *197*

technology: and America as pioneer, 159; and the sublime, 98; and surveillance, 3, 77; unexpected appearance of, 141, 183; and Western myth of primitive solitude, 151

Thompson, Florence, 1

Time (magazine), 124

Tomlinson, John, 19–20

Torgovnick, Marianna, 65

Travels in West Africa (Kingsley), 149

Tuason, Julie, 10

Twain, Mark, 44, 70

type. *See* photography; realism

Underwood and Underwood, 58

United Nations Development Program (UNDP), 5

Urry, John, 22

Vertov, Dziga, 163

Virgin Mary, 2

visual literacy: and geography, 31–41; and *National Geographic*, 11, 22–25, 32–42; and progressive education, 31, 34, 38–39

von Gloeden, Wilhelm, 24, 76, 79–81, 219n47; photographs by, *81*

Waller, Robert, 203, 207

Ward, Robert DeCourcy, 88–89

"war on terror," 3, 5

Wentzel, Volkmar, 160–62, *161*

West, Richard, 76

White, Clarence, 78

Williams, Maynard Owen, 70, 93

Williams, William Carlos, 208

Wilson, Woodrow, 110–11, 114, 116, 124

women: and anti-imperialism, 150; and cultural relativism, 154–57; and science, 153–59; and travel writing, 149–50

World's Work (magazine), 48

World War I: and American magazines, 47; and educating foreign-born U.S. soldiers, 19, 117–18; and First Amendment, 110–11; and hope for world democracy, 115–16; and "Hunnism," 59, 108–9, 110; and immigration, 105–8; and *National Geographic*'s iconicity, 116; and propaganda, 111, 114, 124; U.S. involvement in, 102–3

World War II, 186, 202